Why Syria Goes to War

A volume in the series

Cornell Studies in Political Economy

EDITED BY PETER J. KATZENSTEIN

A full list of titles in the series appears at the end of the book.

Why Syria Goes to War

THIRTY YEARS OF CONFRONTATION

FRED H. LAWSON

CORNELL UNIVERSITY PRESS

Ithaca and London

First published 1996 by Cornell University Press.

Printed in the United States of America

✿ This book is printed on Lyons Falls Turin Book, a paper that is totally chlorine-free and acid-free.

Library of Congress Cataloging-in-Publication Data

Lawson, Fred Haley, 1952–
    Why Syria goes to war : thirty years of confrontation / Fred H. Lawson.
        p.   cm. — (Cornell studies in political economy)
    Includes bibliographical references (p.) and index.
    ISBN 0-8014-2373-2 (cloth : alk. paper)
    1. War—Economic aspects—Syria. 2. Syria—Economic conditions. 3. Syria—Politics and government. 4. Israel-Arab conflicts—Economic aspects—Syria. 5. Syria—Foreign relations—Israel. 6. Israel—Foreign relations—Syria. I. Title. II. Series.
HC415.23.Z9D43   1996
330.95691′042—dc20   96-17769

To Deborah,

who paid the price for me to spend

an exhilarating year in Aleppo

Contents

Figures

Unless otherwise indicated, all data come from Syrian Arab Republic, *Statistical Abstract* (Damascus: Central Bureau of Statistics, various years).

Tables

Acknowledgments

Pride of place on the list of those who urged me to undertake, persevere in, and finally finish this project goes to Peter Cowhey, Peter Katzenstein, Harvey Feigenbaum, James Kurth, and David Laitin, who were there at the very beginning. David was dragged in one more time toward the end and responded pithily as always. Janice Stein prevented me from wrestling with a particularly obdurate dependent variable, and Roger Sparks corrected my economics. Laurie Brand took precious time out from a vacation in Paris to pass along a great many wise suggestions, only some of which I have had the good sense to accept. Encouragement from Hanna Batatu, Gregory Gause, Jo-Ann Hart, Michael Hudson, and Nikolaos van Dam kept me from leaving Syria on the back burner indefinitely. Richard Murphy, Alasdair Drysdale, and Raymond Hinnebusch invited me to participate in a January 1990 seminar on the Syrian armed forces at the Council on Foreign Relations, from which I learned a great deal.

Colleagues and students in the College of Economics at the University of Aleppo, where I was Fulbright Lecturer in International Relations during 1992–1993, will no doubt take exception to much of what I claim about their country and the policies of its current government. But I would have ended up much farther off the mark had they not welcomed me so warmly and taken my ideas and inquiries so seriously. I particularly wish to record my gratitude to and admiration for the president of the university, Muhammad 'Ali Houriyyeh, and the dean of the College of Economics, Ahmad al-Ashqar. Elizabeth Picard shared her extensive knowledge of contemporary Syria whenever I showed up on her doorstep, usually unannounced. Olivier Dubois and his associates at the Institut Français d'Etudes Arabes de Damas permitted me to use the institute's remarkable library, despite my evident linguistic short-comings.

I would never have completed this project without material and moral support from two sources—the first institutional, the second individual. The United States Institute of Peace awarded me a fellow-ship that allowed me to spend the spring of 1989 writing preliminary drafts of several chapters. Roger Haydon of Cornell University Press proffered persistent encouragement and stimulating criticism from the minute he saw the embryonic manuscript. Little did Roger know how long the gestation period would prove to be.

Earlier versions of some portions appeared in *MERIP Reports,* no. 110 (November–December 1982), *International Organization* 38 (Summer 1984), *Orient* 29 (December 1988), the *Journal of South Asian and Middle Eastern Studies* 14 (Winter 1990), and *The Middle East Journal* 48 (Winter 1994). I am grateful to the editors and publishers of these journals for allowing me to incorporate revised sections of my earlier articles into what follows.

F. H. L.

Why Syria Goes to War

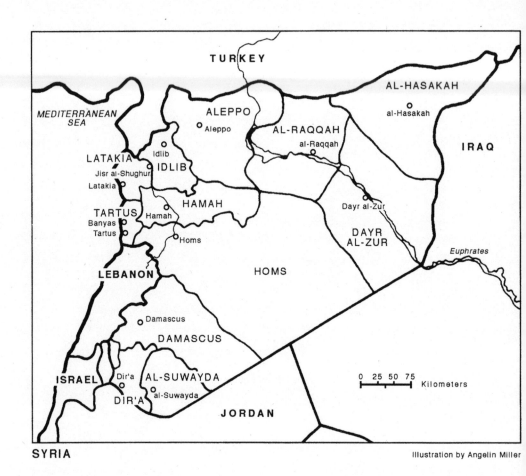

SYRIA

Illustration by Angelin Miller

Linking Domestic Conflict to Foreign Policy

Why do some international crises escalate into war, whereas others do not? Answers to this question currently come almost entirely from specialists in security studies, who tend to play down, if not completely ignore, the political-economic dynamics that surround crises among states. An inadvertent academic division of labor reinforces the long-standing but fundamentally illegitimate split between specialists in the "high politics" of crisis and war and those who study the "low politics" of transformations in the structure of national economies.[1] More insidiously, this division perpetuates the illusion that international crises are driven primarily by broad strategic calculations or matters of principle, most notably the defense of national sovereignty or a "determination to confront aggression,"[2] rather than by underlying struggles among powerful social forces at home.

In this book I argue that there is an intimate connection between the conflicts that shape the domestic political economy and the strategies that governments adopt during confrontations with external adversaries. Earlier literature on the causes of war has explored the link between internal conflict and external aggressiveness, only to discount or reject any such connection.[3] Nevertheless, a handful of recent studies propose more precise linkages between domestic conflict and foreign policy. These works confirm the intuition of generations of writers who have suggested that the presence of severe conflict at home escalates, whereas its absence defuses, international crises.[4]

Unfortunately, current literature on domestic conflict and international crises continues to play down the importance of political-economic dynamics. Leo Hazlewood observes that internal economic difficulties may spark civil disturbances, intraelite cleavages, or popular rebellions, thereby indirectly prompting regimes to adopt aggressive foreign policies. But political-economic factors remain tangential to his argument.[5] Clifton Morgan and Kenneth Bickers doubt there is a systematic relationship between political-economic crises at home and external hostility. They express misgivings about Bruce Russett's suggestion that such a connection might exist and provisionally adopt Russett's disclaimer that "economic downturn per se may be less important in producing a tendency toward engaging in interstate disputes than is domestic political conflict from whatever cause."[6] Patrick James uses purely economic variables such as changes in the consumer price index and the unemployment rate to formulate a mathematical equation linking "latent" domestic conflict to minor conflicts abroad. But such economic factors virtually disappear from his discussion of the impact of "manifest" internal conflict on foreign policy.[7] As a result, the connection between domestic political economy and external crisis behavior remains elusive.

Moreover, current studies of domestic conflict and foreign policy almost entirely ignore the contemporary Middle East.[8] Explanations for foreign policy in this part of the world continue to emphasize the idiosyncrasies of leaders and the constraints imposed upon regional actors by the international environment rather than internal political-economic dynamics.[9] Of no Middle Eastern country is this more evidently the case than the Syrian Arab Republic, whose external crisis behavior is virtually always attributed to the objectives and predispositions of the dominant figure in the country's political elite, the sectarian complexion of the ruling coalition, or the opportunities for action created by the machinations of the great powers. Such accounts not only fail to provide compelling explanations for important shifts in Damascus's policies toward its external adversaries but also paint a picture of the struggles that shape contemporary Syria's domestic and foreign affairs which is at best superficial and at worst profoundly misleading.[10]

EXPLAINING SYRIAN FOREIGN POLICY

Three sets of variables dominate existing accounts of Syrian foreign policy. The first concerns the values and attitudes of the country's leading political figure(s), who since November 1970 has been the president, Hafiz al-Asad. The second deals with the Middle Eastern policies of the United States and the Soviet Union, which are presumed tightly to constrain the activities of regional powers. The third involves the sectarian nature of the regime, whose 'Alawi roots are alleged to have put the governing elite in fundamental conflict with Syria's Sunni majority. Variations on this trio of causal factors have been proposed to explain Damascus's response to each major crisis to which Syria has been a party over the last three decades.

Syrian belligerence toward Israel during the spring of 1967 is generally attributed to the attitudes and ideology of the Ba'thi leadership that seized power in Damascus in February 1966. Charles Yost asserts that the "new and more radical Syrian government . . . enthusiastically supported the claims and machinations of the so-called Palestine Liberation Army which mobilized and inflamed the refugees and carried out some of the raids."[11] Richard Parker observes that conflict between Syria and Israel had been simmering since 1949, "but the temperature went up markedly with the installation of a radical leftist regime in Damascus [which] talked of launching a people's war of liberation to solve the Palestine problem and began to follow a forward policy along the border, encouraging rather than suppressing infiltration and sabotage operations in Israel."[12] In Walter Laqueur's view, "When the [1967] crisis came Syria had the most bellicose government in its entire history."[13] Three factors pushed this leadership to adopt an extremely hostile posture toward the State of Israel: first, the regime's love of ideological pronouncements tended to overwhelm its common sense; second, it was sufficiently weak as to gravitate toward "a militant line on the one issue that was universally popular—Palestine"; and third, it modeled itself after the most salient revolutionary movement of the time, the Viet Cong.[14] Furthermore, Yair Evron suggests that the predominant position occupied by members of the minority 'Alawi community inside the new regime prompted the Syrian leadership to adopt an overly hostile posture toward Israel as a means of assuaging popular suspicions that it was "ready to compromise on Pan-Arab nationalism."[15]

Soviet policy is also accorded a key role in the process that led to the outbreak of the June war. Yost observes that Moscow in October 1966 vetoed "a relatively mild [United Nations Security Council] resolution proposed by six of its members, calling on Syria to take stronger measures to prevent [Palestinian raids on Israeli territory]." This step emboldened the Syrian prime minister to declare that "we are not sentinels over Israel's security and are not the leash that restrains the revolution of the displaced and persecuted Palestinian people."[16] More important, Soviet representatives warned Damascus in April and May 1967 that Israeli commanders were planning to launch a major offensive against Syrian territory. Yost suggests that "the Israelis may have hoped that direct notice to the Soviets might induce them to persuade their Syrian friends to stop the [Palestinian] raids." But Israeli threats "backfired by convincing the Soviets, Syrians and Egyptians that a major retaliatory strike against Syria was fixed and imminent."[17] Moscow thus had little choice but to reaffirm its support for Damascus, while at the same time "spurr[ing] the Egyptians on to vigorous counteraction, the full repercussions of which they did not foresee."[18]

What is most puzzling about this account of the 1967 war is Damascus's evident lack of military preparations along the border with Israel. The Syrian armed forces' unpreparedness for war certainly confused the Egyptian chief of staff, who, according to Parker, "returned to Cairo [in mid-May 1967] to report to Marshal 'Amr that, among other things, the Syrians themselves were not in the state of alert one would have expected of them if they thought an attack was imminent."[19] If the Ba'thi leaders were truly as bellicose as the literature claims, it seems highly improbable that they would have been so lax in shoring up the country's southern security perimeter. Such apparent negligence provides grist for rumor mills, many of which remain in full production.[20] Formulating a completely different explanation for this episode—in which political struggles inside Syria led the regime to implement policies that escalated the crisis but without any single actor necessarily intending to precipitate war with Israel—is long overdue.

Most observers explain Syria's abortive intervention in the civil war that erupted in Jordan in the fall of 1970 as a result of Damascus's relations with Moscow, Washington, and Jerusalem. Henry Brandon reiterates the Nixon administration's view that the tanks that rolled into northern Jordan on 20 September "were Soviet-made and their Syrian crews Soviet-trained; obviously they would not have moved without Soviet approval."[21] The Syrian regime's subsequent decision to cut short the drive into Jordan is generally explained the same way. Henry Kissinger reports that Damascus pulled its troops out of Jordan in the face of unambiguous Israeli threats, with U.S. backing, to take whatever steps might be necessary to preserve the monarchy.[22] Malcolm Kerr argues that a potent but tangled combination of "Israeli and American warnings, Soviet urging, and effective Jordanian opposition" dissuaded Damascus from escalating the conflict, thereby precipitating a regional or general war.[23] Raymond Hinnebusch concurs: although Ba'thi "radicals, in spite of threats from Israel and the United States, sent forces to Jordan to save the [Palestinian] fedayeen and if possible overthrow the monarchy[,] . . . Asad, deterred by the threats, ever aware of the actual balance of power, and unwilling to risk his forces in this adventure, refused to commit air support."[24] Expressions of disapproval from Moscow may even have influenced the Syrian military.[25]

Syria's own interests with regard to the fighting have been adumbrated less cogently. Tabitha Petran asserts that "from the beginning the intervention had a clearly defined geographical limit: it was to be confined to north Jordan." Damascus's objective must therefore have been to provide support for a Palestinian "liberated zone" in this part of the kingdom.[26] Stephen Oren speculates that Syria's poorly developed "sense of identity," which makes little if any distinction between Syria proper, Lebanon, Israel, and Jordan, "explains not only much of her hostility toward Israel but also the motivation for her efforts to intervene in Jordan's civil war in September 1970."[27] R. D. McLaurin, Don Peretz, and Lewis Snider suggest that "the intervention followed from Syrian determination not to be the new home of the guerrilla forces (not to turn a Jordanian-guerrilla conflict into a Syrian-guerrilla conflict), the urge of the 'Alawis to demonstrate their 'revolutionary virtue,' and a direct concern about the Palestine movement."[28] Finally, Yosef Olmert claims that Ba'th party ideology at the time "espoused a totally militant posture directed in particular against Israel and the Hashemite dynasty in Jordan." As a result, ideologues in Damascus found themselves predisposed to take an active part in undermining one of the region's less progressive regimes.[29]

Specialists in Syrian politics add that jockeying between Salah Jadid and Hafiz al-Asad for predominance within the Military Committee of the Ba'th party bore directly on Syrian policy during the crisis. Yaacov Bar-Siman-Tov asserts that

> the Jordanian civil war of September 1970 signalled the last, climactic crisis of the Jadid-Asad conflict. . . . In retrospect, it seems that Asad felt compelled to support the initial intervention, since to do otherwise would have seemed a clear betrayal of the Ba'th commitment to the Palestinian cause. Asad, however, was wary of possible Israeli intervention; he thus sought to keep Syrian intervention minimal. Jadid, for his part, may have sincerely desired to aid the Palestinians. Alternatively, he may have been trying to manipulate the situation in hopes of embarrassing Asad with a military defeat.[30]

This view is shared by many other Syrianists.[31]

The argument that Syria limited its intervention in the Jordanian civil war because of threats from the United States, Israel, and the Soviet Union is unconvincing. Explicit Israeli and American warnings proved insufficient to moderate Syrian policy toward Israel in the spring of 1967; Soviet entreaties failed to persuade Damascus to abandon its support for a war of national liberation on the part of the Popular Front for the Liberation of Palestine and the Syrian-sponsored al-Sa'iqah guerrilla organizations over the subsequent three years. Moreover, Adam Garfinkle claims on the basis of extensive interviews with Nixon administration officials that Washington issued no coherent threat to intervene in support of the Jordanian regime, whether in conjunction with Israel or not; and he questions whether Syrian commanders had time to receive the alleged U.S.-Israeli threats before they ordered their troops out of northern Jordan.[32] Rejecting the argument that Syrian policy changed as a result of outside intervention, Garfinkle concludes that "the most probable explanation for the passivity of the Syrian air force had more to do with internal politics within the Syrian Ba'ath party at the time; it was so fractured that it would not be an exaggeration to say that a slow-motion coup d'état was underway."[33]

Syria's military drive into Lebanon in the late spring of 1976 has generated a sizable literature from specialists in Lebanese and Syrian affairs. Adeed Dawisha explains the intervention as stemming from President Hafiz al-Asad's abiding concern for Arab unity in general and for the "historical indivisibility" of Syria and Lebanon in particular, along with the detrimental impact that a permanently divided Lebanon would have on Syria's strategic position vis-à-vis Israel.[34] Dan Tschirgi lists several additional Syrian "strategic objectives" in sending troops into Lebanon: to prevent the establishment of a radical regime in Beirut, whose activities might draw Syria into an unwanted war with Israel; to prevent the destruction of the Palestinian movement in Lebanon, which could only have hurt the combined Arab position vis-à-vis Israel; and to prevent "the emergence of a power vacuum in Lebanon that might allow Syria to be outflanked by Israel in the event of war."[35] In addition, Asad AbuKhalil asserts that Damascus's actions were "motivated by the Syrian attempt to prevent any side in the [civil] war from prevailing, and consequently from diminishing Syrian power in Lebanon."[36] Finally, Moshe Ma'oz claims that the Syrian government "wished to demonstrate to the United States, Israel's ally, that Syria, acting alone, was able to restore order in Lebanon, and thus prevent Israeli military intervention."[37]

President al-Asad is consistently assumed to have weighed these interests before ordering Syrian troops across the border. Marius Deeb provides a detailed record of the diplomatic maneuverings that preceded the intervention, concluding: "Taking all these elements into consideration, it was not difficult for Syria to intervene militarily in Lebanon to achieve its objectives. President Asad, a master of political tactics, made his moves with superb timing."[38] Eyal Zisser dissects "the secrets of Asad's success in Lebanon, a place where many have failed in the past." Among these secrets are "perseverance in pursuing goals"; "infinite patience and forbearance"; "extreme devotion to the task at hand"; and "infinite caution." Regarding the last of these four traits, Zisser remarks that "Asad by nature does not hurry, and since he lacks a sense of the dramatic or a penchant for theatrics, he is a cautious and prudent man, who thinks through his moves very carefully, who will always check the route he pursues from the outset and along the way. In fact Asad would prefer not to precede [sic] along it at all."[39] Consequently, "Syria's years-long involvement in Lebanon has for the most part been characterized by a lack of Syrian initiative, or more accurately, by a policy of wait-and-see. The only veritable Syrian initiative in Lebanon, was the very decision to enter that country in 1976."[40]

President al-Asad was able to act in pursuit of Syria's strategic interests in the spring of 1976 because Damascus's relations with Washington and Moscow changed. Reuven Avi-Ran claims that "the Americans, in the months preceding the Syrian invasion of Lebanon, no longer attempted to arrest the process of Syrian military intervention, but sought to contain and to neutralize the risks which this process involved."[41] Similarly, Yosef Olmert argues that despite initial warnings from Washington, Moscow, and Jerusalem to refrain from intervening, "[President] Assad decided to invade Lebanon, backed publicly by only one Arab country, Jordan, with Saudi Arabia quietly in support as well." What finally tipped the scale in favor of intervention was a belated "green light" from the United States.[42] Itamar Rabinovich surveys "the various political strategies employed by Syria during the summer of 1976" and concludes that direct military intervention was the best way for Damascus to "bolster its independence vis-à-vis the Soviet Union and . . . obtain American support for its policy in the Arab-Israeli conflict and for its regional ambitions."[43]

Although such explanations appear plausible on their face, they do not satisfactorily account for Syrian policy. First, it remains unclear why the operation was undertaken in June 1976 rather than earlier that year, when both conditions in Lebanon and relations between Syria and the Palestine Liberation Organization had been considerably more propitious. By delaying the operation until June, Damascus found itself alienated from its traditional allies inside Lebanon, criticized by other Arab governments, unable to withdraw without appearing to be a stooge either of the Americans or of the Israelis, and directly undermining its own best strategic interests regarding the Arab-Israeli conflict.[44] The assumption of the rationality of actors inherent in structural arguments is inconsistent with such an evidently suboptimal choice on Syria's part.

Second, existing explanations have trouble explaining why the Syrian regime used regular army units rather than irregular forces to bring the warring parties in Lebanon under control. Damascus had long experience carrying out covert military operations across its western border. By making better use of Syrian-controlled guerrilla units in Lebanon, Syria's leaders could have achieved most if not all of the strategic objectives listed by Dawisha, Tschirgi, AbuKhalil, and Rabinovich—without suffering the political and economic costs associated with overt intervention.

Explanations for the vicissitudes of Syrian-Iraqi relations tend to highlight irreconcilable differences between contending branches of the Ba'th party. Competition between the Syrian and Iraqi wings of the party can be traced to the early 1960s, when rival Ba'thi leaders almost simultaneously seized power in Damascus and Baghdad.[45] Tensions heightened over the next two decades, as the two governments found themselves increasingly at odds over such issues as fees for transporting Iraqi petroleum through pipelines located on Syrian territory and the distribution of Euphrates River water flowing downstream through Syria into Iraq.[46] Syrian-Iraqi hostility was compounded as a result of Damascus's decision to ally with the Islamic Republic of Iran when war erupted between Baghdad and Tehran in September 1980.[47]

Ideological explanations for important shifts in relations between Damascus and Baghdad run up against notable difficulties when trying to account for periodic outbursts of collaboration between the rival Ba'thi regimes.[48] One such outburst followed Egypt's unexpected renunciation of armed struggle against Israel in the fall of 1977; this episode is usually represented as little more than a temporary accommodation in the face of a common threat.[49] But other, even more short-lived reconciliations characterized Syrian-Iraqi relations both before and after the rapprochement of 1977–1978.[50] Arguments based on persistent differences in the political programs advocated by the Ba'thi regimes in Damascus and Baghdad cannot explain such fluctuations.

Other accounts substitute changes in Soviet policy for ideological disagreements as the stimulus for shifts in Syrian-Iraqi relations. On this view, increasing Soviet military and economic assistance after 1980 provided Damascus with the capacity to stand up to Baghdad and Jerusalem at the same time. Syria's brief rapprochement with Iraq consequently collapsed.[51] This argument has trouble accounting for the outbreak of the April 1982 Syrian-Iraqi crisis, however, because the greatest upsurge in Soviet aid took place in the aftermath of the Israeli invasion of Lebanon that June.[52]

Much more promising is Eberhard Kienle's claim that twists and turns in Syrian-Iraqi relations throughout the Ba'thi era can be traced to the fact that neither Syria nor Iraq was sufficiently well-grounded as a nation-state in the 1950s. As a result, neither country's rulers could afford to ignore actual or potential alliances between their primary opponents and political actors based in the other capital.[53] This state of affairs was exacerbated rather than ameliorated by the advent of Ba'thi

9

regimes in Damascus and Baghdad. Both ruling coalitions remained riven by internal splits and threatened by powerful domestic challengers, which led the two regimes to create periodic confrontations with one another to "rally their [respective] Ba'thi supporters, civilian and military alike, many of whom, for different reasons, could be tempted to shift their allegiance to the [other, rival] Ba'th."[54]

Unfortunately, Kienle abandons this line of argument in his discussion of the renewed rivalry that broke out between Damascus and Baghdad after 1979. Instead, he traces growing tension between the two states during these years to "the competition for influence and perhaps supremacy in the politics of the region." But in contrast to the situation from 1968 to 1972, "Iraq initially continued to be the stronger side and accordingly provoked the deterioration in relations in and after spring 1980. Syria, on the contrary, was still weak when the conflict broke open again and would have liked to preserve with Iraq a relationship as co-operative and free from conflict as possible."[55] This comment contradicts the general case, presented so compellingly in other sections of Kienle's study, that increases in domestic instability inside Syria tend to generate conflict, not conciliation, in Damascus's dealings with Baghdad. Furthermore, Kienle himself presents fragmentary evidence that rising political unrest inside each of the two countries played a key role in scuttling the 1978–1979 unity proposal.[56] Syrian military commanders appear to have been particularly concerned that unification with Iraq would undermine the internal stability of the al-Asad regime.[57] It is therefore likely that shifts in Damascus's policy toward Baghdad can be linked to developments in Syrian domestic politics.

Syria's turn toward conciliation in its dealings with Turkey as the 1990s began is usually explained in terms of long-term trends in the distribution of power in the Middle East. Daniel Pipes, for instance, offers "some reasons to be optimistic about Turkish-Syrian relations," the most important of which are the two governments' common interests vis-à-vis Iraq and "Turkey's leverage from its water projects [along the Euphrates, which] may lead to a greater degree of Syrian caution."[58] In addition, a steady expansion in trade between the two countries provides a basis for closer cooperation in strategic and diplomatic affairs.[59]

Growing Turkish power is presumed to engender moderation in

Syria's posture toward Turkey thanks largely to the pragmatism that characterizes the current Syrian political elite. David Kushner observes that "the real turning point in Turkish-Syrian relations, with Syria beginning to demonstrate a readiness to achieve understanding with its northern neighbor, may be linked with the ousting from power in late 1970 of Salah Jedid and his replacement by the Ba'ath faction headed by Hafez al-Assad."[60] Nevertheless, the Syrian leadership has consistently "remained somewhat cool and aloof, even when ready to respond" to Turkish overtures. "The explanation," Kushner suggests, "seems to lie in the particular mind-set which has conditioned Syrian attitudes towards Turkey—and towards other countries, as well—and in the way Syrian regimes have exploited this disposition." Syrian frustration over France's 1939 decision to cede the region around Iskandarun to Turkey, in particular, "has exercised a strong impact on Syrian attitudes."[61]

Most observers expect Syria's policy toward its neighbors to be more conciliatory following the disappearance of the country's primary strategic patron, the Soviet Union. As Alasdair Drysdale and Raymond Hinnebusch remark, "Since Soviet commitments to Syria's security are clearly weaker than they were a decade ago, Asad has to be more cautious in dealing with Israel and the United States."[62] Such caution spills over into Damascus's dealings with other regional powers as well. Eyal Zisser claims that Syria took steps to repair its ties to Egypt at the end of 1989 partly to reduce its isolation in the Arab world but largely as a means of "achieving another central objective—improving its relations with the US."[63] A desire to curry favor with Washington also prompted the Syrian leadership to contribute troops to the United States–led campaign to roll back the 1990 Iraqi occupation of Kuwait. And it convinced Damascus finally to distance itself from clandestine organizations fighting against the Turkish authorities, most notably the Kurdistan Workers' party.[64] These moves succeeded not only in establishing a working relationship with the United States but also in winning greater financial assistance from the Arab Gulf states.[65]

It is not as compelling as it seems, however, to connect changes in Syria's strategic circumstances to shifts in Damascus's foreign policy at the outset of the post–Cold War era. Syrian willingness to join the United States and Saudi Arabia in driving Iraqi forces out of Kuwait was highly overdetermined.[66] The al-Asad regime adapted itself relatively handily to a world in which the Soviet Union no longer existed.[67] And although Damascus accepted Washington's invitation to participate in peace talks with Israel beginning in 1991, it appears to have done so reluctantly, and its positions on virtually all of the issues in dispute moderated little if at all as the negotiations progressed.[68] Thus recent improvements in Turkey's strategic position vis-à-vis Syria could persuade Damascus just as easily to adopt a confrontational posture toward Ankara as a conciliatory stance. Spelling out the domestic political dynamics that tend to push the al-Asad regime along one path rather than the other is important for both conceptual and practical purposes.

POLITICAL ECONOMY AND FOREIGN CONFLICT

As a way of explaining key episodes of foreign expansion in early nineteenth-century Egypt and in contemporary Iraq, I have suggested that states tend to adopt imperialist or aggressive foreign policies whenever domestic opposition to the regime becomes particularly severe.[69] Rulers can generally parry challenges emanating from relatively weak or isolated political rivals by mobilizing resources available at home. But well-organized challengers, or opponents who enjoy institutional arrangements that mitigate against collective action problems among themselves, or a conjunction of challenges arising from several different domestic arenas simultaneously pose a threat that cannot be parried using internal means.

Furthermore, as the level of domestic threat to the regime rises, each of the forces inside the ruling coalition is likely to take steps to secure its own position, which simultaneously jeopardize the interests of its political allies. Growing contradictions within the dominant social coalition increase the likelihood that challengers can succeed in overthrowing the existing political order. Faced with a conjunction of burgeoning opposition and heightened intraregime friction, governments pursue expansionist foreign policies in an effort to capture additional resources that can be used not only to co-opt or suppress the regime's primary opponents, but also to ameliorate fundamental conflicts of interest among the members of the dominant coalition itself.

The domestic challenges that pose the greatest threat to the dominant social coalition are precisely those that arise in the context of crises of accumulation in the local economy. Accumulation crises have the potential to disrupt the orderly expansion and consolidation of a country's industry, agriculture, and commerce, setting the stage for what Peter Bell and Harry Cleaver have called "the development of the working class as a revolutionary subject" or for what Rod Aya has termed a "revolutionary situation," in which wholesale shifts in the distribution of power between the dominant coalition and its most powerful domestic rivals can take place.[70] It is therefore imperative to spell out as precisely as possible the political-economic dynamics that predispose market-oriented economies with substantial private ownership of property to regular crises of accumulation.

Karl Marx's own explication of the workings of capitalist systems is sufficiently opaque to invite a wide variety of competing, if not mutually exclusive, crisis theories. What James O'Connor calls "orthodox" Marxian theories associate accumulation crises with at least one of three broad dynamics: (1) the tendency of the rate of profit to fall, (2) the overaccumulation of capital, or (3) increasingly disproportionate capital accumulation across different departments of the economy.[71] Such theories complement influential but fundamentally heterodox Marxian explanations for crises of capitalist accumulation couched in terms of either a trend toward underconsumption or a secular decline in the ratio of profits to wages (the "profit squeeze").[72] Even more unorthodox views situate the eruption of political-economic crises in the context of growing discrepancies between the requirements of capital accumulation and the demands of regime legitimation.[73] Other writers extend the logic of Marxian crisis theory to economies in which state sectors predominate.[74]

Three recent contributions to the extensive Marxian literature on the origins and development of accumulation crises provide the conceptual underpinnings for the explanation of Syrian foreign policy offered in the following chapters. Each of these lines of argument significantly broadens the scope of conventional radical analyses without abandoning the distinctive features of Marxian political economy. Each is presented cogently and accessibly, and each implies falsifiable propositions that can be confronted with empirical evidence.

13

Financial Contributions to Accumulation Crises

By highlighting the dynamics of production in capitalist economies, virtually all Marxian crisis theories give short shrift to the financial sector. James Crotty argues against an overemphasis on production, claiming that ignoring "money, credit, and financial intermediation" is not only inconsistent with Marx's own theoretical project, but has also hindered subsequent efforts to explain secular trends in market-based, profit-oriented economies.[75] Although money plays little if any part in primitive economies, where barter constitutes the predominant means whereby goods change hands, other economic systems make use of money to transform what Marx calls use value into exchange value. Because one must first sell things in order to acquire the money needed to buy other things, and because such transactions do not occur instantaneously, these two values tend to diverge.[76] When an inordinate amount of time passes between the sale of one item and the purchase of another, money's efficiency as a medium of exchange diminishes, substantially increasing the costs of trade.[77]

During periods of expansion, rising rates of return on investment tend to coincide with stable interest rates, "opening up a gap between [the two rates] which fuels the investment boom." But as the overall rate of return approaches its zenith, the gap narrows: "The interest rate is both pulled up by the strong demand for loanable funds by businesses lusting to take maximum advantage of the high profits of the period, and pushed up by the increasing illiquidity of the economy."[78] As returns on investment peak and then decline, only a small "margin of safety or margin of error separat[es] gross profit flows from required interest payments and principal payments."[79] Since payments are fixed by the credit system, they cannot be altered in response to unexpected downturns in returns on investment or profits. And when "contractual obligations cannot be fulfilled, the credit system comes under duress, confidence shatters, interest rates soar, risk aversion rises dramatically and the forced sale of real and financial assets caused by a desperate effort to obtain money as a means of payment sends commodity and financial asset prices into a tailspin."[80] Meanwhile, increasingly worried capitalists stop making new investments, and the economy stagnates.[81]

What transforms periodic economic downturns into crises of accumulation is the degree of rigidity that characterizes a country's system of credit and contracts at the moment difficulties appear. If sufficient slack or adaptability is present in the credit-contract network, market dynamics can compensate for unanticipated shortfalls in production and sales. But if credit arrangements and contracts are instead pervasive and comparatively inflexible, the damage resulting from such shortfalls is compounded.[82] Since capitalist political-economic orders possess the most extensive and intricate networks of credit and financial contracts, they tend to experience the most severe accumulation crises. Crotty concludes that "the condition of the contract-credit structure is a prime codeterminant of the depth and duration of the economic downturn in Marx's crisis theory. It is the severity of the decline in the profit rate in combination with the condition of the contract matrix that dictates the dynamics of the crisis, downturn and stagnation."[83] Accumulation crises occur when the network of credit and contracts becomes too rigid or too fragile, aggravating rather than dampening periodic dislocations that arise in production and distribution.

Intracapital Competition

Despite their shared class position, capitalists exhibit considerable heterogeneity. Every sector or industry includes some enterprises that make more efficient use of capital than others. Uncoordinated investment in new equipment and productive techniques tends to equalize profit rates across different sectors of the economy, while at the same time generating differential profit rates among firms operating within the same sector or industry.[84] Efforts on the part of more efficient producers to maintain their momentary advantage, in conjunction with attempts by less efficient producers to match the reduced cost structures enjoyed by the more efficient, spark escalating competition for new investment capital. Such heightened competition prevents capitalists from collaborating to reverse the tendency of the rate of profit to fall.[85]

So long as capital can move easily out of less productive sectors, industries, or firms into more productive ones, accumulation proceeds relatively smoothly. But whenever capital concentrates in a limited number of enterprises, the movement of investment into other parts of the economy lags, leading rates of profit to diverge across different sectors, industries, and firms.[86] More efficient producers can then, as Gerard

De Bernis notes, "put new techniques into operation to get around workers' resistance and the 'productivity crisis,' financing these new investments by price rises (inflation) since profit is insufficient." Such tactics enable these producers to boost rates of output and profit, particularly if their operations enjoy economies of scale; "nonetheless the structural stability of the process of accumulation has been broken."[87]

Uneven development among firms active in the same sector or industry thus militates against the emergence of "a stable, sustainable, relationship among capitals," John Weeks points out.[88] Firms that introduce new equipment or innovative techniques of production cannot realize increases in value until their products are sold. Only then, through competition with less efficient firms, do their investments begin to pay off. Until that time, "a rise in the technical composition of capital has occurred but the rate of surplus value has not changed."[89] This dynamic, which Marx calls the law of the tendency of the rate of profit to fall, is partially offset by interactions between more efficient and less efficient producers, resulting in "the reduction of [exchange] values" for commodities produced by all firms.[90]

Yet even the workings of the market tend to exacerbate the instability associated with uneven development. Older producers suffer most when exchange values drop in particular sectors or industries. Eventually, "the money capital which returns after realization of commodities will be less than the money capital advanced for fixed means of production," inflicting substantial losses upon less efficient firms.[91] Producers therefore have no choice but to engage in constant competition to update their means of production.[92] But because markets virtually never operate perfectly, the devaluation of fixed capital suffered by less efficient firms seldom if ever matches the increase in value gained by more efficient ones. Consequently, "overinvestment" is likely to occur, precipitating a particularly severe form of accumulation crisis.[93]

Locating Accumulation Crises

One of the primary ways in which capitalists compete to lower their respective production costs is by investing in equipment and physical plant. This tactic effectively reduces the amount of labor required to produce goods, or in Marxian terminology devalues the commodities produced, while boosting productivity. But it also creates more productive capacity than is needed to satisfy present demand, a dynamic Marx calls overaccumulation.[94] In addition, it takes considerable time and effort to manufacture and install equipment and to construct physical plant. Such activities not only immobilize capital for inordinate amounts of time but also require lengthy periods of (full) operation to recoup the initial investments.[95]

Some capitalists realize disproportionate profits because of the favorable geographical situation of their plants. Others, who find themselves "in disadvantaged locations, . . . could compensate for that disadvantage by adopting a superior technology, and vice versa," as David Harvey explains.[96] They might also take steps to "disturb and alter the conditions under which the preceding spatial equilibrium . . . was achieved."[97] Such measures include extending the area in which their goods are marketed, relocating plants, concentrating operations to achieve economies of scale, and separating the various phases of the productive process so that different kinds of operations are situated more efficiently with regard to inputs of labor and raw materials.[98] The competition among firms that is associated with the emergence and deepening of uneven development in any given industry thus has a notable geographical dimension.

Moreover, capital invested in equipment and physical plant can be reallocated only with great difficulty. As Harvey observes, "producers are firmly pinned down for long time periods through reliance upon fixed capital of long turnover time embedded in the land itself."[99] Since capital is utilized at varying rates in different stages of production, the inertia entailed by investment in equipment and physical plant injects a measure of coherence and predictability into the "frenetic instability" that characterizes capitalist production. At the same time, however, this inertia makes it virtually impossible for firms to relocate without incurring additional costs associated with devaluation at some point in the extended circuit of production and reproduction. The conjunction of these two antagonistic dynamics produces "an even deeper version of that contradiction which plagues the circulation of fixed capital. Capitalism increasingly relies upon fixed capital (including that embedded in a specific landscape of production) to revolutionize the value productivity of labour, only to find that its fixity (the specific geographical distribution) becomes the barrier to be overcome."[100] The establishment of particular plants greatly inhibits the mobility of capital, making it harder for capitalists to respond to shifts in market conditions. In Harvey's words, "the more the forces of geographical inertia prevail, the deeper will the aggregate crises of capitalism become and the more savage will switching crises have to be to restore the disturbed equilibrium."[101]

Moreover, spatial factors accelerate the fall of the rate of profit. Skeptics contend that firms can always reduce labor costs by introducing new technologies, which maintain or even raise profit rates so long as real wages remain constant.[102] But Eric Sheppard and Trevor Barnes posit that whenever technological innovations alter the production functions that characterize specific regions, perhaps by adding the expense of transporting inputs necessary to keep the new equipment operating, then "it is possible that the total cost of production . . . will increase for some sectors in some regions." Sheppard and Barnes go on to infer that under these circumstances, the key "condition [under which it is possible] for technical change to increase profits does not apply, thereby making it difficult to predict profit rates in a changing space economy."[103] In the real world, made up of diverse geographical regions, it is more likely that rates of profit will decline than that they will rise or remain constant.[104] Only if capital is extraordinarily mobile, as Neil Smith notes, can it "remain one step ahead of the falling rate of profit."[105]

Accumulation Crises in Ba'thi Syria

Concepts adduced by recent contributions to Marxian crisis theory can be applied only loosely to the case of Ba'thi Syria. Despite the exceptional comprehensiveness and reliability of the annual statistical series published by the Syrian government, large lacunae remain. Figures indicating rates of return on investment or profits generated by public and private firms represent a particularly glaring omission from the yearbooks. More important, data are nonexistent for virtually all aspects of labor in contemporary Syria, making it impossible to calculate meaningful measures of productivity and profitability. Such gaps heighten the distortions that usually accompany attempts to fit official statistics into Marxian analytical categories.

Moreover, Ba'thi Syria bears only slight resemblance to the paradigmatic capitalist economy hypothesized by Marxian scholarship. In the years since the 1963 revolution, credit has been allocated exclusively by state financial institutions, whose directors pay little attention to the market when they make decisions about investment. Private enterprise has been tightly regulated by agencies of the central administration. Joint-stock companies were nationalized and large agricultural holdings sequestered soon after the Ba'thi regime consolidated power. As a result, many of the specific links in the Marxian chain of argument ring false in the Syrian case.

Private enterprise, however, remained a major component of the local economy even after the nationalizations of the 1960s. Furthermore, both public and private sector firms have throughout the Ba'thi era oriented themselves toward realizing positive rates of return on investment. Ba'thi socialism has consistently aimed at maximizing employment, while at the same time satisfying domestic demand for capital goods and consumer products at heavily subsidized prices. But Syria's public sector managers never abandoned the objective of making a profit. In fact, efforts to maximize profits in state-run companies have become more and more central to the regime's general economic program as the Ba'thi era has progressed.[106]

Insights derived from Marxian work on credit and finance, competition among capitals and the spatial aspects of accumulation therefore provide the inspiration for an analysis of recent trends in the economy of Ba'thi Syria. Elaborating these insights, no matter how imperfectly, not only illuminates the connection between internal crises of accumulation and shifts in Syrian policy toward external adversaries in the years after 1963 but also indicates a path that further investigations might fruitfully take in exploring the relationship between domestic political-economic transformation and foreign policy.

CHAPTER ONE

Provoking Confrontation
with Israel, 1967

Sporadic clashes between the Syrian and Israeli armed forces were a recurrent feature of Middle Eastern affairs throughout the two decades following the 1948 Arab-Israeli war. The terms of the July 1949 cease-fire left Damascus and Tel Aviv each holding strategically important but vulnerable territories along the northern shore of Lake Tiberias, and attempts by either state to enhance its military position within its respective domain constituted a clear and direct threat to the security of the other—a classic security dilemma. On any number of occasions, this situation precipitated violent confrontations between the two countries' armed forces. In February 1960, for example, Israeli settlers advanced into the demilitarized zone around al-Tawfiq, provoking Syrian artillery attacks on the district that in turn provided the pretext for a massive strike against Syrian positions by Israeli warplanes.[1] A combination of overall Israeli military superiority and pervasive disunity within the Arab camp generally limited the scale and effectiveness of Syria's responses to Israel's initiatives along their common border, while Damascus's own moves were as often directed against neighboring Arab capitals as they were against the purported common enemy.[2]

But throughout the spring of 1967, Syria adopted a markedly more belligerent stance in its strategic interaction with Israel. Richard Parker reports that knowledgeable observers in Washington at the time considered the Syrian government to be "following an adventuresome policy on the border that risked a violent Israeli response."[3] Soviet diplomats appear to have concurred: Moscow's ambassador to Syria claims that the leadership in Damascus "was well aware of the risk of forceful Israeli retaliation and had no illusions about the disparity between their two forces. It was concerned about what was likely to happen," he continues, "but was hoping to enflame the Arab world."[4] According to Avner Yaniv, leaders in Damascus decided in the fall of 1966 "to embark upon a strategy which would mirror image Israel's own strategy. Instead of merely reacting to Israeli action or attempting to stop one or another Israeli project, Syria would henceforth initiate military action on a large scale, including an extensive use of air power."[5] Thus on 7 April 1967, when Israeli farmers once again moved armored tractors into the demilitarized zone north of Lake Tiberias, Syrian units retaliated not only with artillery and mortar fire but also with tank and aircraft forays into the disputed area. Israeli armored and air force units counterattacked, bombarding villages lying just across the border in Syria proper and engaging Syrian warplanes in the skies over the suburbs of Damascus itself.

In the wake of this battle, Damascus stepped up its support for guerrilla operations on the part of Palestinian commandos based in Jordan and Lebanon. In addition, the Syrian government dispatched a succession of military missions to Cairo in an effort to persuade the Egyptian leadership to implement the provisions of the mutual defense pact signed by the two regimes in early November 1966. Persistent Syrian pressure, accompanied by reports from Soviet officials that the Israel Defense Forces (IDF) had begun massing for a major offensive along the Syrian-Israeli border, finally convinced Egypt's President Gamal 'Abd al-Nasir to request the withdrawal of the United Nations Emergency Force from the Sinai on 16 May and to close the Straits of Tiran to Israeli shipping six days later.[6] Whether or not 'Abd al-Nasir intended to launch an Arab-Israeli war, the latter move constituted, in Charles Yost's words, "the final fatal step."[7] War erupted on the morning of 5 June in the form of a series of coordinated Israeli strikes against Egypt's primary military airfields.

Syrian belligerence played a crucial role in escalating the confrontation of April–May 1967 into open warfare between the Arab states and Israel. Left to its own devices, the Egyptian regime would no doubt have sidestepped combat with the IDF. Malcolm Kerr remarks that during these months "Nasir had more important things to do than to make war on Israel. He had said a hundred times that the liberation of Palestine must wait—for the unification of the Arab states, for the spread of the socialist revolution, for the preparation of the Arab armies, for the isolation of Israel from the United States. He raised so many conditions that doubts began to arise that he ever intended to liberate Palestine at all. In any case, 1967 was not the year for it."[8] The leadership in Damascus, however, adopted a much more confrontational posture. When Israeli Prime Minister Levi Eshkol told reporters on 13 May that the Israel Defense Forces intended to attack Syrian positions at a time and place of their own choosing in retaliation for Palestinian raids, Damascus persuaded Cairo to activate the heretofore dormant unified Arab command structure to meet future challenges with force.[9] A week later, Minister of Defense Major General Hafiz al-Asad told the local daily *al-Thawrah* that Syrian jets had repeatedly penetrated Israeli airspace during the preceding week and that the regular army, "which had its finger on the trigger," was clamoring for war. "As a military man," al-Asad concluded, "I feel that the time has come to wage the liberation battle. In my opinion it is necessary to adopt at least the minimum measures required to strike a disciplinary blow at Israel."[10] Explaining why the regime in Damascus adopted the policies that precipitated the 1967 war, instead of backing away from the armed confrontation with Israeli forces which erupted that spring, requires an abbreviated look at the domestic struggles that shaped Syria's political-economic trajectory during the early years of the Ba'thi era.

CONSOLIDATING BA'THI RULE, 1963–1965

Little united the diverse collection of military officers that staged the coup d'état of March 1963 save its members' common opposition to the civilian government that came to power in Damascus following Syria's secession from the United Arab Republic in September 1961. This heterogeneous group included not only active members of the Ba'th party but also independent socialist, Nasirist, and other unionist officers; the participants in the coup hailed from the larger north-central cities of Homs and Aleppo, from peripheral districts around Hamah and Latakia, from the more insular communities of al-Suwayda to the south, and from the largely agricultural provinces of Dayr al-Zur and al-Hasakah in the far northeast. In ideology, these officers ranged from scientific socialists heavily influenced by the concepts of orthodox Marxism-Leninism to comparatively moderate reformers willing to co-operate with the country's existing urban and rural bourgeoisie. It is therefore not surprising that the new regime's economic policies vacil-lated between the poles of encouraging the creation of a state-directed socialist society on the one hand and maintaining private enterprise, particularly in industry and commerce, on the other.

During its first months in power, the new regime took two significant steps designed to limit the role of private capital within the Syrian economy. On 2 May 1963, government officials published a decree nationalizing all indigenous banks and insurance companies. The for-mer were subsequently reorganized into five new state-managed finan-cial institutions as a way of concentrating their reserves so they could be used more efficiently.[11] Next, on 23 June, the authorities promulgated an Agrarian Reform Law that superseded a less stringent 1962 law; the new measure set severe limitations on the size of private landholdings, while at the same time easing the terms under which peasants could purchase agricultural land of their own.[12] The ceilings imposed on individual landholdings were lowered three months later, with the re-vised upper limits varying between fifteen and fifty-five hectares for irrigated land and between eighty and two hundred hectares for nonir-rigated land.[13]

Such measures reflected the political-economic program advocated by the more radical wing of the Ba'th, whose supporters were to be found primarily in the party's affiliated trade unions—particularly in Homs and working-class districts of Damascus—and in the poorer agri-cultural areas of Dir'a, al-Suwayda, Dayr al-Zur, and al-Hasakah.[14] Wher-ever officials from these branches of the party held key administrative posts, the private sector found itself subjected to increasing state con-trol. In Aleppo, for instance, the new Ba'thi governor nationalized bak-eries throughout the city during the summer of 1963, a move that was hotly debated at the party's sixth National (Pan-Arab) Congress in early October.[15]

At the same time, however, more moderate members of the regime made a concerted effort to reassure private businesspeople that na-tionalization would not be pursued against "productive industrial busi-ness sectors, which sincerely serve the interests of the people."[16] Thus the new minister of the economy, 'Abd al-Karim Zuhur, justified the nationalization of Syria's private banks both because of the inordinate influence these institutions had exerted over bourgeois politicians before 1963 and because of their directors' reluctance to invest more than a small proportion of their available capital in local productive projects. In line with this less doctrinaire orientation, state officials relaxed the controls that had been imposed on foreign exchange and began allowing banks to sell foreign currency freely during the latter half of the year.[17] By taking steps to pacify propertied interests, especially the country's influential urban merchants and larger manufacturers, moderates based in the central administration were able to win the continued acquiescence if not the active support of Syria's small-scale tradespeople, who were deeply suspicious of the Nasirists within the dominant social coalition.[18]

As 1963 came to a close, friction between the two wings of the regime grew more pronounced. Radical delegates to the sixth National (Pan-Arab) Congress of the Ba'th party pushed a resolution through the convention that committed the central administration in Damascus to the establishment of large-scale collective farms on land expropriated under the terms of the revised Agrarian Reform Law. At the same time, their more moderate colleagues managed to postpone the nationalization of Syria's larger industrial establishments until a comprehensive survey of the country's manufacturing sector could be undertaken.[19] As the party debated these matters, record levels of agricultural output and a dramatic expansion of the private sector began to overtax the state's capacity to administer Syrian economic affairs. The overall growth of the economy, augmented by increasing oil revenues, led to severe inflation in the cities during the fourth quarter of the year.[20] The price rises effectively reduced the wages of public sector workers by around 15 percent, threatening to alienate the regime from one of its strongest bases of support.[21] In an effort to reconsolidate its ties to organized labor, the leadership of the Ba'th adopted measures prohibiting "arbitrary dismissals" and mandating one-week paid vacations for all employees in industrial and commercial establishments that employed more than fifteen workers.[22]

Growing incompatibilities among the forces that made up the ruling coalition during the first quarter of 1964 provided an opportunity for small-scale private tradespeople to initiate a wave of strikes and demonstrations that swept across Syria's north-central cities beginning

24

in mid-February. The first of these incidents involved a clash between Ba'thi and non-Ba'thi students in Banyas; this confrontation was followed by a general strike by independent merchants and craftspeople in Homs. By the last week of March, popular unrest had spread to Aleppo as well. But the most serious disorders broke out in Hamah: a general strike by that city's shopkeepers on 12 April led the regime to promise that it would begin allocating greater amounts of investment monies to the province. When this announcement failed to end the strike, the authorities deployed regular army units in and around the older quarters of the city to quash the rebellion.[23] As the tradespeople's revolt spread to isolated districts of Damascus at the end of the month, the government repeated its two-pronged strategy of offering economic concessions to the strikers—this time in the form of easier credit for small-scale commercial concerns—while employing more forcible means of suppressing their activities by ordering the recently formed cadres of the National Guard to reopen any shops whose owners joined in the protest.[24] In some areas of the city, the regime sanctioned the administration of "workers' justice" against striking shopkeepers by members of the state-supported and armed Workers' Companies (*al-kataib al-'ummaliyyah*), composed of militant trade unionists from the larger cities led by Khalid al-Jundi.[25]

In the wake of these events, forces within Syria's ruling coalition that favored accommodating local capital redoubled their efforts to circumscribe the role of the state in promoting social justice. Salah al-Din Bitar, the newly appointed Ba'thi prime minister, affirmed on 23 May that the private sector would continue to play a major role in the initial stages of the transition to socialism. His generally pragmatic orientation toward economic affairs was buttressed by the fact that the private sector had succeeded in carrying out 141 percent of its investment goals under the Five-Year Plan initiated in 1960, whereas the public sector had met only 56 percent of its objectives.[26] In an attempt to combine public and private enterprise with a minimum of conflict, the cabinet proposed the formation of a "common sector" within the Syrian economy, in which the state would purchase 25 percent of particular firms and assist in managing them in partnership with their private owners. In addition, the regime effectively abandoned its plan to establish state-run collective farms on expropriated agricultural lands by incorporating this project into a broader program of government support for relatively autonomous agrarian cooperatives.[27] Taken together, these moves represented a resurgence of the more accommodationist wing of the Ba'th at the expense of trade unionists and radicals based in the provinces.

But at the same time that Syria's state administrators were carrying out a comparatively moderate program intended to placate the private sector, more radical measures continued to be implemented by doctrinaire socialists within the regime. In Aleppo and Latakia, provincial authorities enjoying close ties to the trade unions nationalized a number of larger industrial concerns as a way of punishing local notables who had sponsored the rebellions of March and April. Among these were seven of the country's largest textile mills, which accounted for almost three-quarters of domestic cloth production. Local party officials instituted a form of self-management in these companies, with factory-level councils—consisting of seven members each, four of whom were elected from among the workers at each plant and the remaining three appointed by the government, the party apparatus, and the appropriate trade union—supervising both day-to-day operations and the distribution of profits. The latter was undertaken according to a formula mandating that 30 percent of the firm's profits be appropriated by the state, 30 percent allocated for expansion of the plant, 25 percent be given directly to the workers, 5 percent set aside for unspecified social needs, and 10 percent used to construct workers' housing.[28] By mid-1964, militant trade unionists were again playing a greater role in formulating economic and social policy at the national level as well. A government decree published that summer sanctioned the formation of a nationwide trade union federation authorized to undertake a wide range of political activities.[29] This move accompanied the adoption of a new labor law that substantially expanded the state's role in championing the rights of organized labor.

During the third week of July, the Military Committee of the Ba'th orchestrated a conference of the party's branch secretaries in Damascus charged with reconciling the more moderate or accommodationist wing of the regime with its more radical components. The congress resolved to carry out this task by enhancing the degree of party supervision over the new trade union federation and other party-affiliated "popular front organizations" (al-munazzamat al-wajihiyyah al-sha'biyyah). To accomplish this goal, the delegates abandoned the

Ba'th's conception of itself as a vanguard party, insulated from the mainstream of Syrian society, and announced instead that the party would assume direct control of the central bureaucracy as a means of administering domestic affairs. At the same time, the party reorganized its local branches into two subbranches: one in which membership would be based on regional identity and one in which membership would be determined by occupation or sector of employment. According to this scheme, "workers, traders and craftsmen, women, university and high-school students and teachers were to be registered in separate subbranches while maintaining their affiliation with the regional ones."[30] These steps provided moderates within the regime with the means not only to isolate and contain their more radical colleagues but also to impose upon them a measure of discipline without transforming the Ba'th into a mass party.

Radical forces resisted attempts by the moderates to subordinate them to the Ba'th party apparatus. Avowed socialists led by Akram Hawrani launched a campaign that August to pressure the government to "democratize" Syria's internal affairs. This faction's demands, Tabitha Petran notes, received "broad support . . . especially among rank-and-file Ba'thists."[31] In mid-September, the party's Regional (Syrian) Command renounced the accommodationist stance of the Bitar cabinet, replacing it with a government led by the leftist General Amin al-Hafiz and composed almost exclusively of party militants. The resurgence of the radical wing of the regime under the aegis of this government was evident in the appointment of a prominent trade union leader as minister of labor and that of 'Abd al-Karim al-Jundi, a hard-line socialist from the Isma'ili community of Hamah province, as minister of agrarian reform.[32]

Private businesspeople reacted to the growing strength of minoritarian radicals and trade unionists within the dominant coalition by withdrawing greater amounts of capital from their operations in Syria and transferring these funds out of the country. By February 1964, an estimated 900 million Syrian pounds had been pulled out of the domestic economy and reinvested overseas.[33] Although precise figures are unavailable, it appears that this movement escalated as the year went by. Petran reports that "the flight of capital out of the country had reached staggering proportions" during October and November.[34] Fragmentary data on capital formation confirm this assessment: after rising steadily

27

during the years from 1957 to 1962, private gross fixed capital formation fell by almost one-quarter in 1963, stagnated in 1964, and then
dropped almost 40 percent in 1965. For 1964 as a whole, gross fixed
capital formation ended up representing only 12 percent of Syria's
gross domestic product, a decline of 25 percent from the proportion
recorded for 1962.[35] The resulting shortage of capital was compounded by the private sector's common practice of borrowing heavily
from state-run banks and insurance companies to cover its current accounts deficits. Consequently, fewer and fewer resources remained
available to fund the expansion of domestic industry. A United Nations
team observed in 1967 that total investment in industry during the
period of the first Five-Year Plan (1960–1965) "encountered a number
of obstacles, including shortages of funds, scarcity of technicians, and
reluctance of the private sector to carry out its share of investments, as
envisaged under its plan."[36]

As the country's economic situation deteriorated during the final
quarter of 1964, state and party officials became increasingly concerned about the possibility that more radical social forces might find
grounds upon which to base a successful challenge to the regime. The
leadership of the Ba'th ordered the party's branch secretaries meeting
in Damascus in early October to devote their energies to finding innovative yet workable ways of resolving continuing difficulties in the
countryside before such problems could ignite popular unrest.[37] Meanwhile, senior members of the Military Committee expressed worries that
the appointment of 'Alawi commanders to key military and administrative posts had tarnished the regime's reputation by lending credence to
criticisms that its programs were rooted in sectarianism (taifiyyah).[38]

In an attempt to stave off popular discontent, the regime adopted a
mixed strategy of augmenting state supervision over the activities of
militant groups, while at the same time implementing some of the less
controversial programs advocated by the radicals. In early October, the
leadership of the Ba'th announced plans to create a General Federation
of Farm Laborers (al-ittihad al-'amm lil-fallahin) as a way of harnessing
the activities of the diverse collection of rural militants that composed
Syria's agrarian movement. At the same time, it proposed a wholesale
reorganization of the overarching workers' federation. These moves
accompanied a sharp increase in the confiscation and redistribution of

agricultural land, particularly in the north-central plains.[39] On 16 December, the government issued a decree reserving for the state all future revenues from the production of Syrian petroleum, a move that in Itamar Rabinovich's apt phrase "nationalized in advance" the country's oil sector.[40] This last action had been a key provision of the platform advocated by Hawrani's hard-line socialists four months earlier.

These measures put Syria's ruling coalition in a virtually untenable political situation by the end of 1964. In the first place, private property owners in both the cities and the countryside had gradually been pushed beyond the point of reconciliation with the regime as a result of the "piecemeal nationalizations" implemented by the radicals in the months after March 1963. Increasingly apprehensive about the regime's ultimate economic objectives, urban manufacturers refrained from setting up new operations and modernizing existing plants. According to Petran, "not a single industrial firm was established in the year after the *coup.*"[41] Furthermore, capital flight continued unabated, leaving the north-central cities and their surrounding agricultural areas precariously short of vital financial resources.[42] These trends generated serious sectoral dislocations within the country's economy and made coherent planning virtually impossible. In the view of those responsible for economic policy making, Syria was left with "all the evils of a liberal regime without its advantages."[43] Moreover, large landowners in the districts around Hamah and Aleppo had begun to forge a tactical alliance with various provincially based farm laborers' organizations to demand less state intervention in rural affairs, while richer merchants and private manufacturers in the north-central cities were providing support for the growing Islamist movement. Consequently, the regime's primary opponents posed a severe threat to its members' continued political predominance as 1964 drew to a close.

In the second place, radical trade unionists continued to resist subordination to the Ba'thi party-state apparatus. Demonstrations and public rallies led by local labor organizers occurred in several of Syria's larger cities throughout the fall and winter of 1964–1965, and the leaders of the General Federation of Workers' Unions made plans to convene a national congress in Homs at the end of October.[44] Although intimidation and coercion by local party cadres ensured the victory of Ba'thi candidates in the workers' federation elections that December, persistent antigovernment agitation on the part of militant labor activists led the regime to scrap some of the concessions it had offered the trade unions during the first half of 1964.[45]

Paradoxically, widespread opposition by militant trade unionists to the extension of state control resulted in a proliferation of artisanal enterprises in Syria's larger cities. As government officials attempted to establish centralized control over the larger labor syndicates in Damascus, Aleppo, and Hamah during the second half of 1964, better-off workers in these districts set themselves up as independent trades-people (*ashab 'amal*). They could thus operate small-scale workshops employing at most two or three other laborers that were exempt from a wide range of government regulations, including the requirement that wage earners become members of the state-sponsored trade union federation.[46]

Finally, members of the ruling coalition occupying important positions within the central administration increasingly came into conflict with those in the higher echelons of the Ba'th party and the armed forces during the last months of 1964.[47] The first of these two factions rallied in support of President al-Hafiz, a Sunni reservist from Aleppo who was only weakly supported by the regular officer corps. The latter coalesced around General Muhammad 'Umran, an 'Alawi from the countryside outside Homs and one of the founding members of the Military Committee of the Ba'th. At the end of October, 'Umran, chafing at the relative insignificance of his official position within the regime—that of deputy premier for industrial affairs—attempted to supplant al-Hafiz as premier and chair of the Presidency Council. This move was successfully parried by 'Umran's erstwhile comrades in the Military Committee, notably Generals Salah Jadid and Hafiz al-Asad. The latter pair favored enlarging the scope of state authority within Syrian society as a way of both providing some measure of coordination between the private and public sectors and reining in the more militant trade unionists, thereby rationalizing the country's economic and political affairs.

RESTRUCTURING THE ECONOMY, 1965–1967

Forces advocating greater state intervention in the Syrian domestic economy, led by President al-Hafiz and the Jadid–al-Asad faction of the

Military Committee of the Ba'th, along with the more radical party cadres, represented by Dr. Yusuf Zu'ayyin and 'Abd al-Karim al-Jundi, instituted a program of comprehensive nationalization in a last-ditch effort to stabilize the regime. The primary nationalization measures, promulgated on 2–4 January 1965 and later referred to as the Ramadan Socialist Decrees, imposed state control over more than one hundred of Syria's largest industrial and commercial enterprises. These firms possessed capital assets estimated officially at 243 million Syrian pounds and employed a total of almost twelve thousand workers.[48] The decrees also increased state participation from 25 percent to 75 percent or more in the fifteen other major companies that made up the "common sector."

These initial nationalizations were soon complemented by a succession of measures extending state supervision throughout the commercial and services sectors of the Syrian economy. In February, the government set up a General Establishment for Consumption (*al-muassasah al-'ammah lil-istihlakiyyah*) to regulate the internal distribution of foodstuffs and other essential consumer items. That same month the state-owned Import-Export Establishment (*al-muassasah lil-istirad wal-tasdir*) was given exclusive rights over the importation of coffee, tea, rice, paper, unrefined sugar, canned meat and fish, iron and steel products, agricultural machinery, tires, automobiles, and other goods.[49] On 3 May, state officials nationalized fifty-five of the country's largest cotton-ginning mills and took control of the exportation of cotton, wheat, and barley. By midyear, the central administration had taken over all of the larger foreign and indigenous electricity-generating companies, petroleum distribution companies, import-export firms, and wholesale trading houses operating in Syria.[50] Government officials announced plans to set up a foreign trading organization and a network of state-run marketing cooperatives to handle the distribution and sale of imported and domestic consumer goods.[51] The cornerstone of this complex, the General Organization for Cotton Ginning and Marketing (*al-haiah al-'ammah li halj wa taswiq al-aqtan*), was incorporated on 8 June.

To ensure the support of the radical trade unionists for the expansion of state control over Syria's economy, the government adopted a series of statutes aimed at improving the standard of living of the country's industrial workers. One of these measures reduced the rent on workers' housing by 25 to 30 percent. Another allotted each laborer in the nationalized and larger nonnationalized firms 150 Syrian pounds or fifteen days' pay "as their share of the 1964 profits."[52] The new benefits were covered by a substantial increase in taxes levied on private joint-stock companies and the owners of real estate. Additional revenues came from major increases in import tariffs and excise taxes on automobiles, alcoholic beverages, and other luxury items.[53] Besides these economic programs, the regime extended a variety of political benefits to its proletarian allies as well. For instance, the practice of establishing governing councils to supervise the operations of nationalized enterprises was extended to each of the companies taken over by the state in January 1965.[54]

But in the end, the nationalization of Syria's largest industrial and commercial firms did little more for the regime than substitute new political difficulties for old, although it provided the central administration with a significantly larger pool of resources upon which to draw. In particular, the Ramadan Socialist Decrees immediately created friction between state officials and well-to-do farmers: the new state-run trading company disrupted the importation of fertilizers, insecticides, and agricultural machinery—particularly tractors and motorized pumps—into the countryside. Such disruption resulted in a sharply reduced rate of capital formation in agriculture during the 1965–1966 crop year.[55] Reduced agricultural investment produced dramatic declines in output for most of Syria's major cash crops that season. Both total production and proportionate yields of wheat, barley, and lentils dropped markedly in the spring of 1966 compared to the first half of the decade. Cotton production fell only marginally, while yields actually improved, no doubt reflecting the relatively longer investment horizon of this particular crop.[56]

More important, the Ramadan Socialist Decrees marked the final step in the alienation of Syria's small-scale tradespeople from the Ba'thi regime. State officials expropriated a number of smaller workshops during the first week of January along with the larger enterprises that were the primary focus of the nationalization program. The small-scale companies, most of which dealt in soap, worsted cloth, and vegetable oils, were later quietly returned to their original owners, but not before their seizure precipitated a wave of sympathy strikes among shopkeepers in Damascus and Aleppo at the end of the month. The regime retaliated against tradespeople who took part in these actions by arresting them and confiscating their places of business. On 27 January, a special military court went so far as to condemn to death eleven men associated with the strikes on charges that they had conspired to return the country to the hands of "reactionary elements."[57]

By the middle of the year, resistance to the nationalization program among smaller-scale traders and manufacturers started to undermine the position of Syria's ruling social coalition. Continued unrest in the north-central cities, combined with growing disaffection among more moderate forcēs inside the regime, led state officials to issue a decree in mid-June turning over 5 percent of the profits of nationalized industrial firms to small shareholders as compensation.[58] When this measure failed to curtail private businesspeople's opposition to its economic policies, the government adopted a statute prohibiting membership in Rotary Clubs and Freemasons' associations throughout the country and threatened those who refused to dissociate themselves from the activities of these organizations with arrest for belonging to a clandestine international society.[59] Resistance to the extension of state control over the Syrian economy nevertheless persisted into the second half of the year, prompting the regime to announce in early December that the construction sector would be left in private hands as a token that large-scale nationalizations were coming to an end.[60]

Syria's Ba'thi ruling social coalition thus came to a turning point in 1965. Until then, the regime had been able to carry out a political-economic program designed to improve the position of smaller independent landholders and industrial workers without jeopardizing the interests of the country's small-scale urban tradespeople and manufacturers, whose activities had been primarily oriented toward the domestic market. But increasing state intervention in Syria's general economic affairs, in conjunction with a persistent shortage of capital in virtually all sectors of the economy, further constrained the operations of the petite bourgeoisie of the cities and towns. Moreover, the agricultural shortfall that became evident during the first weeks of 1966 increased popular discontent throughout Syria's north-central provinces and generated growing support for the various movements associated with the Muslim Brotherhood (*ikhwan al-muslimin*) in Aleppo, Hamah, and Homs. These developments prompted moderate forces within the regime publicly to criticize the "inordinate" expansion of the public sector and seek economic assistance from Western governments. Disagreement among

33

the members of the Military Committee of the Ba'th over how the regime should handle its burgeoning economic and political difficulties precipitated jockeying for predominance among several disparate factions inside the governing elite. This jockeying eventuated in the coup d'état of 23 February 1966, in which military officers loyal to Generals Jadid and al-Asad displaced the government headed by President al-Hafiz.

THE DOMESTIC CRISIS OF 1966–1967

Immediately following the February coup, the newly appointed cabinet led by Dr. Zu'ayyin published a statement informing foreign governments that they need not alter their relations with Syria because the country's domestic and foreign policies would remain unchanged. By the first week of March, however, the party newspaper *al-Ba'th* reported that the "mission" of the new government in Damascus was to improve Syria's economy through "developing and deepening [its] Socialist experience."[61] The turn to more radical economic and social programs was to become a distinguishing characteristic of the regime in the years after 1966. But this trend did not come about by fiat on the part of the new party leadership. It was instead the consequence of a gradual shift in the regime's social bases of support during the first year following the Jadid faction's seizure of power.

Syria's new rulers convened an Extraordinary Regional (Syrian) Congress of the Ba'th party in March 1966 in an effort to clarify the direction of the regime's domestic political and economic programs. According to Rabinovich, this congress "essentially reaffirmed" the policies adopted by previous Ba'thi governments.[62] But its deliberations also reflected a conscious attempt by party leaders to mollify the urban petite bourgeoisie by playing down the minoritarian character of the new governing elite and proposing additional financial assistance to smaller urban tradespeople. These concessions failed to convince the artisanate actively to support the radical Ba'th, and the regime soon turned its efforts to consolidating support among farm laborers and industrial workers instead.

On 6 March, the government proclaimed the end of the first stage of Syria's land reform program, in which excess holdings of agricultural land had been confiscated from richer farmers, and announced the beginning of a second phase, in which the expropriated lands would be distributed among the peasantry. The total area of the land expropriated during 1966 amounted to 45,941 hectares, down significantly from the 220,735 hectares expropriated the previous year. But 70,358 hectares of agricultural land were actually distributed to new owners in 1966, up from the 20,476 hectares redistributed in 1965.[63] By the end of 1966, local committees consisting of representatives of the Ba'th and the party-affiliated farm laborers' federation had been set up to supervise the distribution of confiscated lands.[64] Furthermore, state officials organized lands that had been sequestered during the mid-1960s into a network of agricultural cooperatives. Fifty-nine such units were established in 1966; a further 162 were in place by the end of 1967.[65] Through these cooperatives, state agencies determined crop selection, the allocation of vital inputs such as seeds and fertilizer, and marketing arrangements for the most important cash crops produced in the Syrian countryside. At the same time, the regime set up extensive state-run agricultural projects on reclaimed lands in the far northeastern provinces, where centrally administered irrigation systems were being constructed with the assistance of Soviet advisers.[66]

Industrial policy during the first year or so following the February coup involved a concerted effort on the part of state officials to build up large-scale public sector enterprises in key sectors of Syria's economy. The largest single project envisaged in the second Five-Year Plan (1966–1970) was the construction of a high dam across the Euphrates River at Tabqa in al-Raqqah province; this project had been planned with West German assistance in 1963–1964 but was taken over by Soviet engineers in January 1966 when diplomatic relations between Damascus and Bonn deteriorated. By the end of the year, the project had expanded to include a cluster of irrigation works and an ambitious land reclamation scheme in areas adjacent to the dam.[67] Major investments were also made in pipeline construction, railway extension, and port expansion during these months. More important, the state contracted with Soviet and Czech firms to build a modern fertilizer factory at Homs, with Chinese partners to construct a large-scale cotton spinning mill at Hamah, and with a Polish engineering company to outfit a steel rolling plant at Hamah.[68] These projects accompanied a marked rise in aggregate industrial investment within the country. During the years 1961–1965, annual investment in Syrian industry had averaged about 113 million Syrian pounds; for 1966–1967 this figure rose to around 181 million, reaching a total of more than 252 million in 1968–1969.[69] At least some of this investment went into state-owned light industrial plants as well, particularly to firms producing metal and cement pipe, wire, and other items used in manufacturing and transportation.[70]

In an effort to protect these new public sector enterprises from foreign competition, state officials increasingly restricted the flow of imported goods entering Syrian markets. The government announced in early April 1966 that it would begin levying higher duties on European and Arab products reexported into the country from Lebanon.[71] Three months later, the Central Bank lowered the official exchange rate for the pound, effectively raising the cost of unregulated imports.[72] Early the following January, state officials banned the importation of a broad range of luxury items.[73] Furthermore, state officials made greater use of bilateral barter arrangements with East European governments beginning in mid-1966. Countertrading arrangements, such as the one signed with Hungary in early September, channeled essential imported goods into Syria through state agencies rather than through private hands.[74] By the end of October, a joint Soviet-Syrian economic committee had been formed to discuss the implementation of trade and economic assistance between the two governments.[75] As a result of these discussions, Syria's Import-Export Establishment became the sole agent for Soviet newsprint, machinery, motorcycles, bicycles, fertilizers, and other manufactured goods sold in local markets.[76]

At the same time, however, the profitability of Syria's large state-run enterprises substantially diminished. Gross fixed capital formation in the public sector, which had risen sharply from 1965 to 1966, dropped just as sharply the following year (see Figure 1). The fall in productivity resulted partly from demands voiced by radical trade unionists allied to the regime. Labor organizations pressured the government to provide a variety of expanded benefits to public sector workers during the winter and spring of 1966–1967. Among these were an enlarged profit-sharing scheme and a program administered by the newly established General Federation of Women to set up day care centers for working women and training institutes to improve their industrial and clerical skills. Such outlays kept state-run companies operating at the edge of

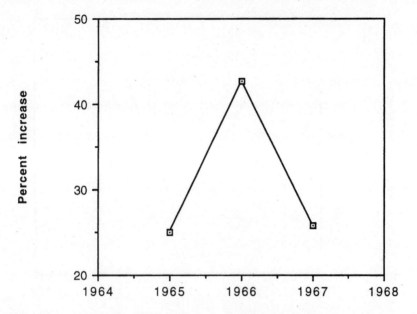

Figure 1. Gross fixed capital formation, public sector, 1965–1967

insolvency throughout the first two years of the Jadid era. They also enhanced the competitiveness of small-scale manufacturers relative to larger public firms, enabling the former to reverse their deteriorating fortunes as 1967 began (see Figure 2).

Private industry exercised its newfound strength within the local economy by withholding investment capital from state-sponsored agricultural and manufacturing enterprises during the first months of 1967. This move severely limited the monies available for new projects designed to further the regime's economic development program. In fact, the second Five-Year Plan called for approximately 60 percent of total agricultural investment to come from the private sector; a virtually identical proportion of investment in public utilities was to come from the same source. Private enterprise was also expected to provide 100 million pounds to finance the public debt and other services during the 1966–1970 period, as well as 125 million pounds to support improvements in transportation and communication.[77] One indicator of the importance the regime attached to privately held funds for the success of the plan lies in its promulgation of a wide-ranging Economic Sanc-

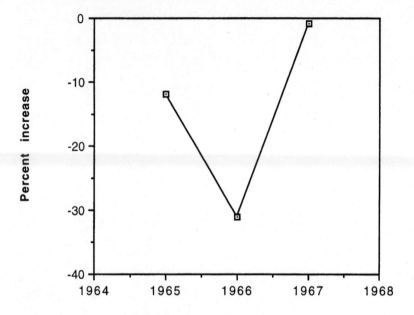

Figure 2. Gross fixed capital formation, private sector, 1965–1967

tions Law in the summer of 1966. The law authorized up to fifteen years' imprisonment for anyone convicted of "economic sabotage," an offense that included the illegal transfer of currency abroad.[78]

Rural opponents of the ruling coalition took advantage of the state's growing financial weakness to infiltrate Syria's agricultural cooperatives and reorient these institutions' operations. Rural laborers allied to the regime often had little choice but to acquiesce in this process. According to Petran, "In the absence of a state policy of adequately financing small peasants, giving them technical assistance, and providing state marketing facilities, poor peasant beneficiaries of the reform often did not have the resources to cultivate the land. So they rented their parcels to yesterday's landlord. The landlord, by concentrating these parcels, continued to be the real exploiter of the land, while the peasants worked as his sharecroppers."[79] Rich peasants' domination in rural districts was further facilitated by the structure of the local Area Lending Committees that allowed larger landholders to appropriate a disproportionate share of the restricted amount of investment credits available in each area.[80] Government officials tried to counteract this trend by increasing the number of state farms in the countryside, but producer collectives proved largely unable to take root outside the far northeastern provinces, where the regime already occupied a dominant position as a result of its control over the centralized irrigation and reclamation works associated with the Euphrates dam project.

Even as it encountered growing resistance from its opponents, the Jadid regime confronted serious challenges from its more radical constituents. At the end of May 1966, the General Federation of Workers' Unions urged its members to arm themselves to defend the achievements of Syria's socialist revolution. In the aftermath of two unsuccessful coups by dissident Ba'thi officers the first week of September, the president of the federation, Khalid al-Jundi, ordered armed workers' companies to enter state-run enterprises and remove "reactionary" managers from their posts. Other units of armed trade unionists patrolled the streets of Damascus to prevent popular demonstrations in support of the coup makers. The vigilantes were called back to their factories on 15 September, when al-Jundi turned over responsibility for preserving domestic order to the party apparatus. Two weeks later, the commander of the new National Guard announced that worker volunteers were being incorporated into this organization. But on 19 October, the government instead opened a network of recruiting centers for a Popular Defense Army (*jaysh al-difaʿ al-shaʿbi*) consisting of trade unionists, farm laborers, students, and other "progressive groups." The trade union federation's leadership claimed that ten thousand of its members volunteered to serve in this paramilitary formation during the first week of recruitment.

Militant trade unionists continued to resist subordination to central authority. As early as mid-September 1966, a pair of prominent labor leaders defected to Jordan, accusing the Syrian state of "exploiting the name of the workers in order to destroy the country."[81] The two charged that the armed workers who had taken to the streets earlier in the month were in fact troops of the regular army's Seventieth Infantry Regiment disguised as proletarians. By the end of the year, the rift between labor activists and the government precipitated behind-the-scenes conflict between more radical cabinet ministers such as Zu'ayyin and al-Jundi on one hand and military officers associated with Jadid on

39

the other. This conflict resulted in the dismissal of twenty-five high-level state administrators on 3–4 December and a crackdown on prominent trade unionists later that month.

Government officials attempted to solve the regime's political and financial difficulties by enlarging the scope of state control over Syrian industry and commerce during the first quarter of 1967. On 1 January, the country's five state-run commercial banks were merged into a single institution, the Commercial Bank of Syria; this move consolidated the banking sector into five overarching specialized enterprises.[82] That March the government reorganized the larger state-run manufacturing enterprises into three comprehensive industrial associations: one for spinning and weaving, one for food processing, and one for chemical and mechanical production. In the course of the reorganization, Syria's forty-five public sector spinning and weaving firms were consolidated into fourteen companies with a combined capital of 100 million Syrian pounds; the twenty-one state-run food-processing enterprises were reduced to eleven with a capital base of 50 million pounds; and the forty-three chemical and mechanical firms merged into twenty-three, capitalized at 84 million pounds.[83]

Simultaneously, the regime adopted a series of measures that concentrated wholesale trade in the public sector. The state's Supply Board took over the distribution of sugar, cooking oil, and salt on Syrian markets at the beginning of March. Four weeks later, police arrested several larger private wholesalers for stockpiling tea during a period of scarcity. Ba'th party members were instructed to keep merchants under close scrutiny in the wake of these arrests and report any irregularities in the availability or pricing of staple goods to the Supply Board.[84] In mid-May, government officials announced that a new state corporation would be set up to import and export pharmaceuticals into and out of the Syrian market, removing this lucrative trade from the hands of private companies.[85]

By the spring of 1967, government attempts to impose greater supervision over Syria's internal economic affairs had driven smaller tradespeople in the north-central cities into active opposition against the Jadid regime. The opposition took two different but related forms. First, private manufacturers and shopkeepers stopped investing in local industry and commerce. According to the best available estimates, total investment for 1967 ended up some 12 percent below the level reached

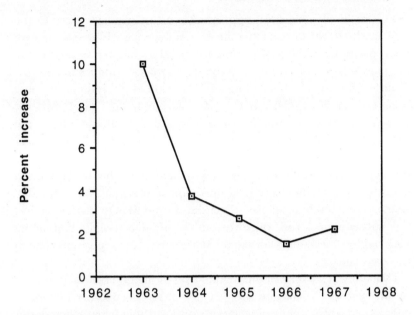

Figure 3. Gross domestic product, 1963–1967

five years earlier, which Eliyahu Kanovsky attributes to "a very sharp drop in private investment."[86] The growing shortage of investment monies fueled a secular decline in gross domestic product (see Figure 3). In addition, local traders cut back severely on the quantity and range of goods they offered for sale; the resulting shortages of foodstuffs and other staples sharply increased retail prices in the larger cities and towns. Between January and May, food prices jumped more than 33 percent, while sales of other essentials on the country's proliferating black market rose dramatically.[87]

Second, small-scale traders and artisans in the north-central cities and towns stepped up their participation in protests organized by Syria's variegated Islamist movement. Sporadic demonstrations against the regime's nationalization program erupted in Aleppo, Hamah, and Homs throughout the spring of 1967. These largely spontaneous protests coalesced into organized opposition to the regime during the first week of May in response to the publication of an article entitled "Molding the Character of the New Arab Socialist Personality" in the army weekly *Jaysh al-Sha'b*. A congress of religious notables gathered in Damascus on

4 May to discuss the most appropriate means of responding to the article, which had asserted that the new Arab personality considers such concepts as "God, religion . . . and all the values which prevailed in the pre-existing society" to be "nothing more than mummies in the museums of history."[88] The leading spokesperson of the religious opposition, Shaikh Hasan Habanka of the Midan quarter of Damascus, delivered a scathing sermon denouncing both the atheism inherent in the article and the regime that sponsored it during his Friday prayer service on 5 May. The sermon prompted a massive demonstration in the capital in which some twenty thousand marchers chanted anti-Ba'th slogans; similar rallies were held in Aleppo and Hamah that same day. Damascene merchants closed their shops on 6 May in protest against the subsequent arrest of forty-four prominent religious notables ('ulama) by state security forces; the strike spread to Aleppo and Hamah two days later.[89]

Escalating resistance to the regime's political and economic policies on the part of artisans and shopkeepers in the north-central cities accompanied a resurgence of sectarian conflict within Syria. Much of this unrest was centered in the Druze areas of the southern provinces of Dir'a and al-Suwayda. High-ranking Druze party officials and military commanders had been cashiered during the last weeks of 1966 in the wake of an unsuccessful coup d'état led by Major General Salim Hatum, the commander of the army's elite commando brigade. Public protests over the dismissals and the detention of several prominent leaders of the Druze community prompted the authorities to dismiss the local council in Dir'a the first week of March 1967 and substitute "progressive elements who believe in socialism and in the welfare of the villages of the Dir'a district."[90] Continuing unrest in neighboring al-Suwayda set the stage for a second wave of arrests in that province shortly thereafter; the local leadership of the Ba'th shut down its branch office in the provincial capital on 5 March. When tensions remained high into early May, the party newspaper al-Ba'th began running stories "denouncing the attempts of local reaction and of hired agents to arouse sectarian feelings" in predominantly Druze areas.[91] At the same time, a number of Ba'thi cadres resigned their posts to show their displeasure at the apparent rise of sectarian antagonism within the army and the party apparatus.[92]

CONTRADICTORY RESPONSES TO THE CRISIS

Faced with both increasing fragmentation inside the dominant social coalition and growing challenges from powerful opponents of the regime, Syria's rulers implemented three largely incompatible programs in the late spring of 1967 in an attempt to reconsolidate their collective hold over the country's domestic affairs. Each of these responses to the regime's internal political difficulties furthered the individual interests of one particular force within the ruling coalition. But each program at the same time worked to the detriment of other components of the regime, thereby threatening the continued viability and stability of the dominant coalition as a whole.

Militants in the Syrian workers' federation and the General Federation of Farm Laborers mobilized these two organizations' paramilitary formations and deployed them into the marketplaces of the larger cities and towns in an effort to break up the strikes and demonstrations that spread throughout the country as the spring went by. Property belonging to striking merchants in Aleppo and Damascus was confiscated by members of the Workers' Companies in early May, prompting the government to issue a decree authorizing the moves retroactively on the grounds that Syria's "biggest capitalists" had been "plotting against the working masses."[93] On 11 May, the minister of social affairs and labor, Muhammad Rabah al-Tawil, told a rally in the capital that "an imperialist-reactionary plot" was subverting "the achievements of the workers, peasants and other small wage-earners" by fomenting "sectarian dissension" among the Syrian population.[94] Further confiscations occurred in the wake of this address.

Operations against rich merchants by the Workers' Companies posed a direct challenge to the monopoly of legitimate violence within Syrian society claimed by the regular armed forces. As early as mid-February, the minister of defense and commander of the armed forces, Major General al-Asad, had openly criticized the growing influence of the Workers' Companies and demanded that their commander, Khalid al-Jundi, be removed from his position as head of the General Federation of Workers' Unions. In mid-March, newspapers close to the Military Committee of the Ba'th accused al-Jundi of misappropriating funds from public sector companies and governing the trade union federation on the basis of personal favoritism and nepotism.[95] At the end of April, the military high command announced plans to integrate the Workers' Companies, along with the farm laborers' militia and several other paramilitary organizations, into the umbrella Popular Defense Army that had been created the previous fall. The new formation was charged with "defending the country in times of war against subversive military activities and external attacks," and its headquarters was transferred from the Ministry of the Interior to the Ministry of Defense.[96] Militia commanders resisted incorporation into the Popular Defense Army as best they could but lacked the strength to stand up to the regular armed forces. In addition, local branches of the General Union of Palestinian Workers took an active part in recruiting both Syrian and Palestinian workers into Popular Defense Army brigades.[97]

In exchange for their assistance in organizing the Popular Defense Army, Syria's military high command loosened its grip on the Palestinian commando units based in the country. Two distinct guerrilla organizations were present in Syria during the first months of the Jadid period: Yasir 'Arafat's al-Fath and the Syrian-sponsored Palestine Liberation Front led by Ahmad Jibril. These units had been given training and staging bases on the outskirts of Damascus, as well as a forward headquarters in Dir'a, from which operations in Jordan and the West Bank could be supervised. But their activities had been closely monitored by the Operations Division of the Syrian General Staff, which enforced a considerable degree of restraint on the commandos throughout the fall and winter of 1966–1967.[98] As the Syrian high command took steps to consolidate its control over the various military and paramilitary formations operating in the southern provinces during April and May 1967, both al-Fath and the Palestine Liberation Front were reinforced and resupplied. The new equipment fostered greater daring among Palestinian commanders. The military wing of al-Fath, al-'Asifah, claimed responsibility for four armed incursions into Israeli territory in the first half of April, as well as for artillery attacks on villages in northern Israel in early May.[99]

Officials in charge of Syria's public sector enterprises took advantage of the army's campaign to consolidate centralized command over the country's paramilitary formations to tighten their own hold over the urban economy. On 9 May, as police forcibly reopened some of the locked shops in the Damascus marketplace, government authorities sequestered the assets of forty-five rich merchants, called Syria's "biggest capitalists" by the party daily *al-Ba'th*. Other prominent merchants had their property confiscated and their liquid assets frozen in the course of the next two days.[100] Moves to augment state control over the local market were stepped up during the first week of June when a series of decrees ordered the rationing of rice, sugar, potatoes, tea, and milk products. Subsequent orders prohibited the movement of flour across provincial boundaries without a government permit.[101]

While the Ministries of Defense and of the Interior took steps to centralize the command structures of Syria's military and paramilitary forces, and those of Supply and of the Economy and Foreign Trade introduced greater control over the local market, officials in the Ba'th party and its affiliated popular front organizations adopted a program of expanding popular participation in public policy making as a way of harnessing popular discontent and channeling it in directions less disruptive than street demonstrations. As early as January, the minister of information, Mahmud al-Zu'bi, observed that "Syria would be unable to carry out political and other reforms unless it first reformed the government machinery." Three months later, officials in the Ministry of the Interior promulgated a revised municipalities law that included provisions designed to decentralize the administration of the country's internal affairs and enhance what it called the "spread of popular democracy."[102] Senior party officials simultaneously orchestrated district elections for top positions within the General Federation of Farm Laborers, in which voting was to be conducted in "a completely democratic manner."[103] These elections took place in April and early May, although the elected representatives did not convene a new general congress until late July. Virtually concurrent elections to the general council of the National Union of Syrian Students threatened to result in a victory for a broad coalition of anti-Ba'th candidates, prompting police to arrest leading members of the Islamist, Nasirist, and dissident Ba'thi wings of the union just before the balloting.

Growing tensions among the various components of the dominant social coalition rekindled smoldering conflicts between the Jadid–al-Asad wing of the Ba'th party and more militant trade unionists during the late spring of 1967. At the beginning of April, the local press reported a widening rift between the Ba'th and the leaders of the Syrian Communist party, whose cadres had consistently supported labor activists loyal to Khalid al-Jundi; the communist newspaper *Nidal al-Shaʿb* openly criticized the Baʿth during the first week of the month for refusing to set up a "progressive national front" to govern the country. The more radical Socialist Workers' party began organizing underground resistance to Baʿthi rule sometime after the first of May. Meanwhile, members of the Nasirist Socialist Unionists' movement distributed leaflets in several of the larger cities calling for an end to the army's control over Syria's internal affairs; in mid-April, this movement went so far as to demand reunification with Egypt "as the only means of liberating Palestine" and restoring democratic rule within Syria. When the leadership of the Socialist Unionists' movement failed to rally to the regime in the face of riots orchestrated by the Islamists in early May, the Military Committee of the Baʿth announced that it "regarded their indifference as tantamount to hostility towards the regime" and ordered the state security police to round up prominent Nasirists throughout the country and place them under arrest.[104] As the rift between senior military commanders and the labor movement widened, the government convened an extraordinary congress of the Inter-Arab Trade Unions Federation in Damascus in mid-May in an effort to generate external support for Syria's central administration and undercut the legitimacy of more radical forces inside the local trade union federation.[105]

Relations between the Military Committee of the Baʿth and influential liberals within the government deteriorated at almost the same time the conflict between al-Asad and al-Jundi reached its zenith. In March 1967, Minister of Information al-Zuʿbi, who had been outspoken in his criticism of the predominance of ʿAlawi officers in the military high command, threatened to resign his cabinet post in response to a series of public statements by al-Asad accusing him of corruption and other misdemeanors against the revolution. Two other cabinet members— Mashhur Zaitun, the minister of supply, and Salih Mahamid, the minister of municipal affairs—joined al-Zuʿbi, forcing al-Asad to back down.[106] Nevertheless, the daily *al-Ishtiraki* complained on 27 March that the structure and procedures of the Ministry of Information failed to "consider the interests of the workers" and other supporters of Baʿthi socialism; the party newspaper *al-Baʿth* published a lengthy proposal for reorganizing the ministry in its 23 April issue.[107] Three days earlier, the paper had run an editorial criticizing attempts to increase popular participation in the regime's popular front organizations—of which al-

Zu'bi was the most vocal proponent—on the grounds that they were resulting in little more than a return to positions of influence of a clique that "had sold its soul to the reaction which hates the revolution."[108]

CONFLICT WITH ISRAEL AND RECONSOLIDATION OF THE REGIME

Escalating the May–June 1967 confrontation with Israel enabled the regime in Damascus to reinforce its domestic political position in three complementary ways. First, reorienting the operations undertaken by the Popular Defense Army and the Palestinian militias allied to it away from Syria's domestic political arena defused rising political tensions in the north-central cities and precluded the Islamist movement from gaining additional followers as a result of violent clashes between tradespeople and the workers' and farm laborers' militias. Second, mobilizing Syria's economy for the war effort allowed state officials to impose greater control over the more militant popular front organizations without prompting accusations that they had abandoned their commitment to revolutionary change. Finally, engaging in a military confrontation with Israel provided the government with legitimate grounds for soliciting greater levels of economic and military assistance from the Communist bloc. Domestic political dynamics associated with the 1967 confrontation with Tel Aviv therefore not only generated concrete benefits for each of the ruling coalition's constituent social forces but also helped to mitigate severe intraregime conflicts of interest that threatened the viability of the regime as a whole.

So long as the units that made up the Popular Defense Army focused their activities on punishing alleged counterrevolutionaries inside Syria, these formations threatened to stir up even greater resistance to the regime among disaffected tradespeople in the larger cities and towns. The newly appointed commander of the Popular Defense Army, Minister of Social Affairs and Labor al-Tawil, publicly advocated a program of rapid nationalization of the country's remaining private enterprises, leading some regular army officers to worry that his troops represented a "red guard" whose primary goal was to rearrange Syria's existing political-economic order.[109] These fears were shared by the small-scale merchants and manufacturers of Aleppo and Damascus,

47

several of whose richer colleagues had borne the brunt of the anti-capitalist campaign carried out by the Workers' Companies in early May.

Officials in the Ministry of Defense manipulated the rising tension with Israel so as to assert their control over Syria's unruly paramilitary organizations. As rioting spread throughout the north-central provinces in early May, induction centers for the reconstituted Popular Defense Army were opened in the larger cities and towns; those who volunteered for service were issued rifles and other small arms, then sent to border areas for further military training.[110] These activities were coordinated by defense committees set up in each province, whose membership consisted of the governor, select Ba'th party cadres, and representatives of the various popular front organizations.[111] In the aftermath of the June war, the provincial committees were combined to form a nationwide Committee for the Defense of the Homeland (*lajnah al-difa' 'an al-watan*). The establishment of this overarching committee greatly facilitated the government's efforts to subordinate the popular front organizations to the party-state apparatus, as well as the regime's moves to merge local administrative agencies and Ba'th party branches throughout the country.[112] Changes in leadership were announced that August for the farm laborers' federation, the workers' federation, and the women's union.[113] Two months later, the Popular Defense Army was formally integrated into the command structure of the regular armed forces, and its commander was appointed a cabinet minister without portfolio.

Moves designed to rationalize the Syrian armed forces were facilitated by the government's burgeoning relationship with Moscow. In the wake of the Ramadan Socialist Decrees of 1965, Soviet and East German officials began providing Damascus with technical expertise and substantial quantities of industrial equipment; an East German adviser was even seconded to the Syrian Ministry of Finance to help reorganize the agency "so that it may conform to the present phase of socialist evolution."[114] But Moscow remained hesitant to increase the overall level of assistance to the Syrian regime, largely because of its perception of "the Ba'th as an inconsistent party relying for support on the lower middle class, the officer corps, and the intelligentsia."[115] Uncertainty about the character of the Ba'thi regime was evident in the Soviet leadership's response to an official visit to Moscow by Prime Minister

Zu'ayyin and Minister of Defense al-Asad in mid-April 1966: the communiqué issued at the close of the visit noted that discussions between the two parties had been characterized by "a frank exchange of opinions."[116] Nevertheless, Soviet authorities agreed to provide Damascus with the $450 million necessary to initiate the massive Tabqa dam project, along with $200 million in armaments. A subsequent request for surface-to-air missile batteries, however, was politely refused.[117]

Moscow's willingness to provide Damascus with greater quantities of military equipment and economic assistance rose in step with the escalating confrontation between Damascus and Tel Aviv. Surface-to-air missiles, fighter aircraft, missile patrol boats, attack helicopters, and even medium bombers arrived at Syrian ports in steadily increasing numbers throughout the spring of 1967.[118] And although the Soviet Union refused to intervene in the 1967 war on the Arabs' behalf, Moscow lost no time in making amends for its caution as soon as the war ended. According to Pedro Ramet, "The Soviets moved quickly to make good Syria's losses. Large shipments of Soviet arms ($300 million worth, including more than 400 tanks and 120 aircraft) were shipped to Syria to compensate for its losses, and perhaps as many as 1,000 additional Soviet advisers flew in soon after the war, complementing the large number already present since before the war."[119] By midsummer, Soviet personnel were assisting Syrian officers in reconfiguring the Syrian armed forces at virtually every level.

Equally important was the economic and technical assistance provided by Eastern bloc companies in support of public sector industry and infrastructure in the months before and after the war. Throughout 1966, Soviet, Czechoslovakian, and Romanian companies played an active part in planning and constructing a wide range of state-owned industrial and agricultural facilities in almost all regions of Syria, while Soviet and Bulgarian companies began building a comprehensive system of highways and railroads.[120] Czechoslovakian officials traveled to Damascus in mid-April 1967 to work out arrangements whereby Prague would purchase substantial quantities of Syrian cotton, crude oil, and phosphates in exchange for advice about how to salvage Syria's floundering second Five-Year Plan.[121] And it was Soviet technicians who brought the vital oil refinery outside Homs back on line in the immediate aftermath of the June war.[122] Syria's burgeoning connections with

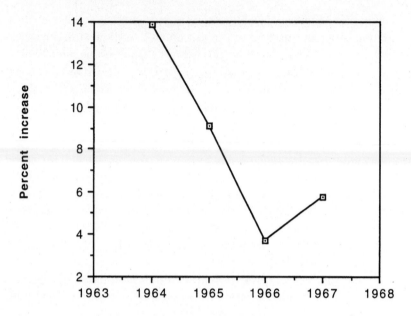

Figure 4. Industrial production index, 1964–1967

the Communist world, combined with an increase in production of war-related goods, sparked a marked resurgence in local industrial production in 1967 (see Figure 4).

As momentous as it proved to be for regional strategic and diplomatic affairs, Damascus's escalation of the May–June 1967 confrontation with Israel was driven primarily by political conflicts at home. Growing splits among the powerful forces that made up the ruling social coalition, compounded by rising opposition to the regime from the country's remaining private tradespeople, generated a severe political-economic crisis inside Syria beginning in the winter of 1966–1967. The crisis precipitated widespread dissent among organized workers and farm laborers nominally allied to the government, which prompted state officials to try to subordinate these forces to the central administration.

But rather than reducing the level of internal conflict, the state's efforts to take direct charge of the Syrian economy further alienated the urban petite bourgeoisie, augmenting popular support for the country's Islamist movement. Each of the forces that composed the dominant social coalition adopted a strategy of its own to parry the Islamist challenge. Trade unionists and rural laborers took steps to break up urban protests by force; officials in charge of the country's infant public sector enterprises imposed stricter state control over the local market; and radical party cadres undertook reforms designed to increase popular participation in public policy making. These programs threatened to fragment the already deeply fissured regime.

Under these circumstances, heightening the confrontation with Israel enabled Syria's rulers to reconsolidate the dominant social coalition, while at the same time attracting new resources from outside which greatly facilitated intraregime coordination. Expanding the state-controlled Popular Defense Army, while simultaneously redirecting its activities toward Israel, sharply reduced the potential for open rebellion on the part of craftspeople and traders in the larger cities and towns. Mobilizing radical workers and farm laborers into the Popular Defense Army in preparation for war also made it much easier for Syrian military commanders to integrate the country's increasingly restive paramilitary formations into the regular armed forces' hierarchical command structure. And the regime's ability to achieve these domestic political objectives was compounded by the military and economic resources channeled to the central administration through the Syrian-Soviet alliance, which solidified as the confrontation with Israel escalated during the late spring of 1967.

CHAPTER TWO

Limiting Intervention
in Jordan, 1970

During the summer and fall of 1970, rivalry between militant Arab states that advocated the continuation of armed struggle to roll back Israel's territorial gains from the June 1967 war and more pragmatic ones clustered around an Egyptian-Jordanian axis, which proposed negotiating a "political solution" to the Arab-Israeli conflict, ignited a brief but bloody civil war in Jordan. The conflict opened with a series of clashes between Palestinian guerrillas and the Jordanian armed forces the first week of June from which the Popular Front for the Liberation of Palestine (PFLP) led by George Habash emerged as the decisive force within the Palestinian national movement. Chafing at the demands Habash's organization made upon his government and forced to look on helplessly as PFLP commandos detained and then dynamited three commercial airliners at an airfield outside Zarqah in early September, King Husain picked up the gauntlet on 16 September by announcing the formation of a military cabinet under the leadership of General Muhammad Da'ud and imposing martial law. As Malcolm Kerr observes, "No one in Jordan doubted what this meant: the gloves were off and the crackdown was imminent. It began the next morning and continued uninterruptedly for the next nine days. Not only Fidayin [guerrilla] strong-points but Palestinian population centers in general—especially the slums in the hills ringing Amman crowded with refugees—became the targets of point-blank bombardment by machine guns, mortars, and artillery."[1]

As Jordan's embattled Palestinian community pleaded for outside assistance and the twenty thousand–strong Iraqi military contingent based in the kingdom remained closeted in its barracks, Damascus ordered a reinforced armored brigade to cross the border into Jordanian territory. On the morning of 19 September, this unit took up positions outside the northern city of Irbid, while Syria's minister of defense, Major General Hafiz al-Asad, monitored developments from a forward command post at Dir'a. Three days later, elite armored and air units of the Jordanian armed forces attacked the Syrians, destroying some 130 tanks and presenting the Ba'thi regime with an unsavory choice between escalating its involvement in the conflict by launching retaliatory air strikes against the Jordanians and pulling its increasingly vulnerable ground units back into Syria. At least with hindsight, al-Asad appears to have had no hesitation in adopting the latter course of action. As he told Patrick Seale in May 1985, "It was a difficult predicament. I was distressed to be fighting the Jordanians whom we did not think of as the enemy. I didn't bring up our own much stronger air force because I wanted to prevent escalation."[2] Seale concludes that this episode provides "a striking illustration of the conflict between Asad's state interests and the interests of the Palestinian guerrillas. He sided with the Resistance, yet had no sympathy for its aim of marching on Amman. His half-hearted intervention drew abuse from the guerrillas who felt betrayed, as well as understandable hostility from Husayn which debarred co-operation between them for years to come."[3]

Syria's evident unwillingness to raise either the level of hostility or the scale of its direct military involvement in the Jordanian civil war contrasts sharply with the unwavering belligerence Damascus adopted in its confrontation with Israel during the late spring of 1967. In both cases, outside powers warned the Syrian leadership against taking steps that might lead to war. But despite any similarities in strategic circumstances, the most cogent explanation for Damascus's evidently deescalatory policy in the case of Jordan lies in the domestic political-economic situation that faced Syria's dominant social coalition during the summer and fall of 1970.

COLLAPSE OF BA'THI SOCIALISM, 1968–1969

In the two years following the June 1967 war, private enterprises gradually chipped away at the public sector of the Syrian economy by making more efficient use of the scarce resources to which they enjoyed

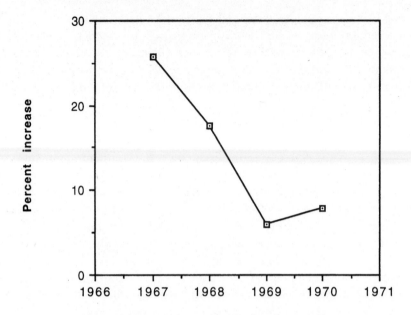

Figure 5. Gross fixed capital formation, public sector, 1967–1970

access. On the basis of fragmentary and often inconsistent data, Eliyahu Kanovsky concludes that "there was a steady rise in the share of the private sector in manufacturing between 1968 and 1970, though official policies did little to encourage such a trend during this period. The share of private sector output in manufacturing rose from 33.8% in 1968 to 38.8% in 1970."[4] This trend was all the more remarkable as the years after 1968 saw a dramatic expansion of the local petroleum industry, all of whose profits are included in the official figures for public sector industrial production from which these percentages were derived. Kanovsky attributes the drop in performance on the part of state-run enterprises to their persistent inefficiencies; this assessment is shared by Ziad Keilany, who reports that state-owned corporations suffered from the twin difficulties of "the practice of replacing experienced owner-businessmen with political appointees loyal to the party" and "the exodus of skilled persons" from Syria during the late 1960s.[5] The deterioration of public sector manufacturing can be seen in the steady decline in gross fixed capital formation in this sector after 1967 (see Figure 5).

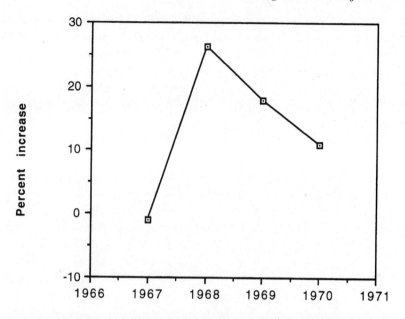

Figure 6. Gross fixed capital formation, private sector, 1967–1970

Consequently, private sector companies began holding their own against the larger state-run enterprises in scattered pockets of the Syrian economy. Private gross fixed capital formation jumped by more than one-quarter from 1967 to 1968 and remained at comparatively high levels over the following two years (see Figure 6). Among the most profitable private companies were those that produced specialized goods such as knitwear and candy, along with firms in the construction sector. Elisabeth Longuenesse shows that the great majority of the re-emergent private companies were relatively small in scale, measured either in terms of capital invested or of the number of workers employed. According to the industrial census of 1970, 31,000 privately owned manufacturing firms were operating in the country but only 550 of these employed more that ten workers; in Longuenesse's words, "There is a multitude of small firms and workshops of which more than a third have only one employee."[6] Privately owned enterprises found themselves constrained not only by what she calls the "harsh measures" imposed by state officials that "slowed the activity of the private industrial sector and discouraged investment" but also by the activities of "loansharks" who represented the only source of operating capital for most small-scale manufacturers. Nevertheless, thanks to the adaptability and flexibility of these companies, as well as to the parasitic relationship many of them maintained with public sector corporations, "the private sector has not continued any less to play a very important role and to dominate certain sectors absolutely" as the 1960s came to a close.[7]

The resurrection of private enterprise after 1967 reignited conflicts inside Syria's dominant social coalition over the proper role of the state in the country's domestic economic affairs. Rapidly expanding small-scale manufacturing and trading concerns demanded greater access to two factors largely controlled by the central administration: internal and external markets for the goods they produced and investment capital. Whether government agencies should loosen their hold over these two economic levers constituted a crucial point of contention between doctrinaire socialists such as the prime minister, Dr. Yusuf Zu'ayyin, on the one hand, and pragmatic advocates of a rationalized political-economic order led by Minister of Defense al-Asad, on the other. The former called for continued efforts to achieve a "socialist transformation" (*tahwil ishtiraki*) within Syrian society through the expansion of the public sector and greater support for cooperatives in agriculture and trade. Such a program envisaged increased worker participation both in the management of state-run enterprises and in the distribution of these firms' profits.[8]

Radicals associated with the Ba'th party apparatus echoed the prime minister's calls for a socialist transformation in the economy by adopting initiatives designed to promote "decentralized democracy" in Syria's administrative affairs. In June 1968, the cabinet published a draft decree mandating the creation of a country-wide network of popularly elected People's Councils to oversee local water and electricity plants, hospitals and clinics, schools, and cultural centers. A prominent party official told reporters that the councils would be granted authority "to plan, legislate and administer Syria's social, economic and cultural activities," subject to the approval of the Regional (Syrian) Command.[9] At the same time, the minister of the economy and foreign trade announced that the government would introduce a "unified budget" as the basis for calculating the revenues and expenditures of all state agencies.[10] More important, the cabinet proposed to set up a Supreme

Planning Council charged with formulating government economic policy, as well as a subordinate State Planning Organization with the power "to take all necessary measures to guarantee the implementation of the projects."[11] In addition, radicals attending the Tenth National (Pan-Arab) Congress of the Ba'th proposed to contain the growing challenge facing the regime from urban tradespeople by creating two new popular front organizations: a Federation of Craftspeople and a Federation of Small Income Earners, under the auspices of the Ministry of the Economy and Foreign Trade and the Ministry of Supply, respectively.[12]

Moderates within the ruling coalition reacted to these initiatives by criticizing the government for devoting scarce state resources to questionable economic development projects, rather than using them to augment the capabilities of the armed forces. Disagreements over the relative importance of economic and military spending resulted in the dismissal of Prime Minister Zu'ayyin at the end of October 1968.[13] The new cabinet reaffirmed the radicals' plan to establish a national network of People's Councils but stipulated that they be organized in a strictly hierarchical fashion, with a higher council to supervise their activities.[14] Radicals who retained their cabinet posts tried to recapture some measure of influence over policy making by implementing the previous government's proposal to create craftspeople's and small income earners' federations. They then pushed through plans to construct a chain of government-operated food storage facilities throughout the country.[15] They also negotiated a series of protocols with East bloc governments designed to expand the role of the state in economic affairs; such agreements were signed with the German Democratic Republic at the end of November and with the Soviet Union in late January 1969.[16]

Hafiz al-Asad's allies, in the meantime, pushed for the adoption of a considerably more liberal set of policies. When this faction captured key cabinet positions in May 1969, it carried out measures designed to deregulate first the commercial sector and then the industrial sector of the Syrian economy.[17] Over the next few months, free trading zones were set up on the northern outskirts of Aleppo and at the port city of Tartus. Then in October the state-run Import-Export Establishment was broken up into five specialized trading companies: for textiles, industrial machinery, pharmaceuticals, metals, and tobacco. These policies culminated in the promulgation of Law Number 348, which reopened

the country to foreign direct investment in both trade and manufacturing.

As intraregime rivalry escalated during the fall of 1968, the managers
of Syria's public sector firms adopted the profit-oriented strategies that
had proven so beneficial for their privately owned competitors. By early
1969, the development priorities generated by the Supreme Planning
Council and State Planning Organization differed little if at all from
those of capitalist enterprises. In his comprehensive analysis of the
regional and sectoral distribution of the large-scale investment projects
initiated by state officials after 1966, Alasdair Drysdale observes that
"considerations of economic viability and profitability, coupled with an
overriding concern with the optimum use of limited financial resources
to achieve national economic growth, lead it for the most part to make
locational decisions that would do credit to a private entrepreneur."[18]
When leftists moved to recapture control of the Supreme Planning
Council in November and December 1968 by appointing as its chair the
deposed prime minister, Zu'ayyin, supporters of the al-Asad faction
formed special party committees to coordinate the activities of government officials with those of the private business communities of the
larger cities.[19]

Increasing concern for productivity and profit in Syria's public sector
created a convergence of interest between managers of state-run firms
and private merchants and manufacturers of Damascus and Aleppo as
the decade drew to a close. The latter benefited from the regime's
policy of concentrating public enterprises in a limited number of
districts so as to create economies of scale in construction and transportation. By setting up firms that specialized in supplying goods and services to the public sector, well-to-do tradespeople—particularly those
based in Damascus—guaranteed themselves steady incomes as de facto
ancillaries to specific state companies. But after 1968, both of these
forces found it more and more difficult to compete with smaller, more
efficient retailers and manufacturers, who were less constrained by intimate ties to the central administration. Mutuality of interest between
the public sector and the Damascene grande bourgeoisie led on the
one hand to greater efforts on the part of the state bureaucracy to crack
down on "black market" operations by unlicensed or unsanctioned private entrepreneurs and, on the other, to the gradual deregulation of
state-affiliated enterprises.

58

It is no exaggeration to say that the regime had by mid-1969 begun to equivocate in carrying out the socialist agenda that had been trumpeted by the Ba'th over the preceding four years. At the beginning of August, the government drew almost $10 million in short-term assistance from the International Monetary Fund; restrictions governing the import and export of more than 190 categories of goods traded with other Arab countries were lifted the following month.[20] That December, the cabinet published details of a new program to provide low-interest loans and other subsidies to small private workshops with annual incomes of less than 15,000 pounds.[21] Two months later, the cluster of state-run import-export agencies sharply reduced restrictions on the importation of a wide range of manufactured items.[22] The state-run Commercial Bank began permitting depositors to open foreign currency accounts later the same spring, on the condition that they be used to finance commercial transactions in line with Syria's increasingly diffuse economic development program.[23]

In January 1970, however, the minister of industry announced that the government was taking complete ownership of all industrial firms that had been only partly nationalized in previous years. This move, he told reporters, was mandated by decisions reached at the Ba'th party's Regional (Syrian) Congress of September 1966, which abolished the practice of partial nationalization.[24] The first week of April 1970 saw a reimposition of trade restrictions on a number of imported commodities, markedly increasing "the list of goods which may be imported only by state agencies." At the same time, the Ministry of the Economy and Foreign Trade warned that it would begin enforcing a 1952 law requiring all Syrian firms acting as agents for foreign enterprises to be totally locally owned.[25] The ministry imposed a comprehensive prohibition on the importation of some three hundred "luxury goods" two weeks later. This decree, which banned the import of cotton cloth, electrical equipment, jewelry, and sweets, was intended to "reorganize foreign trade in accordance with the country's needs and resources," particularly the accelerating demand for hard currency.[26]

Syria's ruling coalition therefore became seriously split over economic policy by mid-1970. The Ba'th party apparatus, supported by the various party-affiliated popular front organizations, continued to pursue a program of state-sponsored, large-scale industrialization combined with administrative control over finance and commerce. This program achieved notable successes in several different arenas during the late 1960s: gross investment increased substantially after 1967, industrial productivity rose by almost 8 percent per year between 1967 and 1972, and the proportion of agricultural land in the hands of small farmers jumped from less than 15 percent in 1967 to more than 50 percent two years later.[27]

But state-sponsored development also created a variety of problems for the regime by the end of the decade. Syria's foreign debt increased dramatically starting in 1967; agricultural production fluctuated wildly after 1965; and greater imports of capital goods produced rapidly growing foreign trade deficits beginning in 1966. Furthermore, it was becoming increasingly evident that the most dynamic sectors of the economy—excepting petroleum extraction—were located in the interstices of the public sector, where small-scale private tradespeople found opportunities to provide goods for the domestic market that larger state enterprises could not supply.[28] Under these circumstances, the radicals' persistent efforts to maintain the public sector at the expense of private interests generated disaffection not only inside the regime but also among smaller-scale urban craftspeople and traders. By late 1969, discontent in the larger cities and towns threatened to erupt into violent resistance against the Ba'thi regime, orchestrated by Syria's reemergent Islamist movement.

THE RESURRECTION OF THE *IKHWAN*

Syria's variegated Islamist movement had throughout the 1960s been led by a prominent secondary school teacher from Damascus, 'Isam al-'Attar. According to a semiofficial history of the movement, al-'Attar consistently hesitated to exploit opportunities to augment and exercise the power of the Muslim Brotherhood (*ikhwan al-muslimin*) during the Jadid era. His political passivism arose in part from his own personal alienation from the great majority of Syria's religious scholars: al-'Attar adopted the comparatively liberal outlook of the rationalist *salafiyyah* movement and sharply criticized such ecstatic practices as those of the mystics (*sufis*), which many of the country's religious notables ('*ulama*) encouraged. Second, according to Umar Abd-Allah, "al-'Attar was criticized for relying too heavily upon his circle of followers in Damascus and not cultivating ties throughout Syria, which had been characteristic of the Brotherhood under [his predecessor Mustafa] as-Siba'i." But third, and most important, "al-Attar never supported the idea of armed *jihad* during the 1960s or 1970s and held adamantly to the position that jihad against the Ba'th would only bring greater suffering to the Syrian people and the Brotherhood."[29] Consequently, the senior leadership of the Islamist movement discouraged the regeneration of the ikhwan al-muslimin as a political force in Syria.

But the humiliating defeat suffered by the country's armed forces at the hands of the Israeli army and air force in June 1967, combined with a profound disenchantment with the principles of Nasirism and Arab socialism more generally that spread across a wide range of Syrian popular opinion, sparked renewed enthusiasm for the Islamists' program, particularly in urban neighborhoods. Militant activists affiliated with the ikhwan, most notably Marwan Hadid of Hamah, took advantage of this sentiment to organize dissident cells committed to armed struggle against the regime in several north-central cities. The militants drew inspiration from the writings of such writers as Sa'id Hawwa of Hamah, who advocated the formation of a party of God (*hizbullah*) to lead the community of believers militant (*jund allah*) in overthrowing Syria's heretical rulers and establishing a just society governed on the basis of Islamic principles.[30] In pursuit of this objective, Hadid and his closest lieutenants moved to Jordan in 1968 and went through basic training at a camp run by Palestinian commandos belonging to al-Fath.[31] Upon returning to Syria, Hadid and his comrades accelerated their clandestine activities, organizing a string of militant cells throughout the north-central provinces. Abd-Allah observes that "although at first they were not taken seriously, probably even by the Ba'thist regime, that was no longer the case in the late 1960s: Hadid was forced to go underground, and it became a crime to know him."[32]

Hadid's success in mobilizing support for the ikhwan prompted the movement's leadership in Damascus to reassess its reluctance to engage in armed struggle against the regime. According to Abd-Allah, rivalry between militants loyal to Hadid and more moderate 'ulama allied to al-'Attar precipitated a "leadership crisis" during 1968–1969, which "culminated in 1969 in a secret general meeting of the Muslim Brotherhood within Syria." As this meeting progressed, a split developed between the Muslim Brothers of Damascus and those of the north, that is, the cities of Hims, Hamah, Halab [Aleppo], al-Ladhiqiyah, and so forth to the north of Damascus. The Damascus group opposed armed confrontation with the Ba'thist regime and followed the line of al-'Attar; furthermore, they were at this time solidly united behind the circle of Muwaffaq Da'bul, Muhammad al-Hawari, 'Ali Mash'al, Zuhair ash-Shawish, Hasan al-Huwaidi, and others. They had some following outside Damascus, but it was small. The Muslim Brothers of Dair az-Zur and Dar'a, for example, were fairly evenly divided between both factions. The northern circle, however, which in addition to Amin Yegen and 'Adnan Sa'id included prominent figures like Sa'id Hawwa, Shaikh 'Abd-al-Fattah Abu Ghuddah, 'Adnan Sa'd-ad-Din, and others, firmly supported jihad and called for al-'Attar's replacement; outside of Damascus, their following was very large.[33]

Hadid and his circle of younger militants appear not to have participated directly in this congress, although their sympathizers among the delegates representing the north-central cities clearly expressed their preference for escalating the level of violence directed against the regime.

Communal tensions generated by the proliferation of underground Islamist cells in the north-central provinces flared into violence in late November 1969, when members of the Greek Orthodox community in Homs rioted to protest the government's attempt to remove the city's archbishop. The prelate, Archbishop Ghofril Faddul, had been elected to his post by a "traditionalist" council, whose members favored a strict separation between religious and political affairs on the part of the church. His proposed replacement, Archbishop Alexei 'Abd al-Karim, was more closely associated with the Damascene branch of the church hierarchy, for whom collaboration with state officials was frequently encouraged.[34]

At the same time that the ikhwan stepped up its activities against the regime, members of the outlawed Movement of Arab Nationalists (MAN) launched a campaign to undermine the ideological hegemony of the Ba'th party among the Syrian intelligentsia. According to reliable reports, the MAN leadership decided in the fall of 1968 to use "arms and corporal liquidation" in its struggle against Ba'thi ideologues. This strategy resulted in the assassination of a prominent student leader at Damascus University in December of that year; on 1 February 1969, the

government newspaper *al-Thawrah* announced that three members of
the MAN central committee had been arrested for the killing.[35] The
leadership of the movement riposted that the murder had been carried
out by a trio of "rightist individuals which had split from the Movement"
and had acted "with the knowledge of the [state] intelligence forces."
At the end of the month, the organization's newspaper *Hurriyyah*
printed a manifesto proclaiming the creation of a new leftist movement
in Syria, the Faction of the Arab Socialist Revolution, whose program
called for democratic reforms in the country's political and economic
affairs.[36] These activities accompanied a revival of the similarly banned
Syrian Social National party, several of whose activists were arrested by
security forces in late 1969 and early 1970.[37]

THE DOMESTIC CRISIS OF 1970

Conflict between Syria's public and private enterprises peaked during the summer and fall of 1970, draining the state treasury of operating and investment capital. As early as the previous November, government officials attempted to augment government revenues by closing
Syria's border with Lebanon, forcing goods that normally entered the
Syrian market by way of Beirut to come in through the state-run ports at
Latakia and Tartus. Transshipment fees for goods crossing Syrian territory were sharply increased at the same time.[38]

By early January 1970, the failure of these measures to solve the
state's financial difficulties led the government to accept a $15 million
loan from Bulgaria earmarked for the purchase of capital goods to
modernize public sector industry.[39] At the same time, an unprecedented barter agreement with Hanoi provided for the exchange of
Vietnamese wheat, rice, coffee, tea, cement, and steel and aluminum
goods for Syrian cotton, leather and glass products, and crude oil.[40]
The minister of the economy and foreign trade, 'Abd al-Halim Khaddam, told reporters in mid-February that a comprehensive reorganization of the country's commercial exchange system was to be implemented as a way of reducing Syria's growing trade deficit.[41] Two weeks
later, the party newspaper *al-Ba'th* reported that the state was planning
to construct a new industrial park at Yabrud, just north of Damascus,
designed to "bring the work to the workers" and thereby reduce the
flow of rural migrants to the capital.[42]

More significantly, Syrian officials attempted to augment the flow of revenues coming into the treasury by exploiting an accident in early May, when a tractor cut the Trans-Arabian Pipeline Company's main artery (Tapline) just inside the country's southwestern border with Israel. The authorities in Damascus initially refused to allow company engineers to repair the break on the grounds that it was too close to the cease-fire line, and heightened activity in the area was likely to spark a military incident. Outside observers speculated that the government was manipulating the episode so it could negotiate a more favorable bargain with Saudi Arabia on the issues of transit fees and transshipment duties. According to these sources, the government found itself in a no-lose situation, at least in the long run: "Syria is already benefitting from the transit fees of tankers calling at Tartous port. The Zahrani refinery in Lebanon, the terminal of the Tapline pipeline, is now dependent on Iraqi oil from the Tartous terminal of the IPC pipeline. And Syria has its own oil and oil policy."[43] Syrian officials hinted at the beginning of June that they might allow the pipeline to be repaired in exchange for an American pledge not to supply Israel with additional F-4 fighter-bombers and a 25 percent increase in Tapline transit fees.[44] Rather than cave in to blackmail, however, the Saudi government closed the kingdom's borders to all goods coming from Syria and hinted that it would redirect the future flow of oil to other outlets. These moves threatened to deprive the Syrian central administration of some $4 million per year in transit revenues, while at the same time costing Jordan and Lebanon even greater amounts of income and subsidized supplies of petroleum. The dispute, despite its potential for raising long-term government revenues, stretched the resources available to the Syrian state virtually to the limit.

Furthermore, state-sponsored land reform had by the summer of 1970 generated growing friction between poorer farmers, who had taken possession of sequestered land, and local-level officials, who had an interest in putting the redistributed properties to the most efficient use. According to Raymond Hinnebusch, "In Hama, a corrupted local party leadership did nothing to aid beneficiaries of state land who fell into debt to moneylenders and the agricultural bank until peasant disturbances captured national attention, spurring the establishment of cooperatives." Similarly, "in Hassaka, a corrupt governor who had collaborated with landlords to undermine the agrarian reform, was protected by a clique of friends in the army and only removed with great difficulty."[45] Pervasive corruption steadily alienated the party-backed Ministry of Agrarian Reform from its primary constituents in the countryside.

Private merchants and manufacturers exploited their unexpectedly strengthened position vis-à-vis the central administration by pushing through two new laws designed to encourage private enterprise. The first of these facilitated the return of Syrian capital back into the country by raising interest rates on deposits of both local and foreign currency deposited in Syrian banks; it also exempted new deposits from any form of taxation for an indefinite period of time. The second permitted all indigenous companies to import industrial equipment, raw materials, and a wide range of foodstuffs into the country, "provided that these imports are paid for in foreign currency."[46] At almost the same time, a Beirut newspaper reported that government officials had issued firm guarantees that private enterprises operating in the country would no longer be subject to nationalization, as well as promising that local investors would be allowed to transfer half of their net yearly profits outside the country beginning in the sixth year of their firms' operations. The first week of July brought news that the minister of the economy and foreign trade was accelerating plans to create an additional duty-free zone alongside the port at Latakia.[47]

Those responsible for managing Syria's public sector companies reacted to these initiatives by taking steps to reinforce their position in several key sectors of the local economy. On 12 July, state officials monopolized the importation of paper products; they simultaneously set up a public company to control the distribution of construction materials throughout Syria.[48] A week later, the government announced the formation of a state-owned company with exclusive rights to exploit the deposits of iron ore that had been discovered in central and northern Syria by Soviet engineers the previous winter. The new company was also given responsibility for contracting with domestic and foreign firms for the construction of a string of steel plants. On 23 July, the authorities announced a comprehensive trade agreement with Moscow, according to whose terms sizable quantities of crude petroleum, cotton cloth, ginned cotton, and other items produced by public sector enterprises were to be exchanged for industrial equipment, chemicals, and specialty steel manufactured by Soviet companies.[49]

State officials simultaneously took steps to shore up their ties to Syria's industrial workers and farm laborers. The party daily *al-Ba'th* reiterated on 8 June the importance of an autonomous public sector for the economic health and security of the nation.[50] On 22 July, President Nur al-Din al-Atassi welcomed a high-level delegation representing the Farmers' Section of the Communist party of the Soviet Union; the team toured state-run rural cooperatives and agricultural research stations throughout the country over the following weeks.[51] In early August, the government announced the formation of a new agricultural cooperative bank, whose board of directors included representatives of the General Federation of Farm Laborers, the General Federation of Workers' Unions, and the General Federation of Agricultural Cooperatives.[52]

Competition between private traders and manufacturers on the one hand and public sector managers on the other precipitated a domestic political-economic crisis as a result of two developments in mid-August that thrust these forces into direct confrontation. The first involved the supply and distribution of locally produced cotton on Syrian markets. Conflicting estimates of the size and quality of the 1969–1970 cotton crop had been published throughout the spring and summer of 1970; by early August it became clear that total output was going to be some 50,000 tons less than the 450,000 tons anticipated at the beginning of the growing season. The shortfall produced not only a smaller quantity of raw cotton for export but also and more crucially a reduced supply of cotton for use by domestic industry. In 1968–1969, 213,562 tons of indigenous cotton had been allocated to domestic manufacturers; for 1969–1970, the figure declined to 206,061 tons.[53] The reduction was made more acute for private tradespeople with the opening of the government's large-scale weaving mill at Hamah earlier that spring, which by itself was capable of handling some 6,000 tons of raw cotton per year. Consequently, the potential for widespread discontent among small-scale artisans and cloth makers in the cities and towns rose to a level unmatched since the mid-1960s, multiplying the threat to the regime posed by clandestine activities of the Islamist movement in these same districts.

Second, the Ministry of the Economy and Foreign Trade published on 13 August a new, unified set of regulations governing Syria's external commerce. The regulations closed a number of loopholes and contradictory guidelines in the existing laws which had provided lucrative opportunities for smaller-scale importers and distributors.[54] Trade with Lebanon was particularly hard hit by the new statutes; the future of this commercial connection was further threatened by the Syrian government's plans to construct new port facilities at Tartus to offload goods that had previously come into the country by way of Beirut.[55]

These twin policies generated widespread discontent among small-scale merchants and manufacturers, as well as sporadic clashes between urban tradespeople and radical trade unionists. Throughout the month of June, the police and state security services arrested hundreds of members of the workers' and students' federations, as well as leftists in the armed forces.[56] Continuing unrest inside the Syrian military establishment prompted reports of an attempted coup d'état in mid-August, allegedly financed by the rival Ba'thi regime in Baghdad.[57] But in sharp contrast to the domestic situation in the spring of 1967, the crisis that erupted during the autumn of 1970 accompanied no broad-based uprising among powerful challengers to the dominant coalition. It therefore prompted a much different set of responses on the regime's part.

CONTRADICTORY REGIME RESPONSES?

Forces that composed Syria's dominant social coalition adopted a disparate collection of measures to deal with the political-economic crisis of 1970. First, state officials took steps—as they had during the 1967 crisis—to mobilize Syrian public opinion against external threats, particularly ones emanating from the State of Israel. At the same time, government planners sharply increased the amount of investment monies earmarked for the development of the country's infant mining sector as a means of diversifying the sources of state revenue over the long run. Third, the government moved to promote closer economic relations with the communist bloc. And fourth, public sector managers augmented production by state-run food processing companies as a way of disciplining the country's small-scale tradespeople.

Growing unrest in the larger cities and towns during the course of 1969–1970 prompted the leadership of the Committees for the Defense of the Homeland and Protection of the Revolution to launch a nationwide campaign to unite the Syrian population to face an assortment of external threats. The committees organized a mass demonstra-tion in Damascus in August 1969 to protest presumed Israeli conni-vance in the fire that was set in the al-Aqsa mosque in Jerusalem by a deranged Australian tourist.[58] The next summer, they sponsored several large-scale rallies throughout the country to agitate against proposed U.S.-sponsored Arab-Israeli peace talks. As tensions subsequently mounted along the Golan Heights, the Popular Defense Army was re-ported to have "carried out a defensive exercise in and around Damascus on 10 July under the supervision of the Army Commander, Hadithah Murad." This exercise was followed by a thirty-five thousand–person rally in the capital.[59]

When fighting erupted between Palestinian guerrillas and the Jorda-nian armed forces in September 1970, radicals inside the Syrian regime attempted to manipulate the country's foreign policy in ways that might enhance their influence within the party-state apparatus. According to reports published in Beirut, Yusuf Zu'ayyin, in his capacity as head of the Syrian-sponsored Palestinian militia, al-Sa'iqah, traveled to Jordan to confer with the leadership of the Palestine Liberation Organization (PLO). He then "allegedly wrote a report in which he suggested Syrian intervention in Jordan. This suggestion was seconded by Salah Jadid, who then shared with Zu'ayyin the leadership of as-Sa'iqa."[60] On 18 September, President al-Atassi urged demonstrators in Damascus to "spare no blood" in defense of the Palestinians in Jordan; two days later, he once again denounced the Jordanian authorities at a mass meeting organized by the General Federation of Workers' Unions.[61] The federa-tion responded by issuing a statement urging "the Arab Palestinian revolution and the Jordanian masses to overthrow the agent military regime and establish a national regime in Jordan."[62] Provincial Com-mittees for the Defense of the Homeland rallied support for the PLO throughout Syria, acting in concert with a network of popular commit-tees for solidarity with the Palestinian resistance formed during the late 1960s.[63]

But at virtually the same time, the regular armed forces closed all branches of al-Sa'iqah on Syrian territory. The military high command announced that district headquarters of the Ba'th party would hence-forth serve as al-Sa'iqah offices because the two organizations had be-come "one and the same."[64] Knowledgeable observers speculated that this move signaled either a turn away from al-Sa'iqah's blanket rejection of any peaceful resolution to the Arab-Israeli conflict or a growing rift between radical supporters of Salah Jadid and moderates associated with al-Asad. Under the circumstances of September 1970, closing al-Sa'iqah's provincial offices may also have set well-defined limits on popular mobilization in support of the Palestinian cause, enabling the regime to prevent unbridled public hostility toward Israel or Jordan from exacerbating popular dissatisfaction with its political-economic program.

While the Committees for the Defense of the Homeland and President al-Atassi were taking steps to mobilize public sentiment against external enemies, state economic planners expanded production of minerals to reduce the regime's reliance on indigenous private capital to fund its increasingly costly industrialization program. Government officials boosted funding for the development of recently discovered phosphates deposits in southern Homs province by more than 65 percent. The 500-million-ton phosphates field was expected to begin production for export at the end of the year.[65] Meanwhile, the value of completed contracts for Syrian petroleum exports jumped from some 80 million Syrian pounds in 1969 to more than 150 million in 1970; total oil production for 1970 was expected to yield a net profit of around 220 million pounds.[66]

Besides generating increased export revenues for the central treasury, the exploitation of Syria's mineral deposits laid the foundation for a substantial expansion of the role of the public sector in the country's economy. Phosphates produced in the mines of the eastern desert were to be shipped overseas from a newly constructed pier at the state-run port of Tartus. Whatever product was not exported was earmarked to provide raw materials for a new state-owned triple superphosphate fertilizer plant on the outskirts of Homs, whose output was to be distributed throughout the country by state agricultural agencies.[67] As the autumn of 1970 began, government officials neared agreement on the most ambitious public sector enterprise of all: a modern steel-rolling mill, to be constructed under the supervision of communist bloc engineers. Plans for this project were finalized with Polish experts in late July, and the plant—capable of producing 100,000 tons of finished steel rods per year—was completed at the beginning of December.[68] Such enterprises—along with the Chinese-built textile mill that opened in Hamah in late October—gave public sector managers an unprecedented capacity to manipulate the flow of vital inputs into the industrial and agricultural sectors of the local economy, severely undermining the position of Syria's private import-export firms and wholesale trading houses.

This trend was buttressed by the blossoming relationship between public sector firms and the Eastern bloc. A Polish company set up Syria's first telephone assembly plant in 1970; North Korea provided a low-interest loan and shipments of bulk steel to subsidize the start-up costs of the Hamah steel complex; trade and financial assistance agreements with East Germany were signed in May, followed a month later by the creation of a joint commission on economic and technical cooperation between the two governments.[69] In late July, authorities in Damascus ratified a protocol with Soviet representatives calling for further increases in state-sponsored trade between their two countries, which had already grown from some 11 million rubles in value in 1964 to more than 43 million rubles' worth five years later. Final figures for 1969 showed the USSR to have become Damascus's leading trading partner, with Syrian exports to the Soviet Union increasing by 16 percent and Syrian imports from the Soviet Union jumping by more than 82 percent over the previous year.[70] The Eastern bloc accounted for almost 35 percent of total Syrian exports and some 9 percent of Syrian imports in the same period.[71] Rising trade accompanied a succession of official visits by Soviet, East German, Hungarian, Bulgarian, Czechoslovakian, and North Korean technical advisers to Damascus during the course of 1970; each delegation offered suggestions for consolidating Syria's expanding public sector.

Nowhere was the expansion of state enterprises more significant than in the vital area of food processing. The state-affiliated Union of Food Processing Industries announced in mid-September that the greatest proportion of the 56 million Syrian pounds allocated by the authorities for investment in manufacturing during 1970 was to be devoted to augmenting processed food output by public sector firms.[72] This move followed the promulgation in late July of "a law broadening the activities of the Agricultural Credit Bank of Syria to include loans for sectors not directly related to agriculture, such as fisheries, refrigeration, animal husbandry and various transport and marketing concerns connected with the co-operatives."[73] A month later, the government sharply restricted the importation of baby formula, powdered milk, and fresh eggs into local markets.[74] Taken together, these measures not only undercut private food processing and importing companies but also strengthened the hand of the central administration in its dealings with private capital virtually across the board by giving it control over the foodstuffs consumed by owners and laborers alike.

Consequently, and in a way markedly different from their response three and a half years earlier, the forces that made up Syria's ruling coalition met the domestic crisis of 1970 by implementing a set of policies that furthered their respective parochial interests without at the same time generating intractable intraregime contradictions. Efforts on the part of the Committees for the Defense of the Homeland to mobilize anti-Israeli, and later anti-Jordanian, sentiment broadly complemented those aimed at enlarging the role of the central administration in supervising the provision of essential foodstuffs to the general population, while steps designed to promote minerals production for export fit in well with moves on the part of public sector managers to expand Syria's barter trade with the Eastern bloc. In early September, Minister of Oil, Electricity, and Mineral Resources Ahmad Yusuf Hassan underlined the importance that the regime attached to improving intersectoral coordination by hosting a delegation of economists from the United Nations Industrial Development Organization, which was visiting Damascus to recommend ways of enhancing the efficiency of the General Institution for Industrial Planning and Studies.[75]

Such policies enabled Syria's public sector to recover some of the ground it had lost to private enterprises. Rapidly expanding oil production raised the public sector's share of total industrial production to almost 62 percent in 1971, up from 59 percent a year before.[76] Meanwhile, gross private investment fell from 42 percent of total investment in 1969 to 30 percent in 1970, inching back up to 33 percent the following year.[77] Volker Perthes observes that throughout the 1970s "the state retained a leading role in industry and foreign trade while, in turn, it opened the country to the world market. In essence," he continues, "Syrian infitah [economic liberalization] meant a huge program of public economic investment."[78] It is indicative of the state's political-economic resurgence that the central administration's contribution to net domestic product steadily rose during this same period (see Figure 7).

By the late fall of 1970, forces associated with the public sector

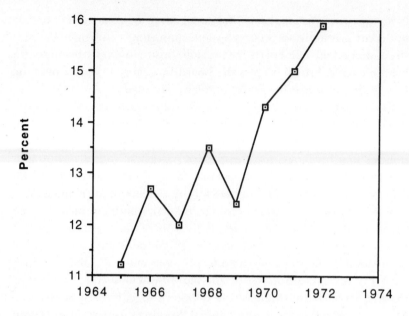

Figure 7. State expenditures as proportion of net domestic product, 1965–1972

seemed poised to recapture a predominant position within the Ba'th party apparatus. In the midst of the stormy emergency session of the Tenth National (Pan-Arab) Congress of the Ba'th that convened in early November, the workers' federation newspaper *Kifah al-'Ummal al-Ishtirakiyyah* printed a manifesto criticizing the armed forces for exerting inordinate influence over the country's internal affairs. The expansion of these forces following the 1967 war "was accompanied by a negative and dangerous phenomenon, namely, the continual and growing role of some of the military commands in the public life of the country, and—by factional groupings—their forming a power center." This situation, the paper continued, represented "an unnatural encroachment upon the party's institutions which encircles the party and feeds it with various connections and illegitimate privileges and interests."[79] The document was signed by the heads of the General Federation of Workers' Unions, the General Federation of Farm Laborers, the National Union of Syrian Students, the Youth Federation of the Revolution, and the General Federation of Women.

Backed by such a broad coalition of popular front organizations, the

72

party's assistant secretary-general, Salah Jadid, dared on 9 November to make a speech to the congress sharply critical of Minister of Defense al-Asad, who reportedly stormed out of the hall in the middle of the address. When the defense minister returned to the congress two days later, units of the Popular Defense Army and al-Sa'iqah opened fire on his entourage, forcing him to retreat to the ministry's fortified compound.[80] The party daily *al-Ba'th* observed on 13 November that delegates to the congress had reaffirmed their intention of "building the popular democracy" in the spirit of the comparatively radical congresses of September 1966 and September 1967.[81]

Foreign Nonintervention and Regime Transformation

As soon as the extraordinary party congress adjourned, regular army units loyal to al-Asad arrested Assistant Secretary-General Salah Jadid, former prime minister Zu'ayyin, President al-Atassi, and key officers of al-Sa'iqah. On 16 November, a newly formed Provisional Regional (Syrian) Command of the Ba'th broadcast a statement over Radio Damascus outlining its reasons for overthrowing the "domineering, maneuvering leadership" that had "gradually put out the flame of struggle which had inspired the hearts and minds of our fighters and masses" in the wake of the February 1966 "movement of change."[82] The leadership of the "corrective movement" (*harakah al-tashih*) then appointed new heads to each of the party-affiliated popular front organzations, as well as new commanders for the Popular Defense Army and al-Sa'iqah. The appointments sparked a wave of strikes and demonstrations on the campus of Damascus University, among workers building the Tabqa dam, and at public sector factories in several of the larger cities and towns.[83]

Support for the "corrective movement" was strongest among Syria's merchants and craftspeople. Shops in the Damascus marketplace displayed signs applauding the movement in its very first days, while preachers in the capital's mosques called its platform a means both of ensuring "the unity of the progressive forces" and of "meeting the basic needs" of the population.[84] A number of party branches quickly pledged their allegiance to the new leadership as well.[85] Buttressed by such expressions of popular support, Provisional Prime Minister al-Asad

73

called at the headquarters of the General Federation of Workers' Unions on 24 November in an attempt to persuade its officers to join the "corrective movement." Senior party officials simultaneously organized public meetings throughout the country to brief the rank and file concerning "the nature of the latest developments."[86] By mid-December virtually all resistance to the movement inside the Ba'th had evaporated, and al-Asad finally had to appeal to well-wishers "to stop sending more delegations and cables, so that he could be 'free to work.' "[87]

Later observers have linked the al-Asad coalition's success in ousting the more radical wing of the Ba'th to structural features of the state-party apparatus constructed by the regime during the late 1960s. Hinnebusch, for example, claims that "despite their control of the party apparatus and its 'popular organizations,' the radicals could do nothing but mobilize ineffectual demonstrations, no match for the army with its monopoly of the ultimate resort. The fragility of the Ba'th's mobilizational effort was exposed by its failure to offer any real resistance to Asad's military coup: unable to transcend a style of 'action from above,' its organizations remained, at once, too bureaucratic and too riddled with personalistic cliques to mobilize the intense popular activism which might have made a difference in the internal power struggle."[88] Such a conclusion is more self-evident in retrospect than it was in the fall of 1970.

Foreign policy played a central role in the outcome of the struggle between supporters of Salah Jadid and allies of Hafiz al-Asad. At the very time that party-affiliated popular front organizations and the Popular Defense Army were mobilizing public sentiment in favor of intervention in the Jordanian civil war, regular army and air force commanders expressed strong opposition both to direct Syrian involvement and to the propaganda campaign directed against the regime in Amman. When Syrian armor was ordered into the area north of Irbid to back up al-Sa'iqah units already on the ground, Minister of Defense al-Asad, acting in his capacity as commandant of the air force, adamantly refused to order ground-support aircraft to provide the brigade with air cover.[89] Those close to Salah Jadid blamed the regular armed forces for the ensuing debacle, but high-ranking military commanders riposted that the intervention had been ill-considered from the beginning, and it was only their actions that prevented the country from being sucked into a quagmire.[90]

More crucial in accounting for Syria's deescalation than such conflicting postmortems is the clear absence of overriding incentives for the ruling social coalition to escalate its involvement in the fighting raging just across the border. Despite the political-economic crisis that gripped the country in the fall of 1970, the comparatively moderate internal threat to the regime posed by domestic political challengers sharply reduced the importance of whatever minor intraregime conflicts of interest arose as a result of the policies that were implemented to meet the crisis. It is even possible that the relatively low level of internal threat provided the dominant coalition the luxury of formulating and carrying out programs that were exceptionally complementary. In Hinnebusch's words, "The state whose helm Asad inherited was a far sturdier structure than the fragile entity the Ba'th had seized in 1963. But, besides the creation of new structures, the transformation in the social composition of the state, the re-orientation of policy to serve its mass base, and the leveling of the social terrain on which it rested were crucial in giving the state a wholly new power, autonomy of the dominant societal forces, and impact on Syrian society."[91] In this particular instance, *pace* Charles Tilly, state making advanced through a notable abstention from war making.[92]

CHAPTER THREE

Expanding Intervention
in Lebanon, 1976

Syrian involvement in the Lebanese civil war dates from the very first weeks following the outbreak of fighting between Palestinian guerrillas and the Maronite al-Kataib militia in mid-April 1975. Damascus dispatched Foreign Minister 'Abd al-Halim Khaddam to mediate between the combatants that June, then sponsored the formation of a Committee for National Dialogue three months later as a forum for debating the reforms necessary to bring the continuing violence to an end. When none of these mediation attempts showed any sign of succeeding, Syrian officials offered a comprehensive reform package of their own and ordered units of the Syrian-sponsored Palestine Liberation Army to move into central Lebanon as a signal to the Maronite-dominated Lebanese government that they wanted the proposal to be taken seriously.[1]

Subsequent negotiations between Lebanon's President Sulaiman Franjieh and Syria's President Hafiz al-Asad merely widened the gulf separating supporters of the Lebanese status quo ante from groups that demanded fundamental political and social change. Fighting between al-Kataib militias and dissident Lebanese army units led by Lieutenant Ahmad al-Khatib erupted in mid-March 1976, prompting Damascus to deploy squadrons of warships to interdict shipments of arms and ammunition through the ports of Tyre, Sidon, and Tripoli. During the first week of April, a Syrian armored battalion took up positions straddling the main Beirut-Damascus highway, just inside Lebanese territory. This initial military intervention guaranteed the success of Syria's preferred candidate, Elias Sarkis, in the Lebanese presidential election held the first week of May. But it failed to halt the fighting between al-Kataib and forces allied to the Lebanese National Movement, which claimed some one thousand casualties in a series of clashes during the middle of the month.[2] The last week of May, troops belonging to al-Khatib's Lebanese Arab Army attacked a string of Maronite villages around Tripoli, raising the specter of all-out war between al-Kataib on the one hand and Palestinian and Lebanese National Movement militias on the other.

Faced with a rapidly disintegrating political and military situation throughout Lebanon, the Syrian government on 1 June launched a two-pronged offensive toward Akkar and Tripoli in the north and Zahle and Beirut, carried out by armored and infantry units of its regular armed forces. The offensive ground to a halt nine days later after fierce battles on the outskirts of Beirut and Sidon to the south. But serious fighting continued throughout the remainder of the month between Syrian forces and Palestinian-Lebanese National Movement commandos as diplomats in Cairo debated the role and composition of an Arab peacekeeping force. The negotiations produced no mutually acceptable resolution to the conflict and soon collapsed.

Sporadic fighting persisted throughout the summer. Then, in mid-October, a second, more massive Syrian offensive overran all of central Lebanon, along with the country's most important urban centers. This second operation not only put Damascus in a position to dominate Lebanese affairs to an unprecedented degree but also upset Syria's delicate strategic equilibrium with Israel. Why the Syrian leadership undertook such a risky and costly military campaign during the late spring and summer of 1976 can best be explained in terms of ongoing conflicts among powerful forces inside Syria itself.

REORIENTING THE BA'TH

As its first move after taking control of the party-state apparatus in November 1970, Syria's new governing elite appealed to private businesspeople to assist it in solving the country's persistent economic difficulties. In front of a delegation of wealthy Damascene merchants on 6 December, President Hafiz al-Asad announced his intention to do all he could to enhance the role of the private sector in Syria's commerce and industry. In addition, the president promised to initiate a wholesale reorganization of the public sector with a view to improving its overall efficiency. The newly appointed minister of the economy and foreign trade, Mustafa Hallaj, echoed these sentiments in a meeting with prominent businessmen from Aleppo the same day. In his words, the new regime intended to "create genuine co-operation between the public and the private sectors."[3] In a subsequent speech to a rally in the capital, al-Asad went even further: "We shall deepen the socialist steps the revolution has realized. We shall strengthen the public sector, eliminate its defects, work to develop its establishments and provide it with all available know-how. . . . At the same time, we shall give every opportunity to private initiative with which our people abounds, within the legal laws and decrees."[4] Changing the rules according to which the Syrian economy operated constituted the first stage of a general reorientation undertaken by the new leadership of the Ba'th after November 1970.

In January 1971, state officials altered Syria's foreign trading regulations to make them more accommodating to private importers. The new laws permitted any private sector trading company to bring up to 100,000 Syrian pounds' worth of raw materials, machinery, and spare parts into the country duty-free.[5] This measure stimulated private interests to undertake 1,178 new ventures during the first ten months of that year, employing approximately 3,900 workers at a total cost of 74 million pounds.[6] By the first months of 1972, state officials had eased restrictions on the importation of sugar, rice, and flour in the face of severe shortages of these staples on local markets. Further deregulation in the foreign trading sector of the country's economy took place that April, opening the importation of electrical equipment and other spare parts to private concerns.

At the same time, the central administration encouraged the expansion of private industry. Between mid-1971 and mid-1972 the Ministry of Industry issued more than 100 licenses to individuals or private companies to set up new industrial ventures. The majority of these ventures was in the areas of construction, clothing manufacture, and plastics making, and virtually all were comparatively small, with an average capital of 500,000 pounds. By the end of 1972, 1,237 licenses had been granted to small-scale industrial projects.

Private enterprise responded hesitantly but positively to the new lib-

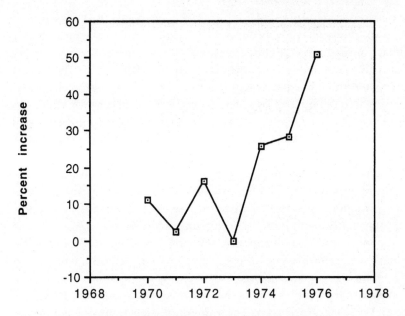

Figure 8. Gross fixed capital formation, private sector, 1970–1976

eralization measures. Gross fixed capital formation in private firms remained virtually unchanged from 1970 to 1971 but increased by some
15 percent the following year (see Figure 8). The private sector accounted for 29 percent of Syria's total foreign trade in 1971, and most
of the goods it imported consisted of textile-making equipment, fruits,
vegetables, and canned foodstuffs. Figures for 1972 indicate that private firms provided 35 percent of aggregate manufacturing production
and employed some 62 percent of the country's workforce. Elisabeth
Longuenesse reports that by 1973 the private sector "produced 85
percent of the chocolate, 51 percent of the cotton and silk, 94 percent
of the knitted goods, 70 percent of the socks, 56 percent of the paint,
45 percent of medical supplies, 78 percent of the soap, etc." for the
country as a whole.[7] These proportions are all the more remarkable
given the priorities of the third Five-Year Plan (1971–1976). According
to this plan, 79.2 percent of total investment was earmarked for large-
scale public industry, particularly state-affiliated enterprises situated in
the larger cities.[8]

With the blossoming of the private sector, membership in the state-sponsored trade union federation steadily declined. In Damascus and Aleppo, the proportion of workers belonging to the federation's subsidiary organizations shrank dramatically in the decade between 1972 and 1982. Increasing mobility of industrial workers during these years prevented the labor movement from recapturing the influence it had exercised in the mid-1960s while enabling state officials to "keep things under control" in Syria's most important urban areas.[9] A different trend became evident in peripheral regions of the country: the ten years after 1972 saw a 400 percent increase in the size of the labor unions in Tartus and al-Hasakah and a 300 percent jump in membership in Dayr al-Zur. In these three provinces, where small landholders and petroleum and transportation workers formed major bases of support for the regime, laborers continued to join the trade union federation.

Liberalization thus dampened the potential for overt conflict between Syria's newly reconstituted ruling coalition and the labor movement during the early 1970s. But deregulation soon created serious coordination problems among the various sectors of the country's economy. As early as April 1971, government officials reintroduced restrictions on the importation of fruits, vegetables, and consumer goods from Lebanon as a means of stemming the flow of Syrian currency to Beirut and protecting nascent private food and consumer goods producers within the country.[10] By the first half of 1972, increases in state spending to finance current development projects and fund future ventures precipitated sharp increases in prices on local markets.[11] This trend forced the government to cut back on actual expenditures for state-sponsored projects during fiscal 1972–1973, with the exception of large-scale capital goods plants such as the new cement factories at Damascus, Aleppo, and Hamah.[12]

Conflict between the private and public sectors of the Syrian economy escalated over the following three years. The government issued a series of decrees in March 1974 relaxing the procedures regulating currency exchanges and providing incentives for foreign investment to enter the country; subsequent changes in the law made it possible for private companies based in Syria to contract with outside investors to set up joint commercial and industrial ventures, as well as for foreign firms to bid on Syrian government projects through local brokers.[13] In the first months of 1975, American petroleum exploration and hotel management companies were invited to begin operating in the country; a

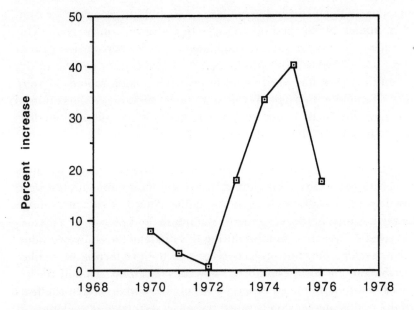

Figure 9. Gross fixed capital formation, public sector, 1970–1976

handful of other Western firms was given permission to undertake joint ventures with indigenous public sector enterprises in the middle of the year.[14] These tentative openings to the international market were reinforced that summer by a formal agreement signed between Damascus and Washington which guaranteed the inviolability of American investments in Syria.

Nevertheless, state officials continued to fund a wide range of large-scale, capital-intensive industrial projects throughout the early and mid-1970s. In July 1974 the government announced that it would begin work on several key public enterprises: a sodium carbonate factory capable of producing 100,000 tons of this compound annually, a foundry capable of converting 100,000 tons of scrap iron into usable metal each year, a factory designed to manufacture 10 million electric light bulbs annually, and one capable of producing 25 million pencils per year.[15] Major additions to the existing state-run ceramics and phosphate plants were proposed around the same time.

The regime's continued concentration on large-scale, mechanized industry demanded considerable sustained investment on the part of the state. In the textile industry alone, total public investment rose from 23.1 million Syrian pounds in 1971 to 311.2 million in 1975. This fourteenfold increase was accompanied by a 184 percent increase in the value of Syrian cloth production during the same period. In the chemical sector, the government invested 28 million pounds in 1971 and 833 million by 1975. At the same time, the value of the country's chemical production rose from 171 million to 324 million pounds.[16] These trends are illustrated in Figure 9.

After 1974, contradictions arising from the simultaneous expansion of the private and public sectors deepened as Syrian economic planners began to encourage both Western firms and local monied interests to participate directly in the growth of the country's capital-intensive heavy industry. Fertilizer, cement, aluminum, and phosphate factories received the greatest stimulus during this phase of the country's industrial development. But projects related to the production of textiles, petroleum, and iron continued to occupy a central place in the regime's thoroughly mixed economic program. Nowhere were the effects of the underlying tension between these two sectors more evident than in the relationship between Syria's cotton and petroleum industries.

COTTON, PETROLEUM, AND THE CRISIS OF 1975–1976

Cotton production and the manufacturing activities associated with it traditionally represented a major component of the Syrian economy. During the 1960s and early 1970s, cotton growing and the manufacture of cotton goods provided work for more people than did any other industry. The number of independent, small producers and sellers of cloth and yarn actually rose as the regime's program of setting up large-scale, state-run textile complexes proceeded after 1965.[17] But around 1974, cotton's preeminent place in the country's economy was finally overtaken by petroleum-related products. Whereas cotton-related items accounted for 51.6 percent of the total value of Syria's exports in 1973, crude petroleum accounted for 69.1 percent by 1975.[18] The virtual reversal in the importance of these two industries significantly altered the distribution of power within Syrian society.

Cotton-related activities clustered in the north-central and far northeastern parts of the country. During the 1970s, the great majority of

Syria's cotton was grown on newly reclaimed agricultural land in the easternmost provinces, especially to the north of Dayr al-Zur. Economic activities in the lands adjacent to the Euphrates River and throughout the rest of the northeast, known collectively as al-Jazirah, were for the most part dominated by the rich merchants and businesspeople of Aleppo.[19] These individuals controlled not only the export of raw and ginned cotton, which dipped during the 1974–1975 and 1975–1976 crop years, but also the milling and weaving of cotton goods, which remained very profitable throughout the early 1970s.[20] Besides Aleppo, other cities in the north-central part of the country also had a major stake in cotton production. The state-run textile complex at Hamah ran at virtually full capacity during the middle years of the decade, as did two additional ginning mills at Idlib and Homs. These factories, along with smaller operations located in the towns and villages, provided work for landless farm laborers in the districts around Hamah—where such laborers were particularly numerous—and other north-central cities.[21] These marginal workers were hurt severely as the amount of land devoted to cotton declined and the output of small-scale textile work-shops fell off during 1975–1976.

Three related trends illustrate the decline of the established cotton industry in Syria's north-central cities during the mid-1970s. First, the total acreage devoted to cotton production dropped from almost 220,200 hectares of irrigated land and 30,300 hectares of nonirrigated land in the 1971–1972 crop year to 185,100 and 23,000 in 1975–1976, respectively. By the late spring of 1976, there were clear indications that the amount of land planted in cotton was going to fall substantially for the 1976–1977 season as well.[22] This trend was especially marked in the provinces of Hamah, Homs, and Aleppo, reinforcing the drift of cotton production northeastward to the areas around Dayr al-Zur, al-Raqqah, and al-Hasakah.

Second, changes in cropping patterns led to a shift away from the small-scale, labor-intensive cotton farming that had remained viable in north-central Syria throughout the early 1970s. Small-scale cotton pro-duction was increasingly undermined after 1974 by the expansion of very large, capital-intensive agricultural enterprises centered in the far northeastern provinces. This shift is evident from the figures for gross fixed capital formation in the country's agricultural sector, which show an increase from 397 million Syrian pounds in 1974 to 734 million the following year. Production shortfalls reduced this figure to 605 million pounds in 1976, but it rose steadily thereafter.[23]

Finally, beginning in 1975 a higher proportion of Syria's total cotton crop began to be funneled into factories operated by the state-controlled General Organization for Textile Industries (Unitex). This organization had begun building four very large spinning factories at Dayr al-Zur, Homs, Idlib, and Latakia during the winter of 1975–1976.[24] The construction of additional weaving mills, dyeing plants, and clothing factories to be operated by Unitex complemented the modernization and expansion of the country's capital-intensive, export-oriented cotton industry.

Changes in the size and organization of the cotton-related sector of Syria's economy during the first half of 1976 dramatically increased the potential for social conflict in and around the north-central cities. Reductions in the amount of acreage devoted to cotton production created a significant rise in the level of unemployment in this region, not only among agricultural laborers but also among the urban craftspeople whose livelihoods depended upon obtaining adequate supplies of cotton and other industrial crops. Between 1970 and 1976, the official rate of unemployment in Hamah province increased more than 28 percent, from 4.6 percent to 5.9 percent of the total labor force; in Idlib province the rate rose more than 23 percent, from 5.6 percent to 6.9 percent of the total labor force; in al-Raqqah province it jumped more than 32 percent, from 3.1 percent to 4.1 percent of the total labor force.[25] At the same time, small-scale farmers in Homs, Hamah, and Aleppo found themselves increasingly unable to compete with the capital-intensive, state-supported agrarian enterprises of the far northeast. Their disadvantageous position relative to those who controlled such enterprises severely weakened the position of independent small-holders in the north-central provinces vis-à-vis larger landholders in their own districts as well. Urban artisans and shopkeepers found themselves in a similar position relative to the state-controlled ginning and manufacturing operations that were being set up in north-central cities during 1975–1976. Taken together, these circumstances created the distinct possibility that a broad range of social forces with ties to cotton production and manufacturing in north-central Syria might ally themselves in opposition to the regime during the spring of 1976. And this possibility heightened as a result of concurrent developments in the petroleum sector.

Throughout the 1970s, Syria's oil industry centered on the north-central city of Homs. Two oil refineries and a petrochemical fertilizer plant had been set up outside the city by 1972. The government announced plans in March 1976 to cooperate with the French in building a second fertilizer plant at Homs to make further use of the various by-products of the petroleum refining process; capacity at the newer of the two refineries was doubled a month later with the addition of a pair of new distillation units.[26] These operations created a considerable population of industrial managers and skilled workers in Homs province, complemented by the transportation and pipeline workers tied to the petroleum sector in the adjacent districts of Tartus and Banyas.[27] By 1977, almost twenty thousand workers were employed in Syria's petroleum industry. Approximately three-fifths of these were involved in production and distribution activities outside Homs province; around eight thousand workers were engaged in refining and transit operations at the two refining centers of Homs and Banyas.[28] Moreover, several thousand construction workers were also employed at the Homs refinery complex during the mid-1970s, repairing the damage inflicted on the installation by Israeli warplanes during the October War of 1973. Additional construction workers were hired to build other petrochemical plants at both Homs and Hamah during these years.[29]

Homs's petroleum-related labor force was on the whole more dependent on the regime than were other industrial workers in Syria's north-central provinces. State officials maintained tight control over petroleum and petrochemical laborers by incorporating them into the General Federation of Workers' Unions, and these workers enjoyed relatively high wages compared to the artisans and shopkeepers of Hamah and Aleppo. But oil workers faced an uncertain future as a result of the Iraqi government's announcement in early April 1976 that it intended to stop shipping oil across northern Syria.[30] Since Saudi crude oil was already being channeled into the state's newer refinery at Banyas and potential alternative sources of supply such as Libya and Nigeria also enjoyed closer connections with that coastal refinery than with the inland facility at Homs, petroleum workers in Homs faced a likely cutback in employment at their complex by the end of the spring.

Under these circumstances, the pivotal position of Homs's oil workers within Syria's domestic economy made the possibility of unrest on their part severely threatening to the regime. In the first place, these laborers' strategic location with regard to local oil refining and fertilizer production enabled them to disrupt domestic heavy industry and large-scale agriculture, both of which depended heavily upon petroleum-related products. Second, these workers could deprive the regime of the petroleum exports that made up the country's primary source of foreign exchange. Third, the revenues derived from oil exportation provided a substantial portion of the investment monies necessary for continued growth in the capital-intensive industrial and agricultural sectors.[31] Thus the possibility that petroleum workers in Homs might join other forces in Hamah and Aleppo in active opposition against the government posed a severe threat to the position of Syria's dominant social coalition by the late spring of 1976.

INTRAREGIME CONFLICT AND THE REVIVAL OF THE IKHWAN

In allying itself with the commercial and industrial bourgeoisie of Damascus, Syria's central administration became committed after 1970 to a liberalizing economic program predicated on the development of capital-intensive industry. David Carr has noted that the industrial program undertaken during the mid-1970s involved "a concentration of investment and manpower resources on a few new very large projects. At the same time, the Syrian government has given increasing attention to the 'modern' engineering and chemical industries at the expense of the traditional foodstuffs and textiles industries."[32] That this orientation permeated policy-making circles at this time can be illustrated by three more or less typical projects. Peugeot announced in mid-August 1975 that it had contracted with the government to construct an assembly plant, to be situated somewhere near Tartus, capable of turning out ten thousand automobiles per year. In the spring of 1976, a French firm won a $45 million contract to build a mechanized public sector glass factory in Damascus. This award was followed five months later by arrangements with Yamaha of Japan to set up a motorcycle assembly plant in the capital that would use chassis manufactured locally.[33] Such large-

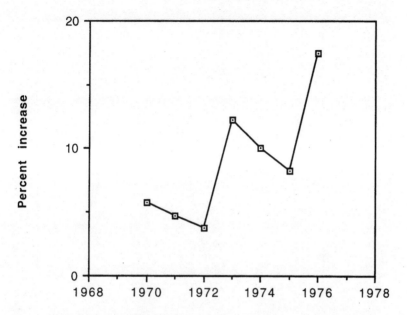

Figure 10. Industrial production index, 1970–1976

scale industrial projects required substantial quantities of capital both for the purchase of raw materials and other inputs once construction was completed and for future modernization and expansion.

But by the spring of 1976, capital was becoming increasingly scarce throughout the Syrian economy. As early as 1974, the country started to suffer from the peculiar mix of economic difficulties associated with "stagflation."[34] These conditions grew more pronounced over the next two years. It was reported that Syria suffered from an inflation rate of almost 30 percent by 1976; at the same time, industrial production had begun to decline (see Figure 10).[35] Increases in gross domestic product, which had registered notable gains after 1972, peaked in 1975 (see Figure 11). As a result, access to larger amounts of capital became necessary to ensure that industrial expansion and increases in productivity could keep pace with inflation. A sizable proportion of new investment monies was made available in the form of aid from wealthier Arab governments during the oil boom years of 1974–1975. But inputs from external sources proved insufficient to offset the detrimental effects of "a downward trend in the 'true' domestic savings ratio from 1973–

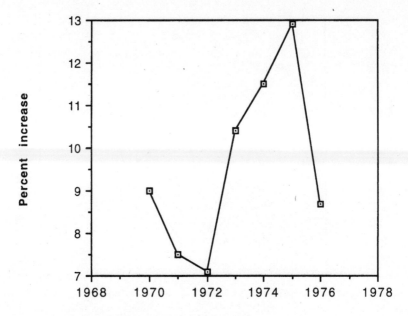

Figure 11. Gross domestic product, 1970–1976

76."[36] Furthermore, Saudi officials unexpectedly terminated the kingdom's economic assistance payments to Damascus at the end of January 1976, forcing the government to recalculate its proposed budget allocations for industrial development.[37]

These developments not only hurt the regime but also undermined the long-standing local predominance of influential agricultural, commercial, and industrial elites—whose continued acquiescence was essential for the regime's political stability—in Syria's north-central provinces. As cotton acreage steadily shrank during 1975–1976, richer cotton-growing landowners in northeastern parts of the country found themselves unable to switch to fruit and vegetable production for export as well-to-do landlords in the southern provinces of al-Suwayda and Dir'a could.[38] Larger commercial farmers in Aleppo and Hamah provinces were thus put at a substantially greater distance from, if not in actual opposition to, the regime in Damascus. At the same time, the larger-scale manufacturers and merchants of Aleppo and Latakia who could be co-opted or pacified by the regime as long as new industrial and commercial projects were being set up within their domains could

88

no longer be expected to collaborate with the central administration as investment capital dried up. Thus the spring of 1976 saw a heightened potential that farm laborers and smaller manufacturers in the districts around Hamah and Homs might ally with out-of-work petroleum and construction workers. And this trend took shape at the very time that provincial elites, whose continued neutrality was vital for the security of the regime, were growing restive.

Deepening coordination problems among the various sectors of the Syrian economy, in conjunction with the increasing alienation of richer businesspeople in the north-central cities and towns, sparked an upsurge of activity on the part of Syria's Islamist movement during the late winter and spring of 1976. In February, following the death of Marwan Hadid in a government prison, rioting broke out in several northern districts. The most serious disturbances occurred in the central neighborhoods of Hamah, where government forces clashed on several occasions with students and tradespeople. During one of these riots, the chief of Syria's state security forces was killed.[39] Urban unrest continued to smolder during March, exacerbating long-standing tensions between the Christian and Muslim communities.[40] The trend culminated in a wave of mass arrests at the end of April.[41]

According to sources close to the Muslim Brotherhood, such confrontations greatly increased popular support for the ikhwan throughout Syria's north-central provinces. Not only did the organization's membership grow during the winter of 1975–1976, but the new cadres were described as being of better "quality, as these new members were highly committed and ideologically conscious."[42] The official publication of the Syrian ikhwan, *al-Nadhir*, gives 8 February 1976 as the date when the leadership of the movement proclaimed the start of a general struggle (*jihad*) against the al-Asad regime. This step coincided with a reported reconstitution of the outlawed Egyptian ikhwan at the end of March.[43]

CONTRADICTORY REGIME RESPONSES

Syria's ruling social coalition made no unified or coordinated response to the threats confronting its members in the spring of 1976. Instead, each of the social forces that constituted the regime adopted a distinct program designed to improve its own position relative to that of its opponents. State officials ordered the military and police into the north-central cities of Aleppo, Hamah, and Homs on several occasions during April to suppress dissident organizations by force. Meanwhile, public sector managers based in Damascus, who controlled the heavy industrial sector of Syria's economy, stepped up their investment in large-scale construction and manufacturing projects in the north-central provinces as a way of integrating the region's independent producers into tightly organized, hierarchically structured institutions. Finally, Damascene import-export merchants imported substantial quantities of foreign-made goods into the country in an effort to undercut indigenous, small-scale manufacturing. These measures—adopted by each partner in the ruling coalition individually—effectively weakened the respective positions of the most powerful challengers to the regime. But they also put one another's political and economic interests in jeopardy, thereby threatening the collective position of the dominant coalition.

Throughout the early 1970s, the al-Asad regime turned to the Syrian armed forces and state security services to suppress political dissidence in the north-central provinces. In February 1973, elite army units surrounded the city of Hamah, where violent demonstrations had flared in response to the deletion of any reference to Islam in Syria's newly revised constitution. State security forces moved into Homs two months later to put down rioting in that city.[44] Fighting between the country's military and Islamist militants surfaced again in July 1975, when security forces arrested "a number of members of the right-wing Muslim Brotherhood" for plotting to overthrow the regime and other "anti-government activities."[45] Three weeks later, army units mobilized when mass demonstrations broke out in Aleppo, ostensibly to protest the serious water shortages plaguing the city.[46] But the state's use of military forces to suppress dissident organizations reached a peak during the months immediately before the Syrian intervention in the Lebanese civil war.

In response to widespread rioting in Hamah during February 1976, elite units of the Syrian armed forces under the command of the president's brother were ordered into the country's north-central cities. Their mission was to break up the organizational structures of any clandestine groups operating in the region, using any means necessary.[47] To this end, large-scale arrests were carried out in Hamah during the last two weeks of the month. Such operations were for the most part entrusted to the Defense Brigades and the Special Elite Forces. But these two units were reinforced by some five hundred regular army troops, and the Forty-seventh Armored Brigade headquartered in Hamah was put on alert. Two months later, army and security units arrested two hundred followers of Hafiz al-Asad's former rival, General Salah Jadid, along with "some figures associated with a rightist Muslim sect," no doubt the ikhwan.[48] At the same time, the head of the Kurdish Democratic party—whose primary supporters were to be found among the farm laborers of the country's far northeast provinces whose lands had been sequestered by the regime to build "model state farms" beginning in 1973—was transferred from his place of detention in the north to a hospital in the capital. The transfer coincided with a government effort to force the Syrian Communist party to disband its youth and women's organizations.[49] In short, state officials undertook an extensive program of military coercion and intimidation in the spring of 1976, directed against a wide range of political organizations opposed to the regime.

The use of Syria's armed forces to suppress political opposition weakened the organizations whose members were actively challenging the regime's control over the north-central provinces. But it also provoked heightened political violence in Homs, Hamah, and Aleppo, sharply polarizing these communities. The open split between supporters and opponents of the regime became apparent in the wave of bombings and assassinations that swept across Syria's north-central cities during the spring and summer. It also prompted small bands of well-armed fighters to carry out carefully planned strikes against government facilities and state-run industrial plants throughout the region.[50] That August, for instance, a key section of the main oil pipeline near Homs was cut by a bomb blast, seriously disrupting operations at the refinery there. A rocket attack on the headquarters of the state security agency in Hamah followed, for which a previously unknown group, the Syrian Revolutionaries' Organization, claimed responsibility.[51] Such incidents became less frequent as Syria's central administration consolidated its position in both Lebanon and the north-central provinces after October 1976, although attacks against government installations never stopped altogether.[52]

While military commanders deployed Syria's armed forces to suppress opposition movements in Aleppo, Hamah, and Homs, managers of the country's public sector enterprises began carrying out a concerted program of large-scale industrialization in the north-central provinces as a way of subjecting the region's independent artisans and craftspeople to some form of centralized regulation. State officials expanded the government-run cotton-spinning mill at Hamah during the first months of 1976, and construction was initiated on three new mills at Idlib, Latakia, and Qalamun. At about the same time, plans were drawn up to build an aluminum-rolling plant at Latakia with the cooperation of a Japanese consortium, to construct a massive cement factory at Hamah, and to install a pair of new distillation units at the Homs refinery complex.[53] Each of these projects required a sizable number of construction workers, as well as skilled and unskilled labor to run the plant once it was completed. And for them to operate at a profit, the labor force would have to be relatively tame, if not docile.

But by the spring of 1976, the state's reliance on military force in its escalating conflict with the Islamist movement created anything but stable conditions throughout most of north-central Syria. Military commanders and public sector managers consequently found themselves working at cross-purposes. By transforming the long-standing political struggles that pervaded local society in Aleppo, Hamah, and Homs into overt and violent confrontations pitting the security forces against the local population, those in charge of the armed forces made it increasingly difficult for those responsible for public sector industry to achieve the objectives they set for themselves.

This contradiction inside the ruling coalition was exacerbated by the actions of Syria's major import-export concerns. Beginning in 1974, richer Damascene merchants sharply raised the level of imported consumer goods coming into the country's urban markets to undercut the operations of small-scale manufacturers and craftspeople. The rise in imports generated an aggregate trade deficit of some $450 million for 1974, which surged to over $650 million the following year.[54] More specifically, the total tonnage of imported yarn and thread entering Syria jumped by 41.5 percent between 1975 and 1976, while the total tonnage of cotton cloth imported into the country in 1976 was virtually double the quantity brought in the year before.[55] Consequently, wholesale prices for locally produced cotton yarn dropped on markets in both Aleppo and Damascus.[56]

In addition, by effectively reducing the demand for domestic light manufactures, and hence for indigenously produced raw materials, the increase in imported manufactured goods created substantial incentives for large-scale agriculturalists to shift from growing staples and industrial crops to producing fruits and vegetables for sale overseas, particularly in Europe. The resulting shortage of foodstuffs on local markets greatly amplified the political difficulties facing Syria's ruling coalition. During 1975, for instance, Syrian wheat production dropped 5 percent from its level the preceding year; barley production fell 8.8 percent, while the output of lentils and olives was down 20 percent and 27 percent, respectively.[57] The fall in local agricultural output had a particularly heavy impact on Syria's already restive north-central urban areas, since it was the artisans and tradespeople of Aleppo, Hamah, and Homs who could least tolerate even small increases in the cost of agricultural produce, both because of the steadily rising cost of industrial crops such as cotton and because of the intrusion of state-run enterprises into the region's economy.

By early 1976, the activities of Syria's larger import-export merchants began to hurt not only small-scale manufacturers of household and luxury items but also the country's expanding state-supported heavy industrial sector. In the first place, large-scale commercial firms lost one of their primary suppliers of reasonably priced, light manufactured items as fighting escalated in Lebanon.[58] This development forced Damascene merchants to turn to more expensive European goods to maintain their predominant position in the country's foreign trade. But financing imports from Europe required substantially greater amounts of credit than their previous operations had. The turn to extraregional manufactures caused demand for Syria's already severely limited reserves of capital and foreign exchange to skyrocket.[59] Government officials hinted in early February that they would begin allowing foreign banks to open subsidiaries in the country's seven free trading zones as a means of ensuring local traders greater guaranteed access to credit.[60]

Second, foreign trading houses started to import a variety of capital goods in addition to lighter consumer items. Private interests contracted with Britain's Ministry of Overseas Development, for example, to supply some 47,000 pounds sterling worth of tool-and-die-making machinery in early April.[61] Such arrangements enabled large-scale private companies to upgrade and expand their operations, but at the same time put them into direct competition with Syria's state-run factories. As competition intensified, short-term interest rates within the country rose and prices for locally made industrial goods plummeted. These two trends effectively reduced the returns on investment in Syria's larger, capital-intensive manufacturing plants, compounding the regime's difficulties in coming up with sufficient amounts of capital to cover the costs of newly proposed ventures.[62]

Moreover, in early 1976 the activities of Syria's import-export concerns reversed the country's balance-of-payments situation, turning it from net surplus into net deficit. The regime thus suffered a worsening overall financial situation at the very time that the cost of servicing Syria's existing foreign debt was rising most rapidly.[63] Debt payments became more and more difficult to make as government revenues from oil production failed to achieve anticipated levels during the course of 1975–1976.[64] By the second quarter of 1976, the country's dominant social coalition confronted serious intraregime tensions, not only between powerful military commanders and the managers of public sector industry but also between state industrial managers and richer merchants enjoying close ties to the government.

FOREIGN INTERVENTION AND DOMESTIC POLITICAL RESOURCES

Syria's ruling coalition became unable in the late spring of 1976 to dominate its opponents by using domestic resources alone. Direct military intervention in Lebanon, intended to impose a solution to the escalating fighting there, thus grew more and more attractive to the Syrian regime. Such a move could provide Syria's rulers with additional resources that they could use to their own domestic political advantage. Of these, the most important were the capital held by Lebanese financial institutions, the light manufactures produced by Lebanese companies, and the docking facilities at the port of Beirut.

Large-scale investment projects within Syria had depended heavily upon Lebanese capital for financing before the outbreak of the civil war in April 1975. This dependence was particularly pronounced in Syria's private sector, which found itself at a clear disadvantage relative to government-run enterprises by the mid-1970s.[65] During the years from 1972 to 1976, private firms drew more and more of their available credit from the state-run Commercial Bank of Syria, creating greater competition for domestic capital at the same time the government was commited to maintaining a fixed national interest rate.[66] This trend made Beirut's financial institutions, which continued to augment their locally held assets even as their overseas investments soared, an increasingly important alternative source of financing for Syrian developers.[67] Furthermore, beginning in mid-1975, Lebanon's major banks experienced serious problems of excess liquidity, largely as a result of changes in the structure of their relationships with Western banking institutions.[68]

These difficulties were exacerbated in two ways as fighting in Lebanon escalated. On one hand, Beirut's financial community could not find domestic outlets for its holdings as long as the country's internal security remained precarious. On the other, armed bands raided the city's larger banks to steal the fortunes contained in their vaults more and more frequently as the Lebanese central administration crumbled. So by the spring of 1976, Beirut constituted an immense pool of finance capital that remained virtually unusable as long as the civil war persisted. By forcing an end to the growing anarchy in Lebanon's major cities, Syria's armed forces could create conditions that would allow the activities of the country's banking sector to return to normal. And to the extent that normality returned, Lebanese investment capital would once again become available to Syrian enterprises. These monies could not only relieve the country's desperate shortage of credit but also compensate for the loss of foreign exchange that resulted from the cutoff of Iraqi oil-transit revenues.

In addition, putting an end to the fighting in Lebanon could restore the stability necessary for Lebanese light industry to resume production. A resumption of manufacturing inside Lebanon would enable Syria's large-scale commercial interests, especially those based in Damascus, to renew their long-standing connections with Lebanese manufacturers, a move that could be expected substantially to reduce the demand for commercial credit within the Syrian economy. At the same time, such a step would help relieve Syria's growing balance-of-payments difficulties by substituting comparatively cheap regional goods for more expensive ones produced in the Western industrial economies. Moreover, bringing an end to the fighting could enable Lebanese light industry to resume its traditional role in the Syrian economy, buttressing Syria's heavy industry by keeping consumer goods available on local markets.[69] The political importance of maintaining the flow of these items into the country is indicated by a measure promulgated by the Syrian authorities in mid-February 1976, which exempted imports from Lebanon from all taxes, duties, and storage charges at Syrian ports of entry.[70]

As the civil war intensified, not even measures such as this one could ensure a steady flow of Lebanese light manufactures into the Syrian market. Taking more active steps to restore order in Lebanon became the most secure way to provide Syria's rulers with the consumer goods necessary to allow large-scale factories in Damascus and other Syrian cities to continue to concentrate on heavy industrial output.

Finally, overt military intervention in the Lebanese civil war could reestablish Syria's access to the largest and most efficient harbor in the area, the port of Beirut. Continued fighting in Lebanon virtually severed this vital link between southern Syria and the outside world by the end of 1975. Consequently, congestion at the state-run ports of Latakia and Tartus, which had resulted in waiting times of almost two months even before the outbreak of the civil war, increased dramatically.[71] Delays at Syria's two main harbors severely disrupted the country's foreign trade, while at the same time making the financing of commercial transactions much less predictable. Furthermore, diverting goods through the more distant ports at Tartus and Latakia significantly increased the costs of doing business for Damascene merchants, forcing them to borrow greater amounts of float capital from the state's already overextended financial institutions. Finally, the connection between Damascus and Beirut became particularly vital to the Syrian regime whenever the likelihood of social disorder in north-central Syria increased because the main transportation routes linking Tartus and Latakia to the capital ran through Hamah and Homs. Beirut thus represented not only a "lender of last resort" and an important source of light manufactured goods for Syria's ruling coalition; it also constituted the hub of a crucial transportation and communications network, whose reopening was economically and politically imperative for the regime in Damascus.

Syria's military intervention in the Lebanese civil war can best be seen as an attempt by the social forces that constituted the country's ruling coalition to shore up their collective political position in the face of severe domestic challenges. Far from providing the Syrian leadership with "new opportunities" to achieve its presumed "historic ambition" of incorporating Lebanon into an overarching entity governed from Damascus,[72] the escalation of communal fighting in and around Beirut during the spring and summer of 1976 aggravated a wide range of political-economic difficulties confronting the al-Asad regime. These problems involved not only growing activism on the part of forces out-side the ruling coalition but also and more importantly deepening contradictions among its primary constituents. Dispatching units of the regular armed forces to restore a modicum of stability across the border in Lebanon mitigated fundamental conflicts of interest inside the re-gime both by harmonizing its members' disparate responses to their respective domestic opponents and by providing them with the re-sources they needed to prevail.

CHAPTER FOUR

Defusing Confrontation with Iraq, 1982

Syrian-Iraqi relations vacillated wildly during the two decades after 1970. In the first months following the coup d'état that brought Hafiz al-Asad and his colleagues to power in Damascus, the Ba'thi regimes of Syria and Iraq collaborated on a number of fronts, the most salient of which included oil policy, the promotion of radical movements and causes within the Arab world, and the ongoing confrontation with the State of Israel.[1] Iraqi overtures to Turkey, combined with recurring disagreements between Damascus and Baghdad concerning the best way to prosecute the struggle against Israel, precipitated a gradual deterioration in relations between the two states beginning in the mid-1970s. Growing conflict over the most equitable way to share the vital waters of the Euphrates River eventually "turned already sour relations into those of coherent hostility," as Amatzia Baram notes, by the spring of 1975.[2]

Egyptian President Anwar al-Sadat's peace initiative produced a short-lived rapprochement between the two governments as the 1970s drew to a close, but the spring of 1980 saw a dramatic return to open hostility as first Baghdad and then Damascus accused the other of arming and financing groups working to undermine its internal political stability. The outbreak of war between Iraq and the Islamic Republic of Iran that September elicited unabashed support for Tehran on the part of the Syrian leadership. During the first weeks of the fighting, Bruce Stanley observes, "Syrian airfields were made available for Iranian strikes against western Iraq. Syria engaged in violations of Iraqi airspace as a way of keeping Baghdad unsure about Syrian military intentions, thus retaining Iraqi troops on the Syrian border. Syria gave material and financial support to opposition groups within Iraq, particularly the Kurds in the north."[3] It has been reported that Damascus provided the Iranian armed forces with war matériel and military advisers during the initial phase of the conflict.[4]

As the Iran-Iraq War dragged into its second year, relations between the Syrian leadership and its Iraqi counterpart steadily worsened. President al-Asad used the occasion of the nineteenth anniversary of the March 1963 revolution to accuse the Iraqi regime of sponsoring the wave of unrest that swept Syria in the winter of 1981–1982. Ba'th party members suspected of harboring pro-Iraq loyalties were summarily arrested throughout the country in the wake of the president's speech.[5] But even this episode did not represent the lowest point in relations between the two governments. According to Amatzia Baram, "April 1982 saw the nadir. On 8 April, Syria closed its border with Iraq, allegedly to prevent the infiltration of saboteurs and weapons from Iraq in support of the Muslim Brotherhood's underground and other Iraqi-sponsored movements inside Syria. On 10 April . . . the Kirkuk-Banias pipeline was shut down by Damascus. Finally on 18 April, Syria broke off diplomatic relations with Iraq, and Walid Hamdun, a deputy premier, promised to help the Iraqi people in toppling the regime in Baghdad."[6] Damascus backed up this threat by reinforcing infantry and armored units stationed along the Syrian-Iraqi border and ordering them to initiate military exercises in clear view of Iraqi troops on the other side of the boundary.[7] Caught between the need to guard against a Syrian attack and the growing fragility of its own forces' tactical position in southwestern Iran, Baghdad reiterated calls for a cease-fire with Tehran, while redoubling its efforts to eliminate remaining pockets of Iranian resistance in Khuzestan. The Islamic Republic responded by launching a major offensive in the area between al-'Amarah and Khorramshahr at the end of the month.

Nevertheless, Damascus opted not to follow through on its threat to open a second front in the Iran-Iraq War during the spring of 1982.[8] By the beginning of September, when Arab heads of state gathered in Fez, Syrian officials had noticeably softened their posture toward Baghdad. President al-Asad permitted the rulers of Jordan, Morocco, Kuwait, and Saudi Arabia to mediate between himself and Iraqi President Saddam

Husain during the course of the summit. Damascus even hinted that
the best way to resolve the Iran-Iraq War would be for Syria and Iraq to
merge into a unified Ba'thi entity. President al-Asad promised to meet
with Saddam Husain later that fall to work out the details of unification
between the two countries and discuss other areas of future political
and economic cooperation.[9] To no one's surprise, the unity scheme
failed to materialize. But that it was proposed at all highlights
Damascus's willingness to defuse the confrontation with Baghdad. The
fact that the April crisis ended without escalating into open warfare is
intimately connected to political-economic developments inside Syria
during the spring of 1982.

ANTINOMIES OF BA'THI LIBERALISM

Moves by state officials and the rich merchant community of
Damascus to reduce government supervision over Syria's commercial
and financial affairs generated a marked downturn in the local economy at the end of the 1970s. Even though real gross domestic product
increased from around 4.2 billion Syrian pounds in 1977 to just under
5.8 billion pounds in 1982,[10] the rate of increase in the country's gross
domestic product plummeted between 1976 and 1978 (see Figure 12).
Similarly, even though gross fixed capital formation in the private sector
doubled between the mid-1970s and the early 1980s, a marked drop in
the rate of increase occurred from 1976 to 1979 (see Figure 13). Capital formation in the public sector dropped even more precipitously (see
Figure 14). The greatest beneficiaries of these trends were the members of what Elisabeth Longuenesse calls "a parasitic class of new capitalists . . . based on monopolization and commerce," whose connections to
the central administration enabled them to dominate the distribution
of goods coming into the country both through the government-run
ports at Latakia and Tartus and across the border from Lebanon.[11] By
the end of the decade, many of the richest individuals that made up this
"new class" had become successful entrepreneurs, investing in transportation, tourism, and construction projects, as well as in urban and rural
real estate.[12]

But the new commercial elite of Damascus was not the only urban
force to profit from the economic difficulties of the late 1970s. Inde-

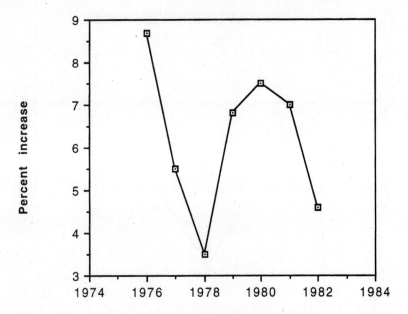

Figure 12. Gross domestic product, 1976–1982

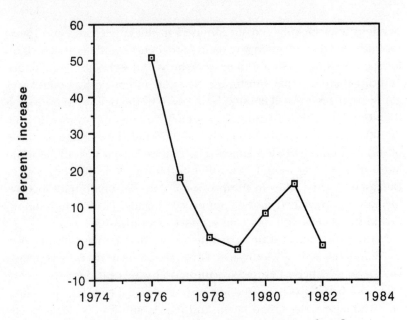

Figure 13. Gross fixed capital formation, private sector, 1976–1982

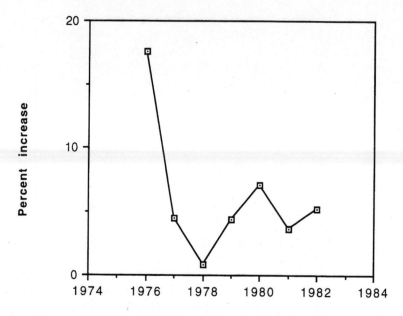

Figure 14. Gross fixed capital formation, public sector, 1976–1982

pendent tradespeople and shopkeepers in the larger cities and towns took advantage of shrinking demand for expensive and luxury goods on local markets by enlarging their workshops and stores to manufacture and distribute cheaper substitutes. Some members of the petite bourgeoisie managed to sell enough by the turn of the decade to transform their operations into medium-sized establishments employing one hundred to two hundred workers each.[13] Others failed to achieve this level of success but nonetheless amassed considerable fortunes, all the while harboring a deep-seated resentment toward both the regime in Damascus and its allies in the provinces. Less fortunate tradespeople increasingly gravitated to the country's variegated Islamist movement, providing its cells with financial support and cadres.[14]

At the same time, private agriculture expanded dramatically in many districts of the Syrian countryside. Throughout the north-central plains, lands that had been devoted to cotton and wheat production during the 1960s began to be planted in a variety of cash crops. The quantities of watermelons, dry broad beans and lentils, sunflowers, sugar beets, green plums, and pistachios cultivated in these areas rose markedly during the second half of the 1970s; the total amount of acreage devoted to millet and potatoes correspondingly dropped.[15] The spread of cash crops accompanied the reemergence of a class of richer land-holders in the region around Aleppo, Hamah, and Idlib. Richer agriculturalists gradually displaced the area's smaller independent farmers and reestablished pockets of capital-intensive, cash-crop agriculture in the north-central provinces as the 1970s drew to a close.[16]

Some of these resurgent larger landholders represented branches of the pre-1963 landowning elite. But most had been the beneficiaries of the land reform programs carried out during the Ba'thi era and thus constituted a new class of capitalist farmers. As Françoise Metral observes,

> it is mechanization, intensification and modernization of farming techniques that, because they have required increased use of machinery, capital and various forms of technical knowledge, have brought about a rapid development and change in capitalist-based agricultural production. . . . The peasants of the Ghab [valley northwest of Hamah] seem completely at ease with these apparent contradictions, and their actions are gauged to respond to them as effectively as possible. Although they are beneficiaries of a state-controlled system, all their efforts are mobilized with an eye for gaining access to an open market economy.[17]

The symbiotic relationship between public sector agricultural agencies and resurgent private landholders enhanced the overall efficiency of Syrian agriculture during the late 1970s and early 1980s. In Metral's view, "The coexistence of the public and private economic sectors, when added to the tolerant attitudes and even complicity of the administrative authorities, has given the system a certain degree of flexibility, leaving channels open for local initiatives." Such "adaptations" provided increased revenues to the central treasury, as well as enabling the cooperatives to respond more quickly to changes in foreign and domestic demand.[18] Consequently, agricultural production skyrocketed in the five years after 1974, as did gross fixed capital formation in agriculture (see Figure 15).

Although the expansion of cash-crop farming generally broadened the base of support for the al-Asad coalition, the reconsolidation of a class of richer private farmers in the countryside entailed at least two consequences that were much less favorable to the regime's interests.

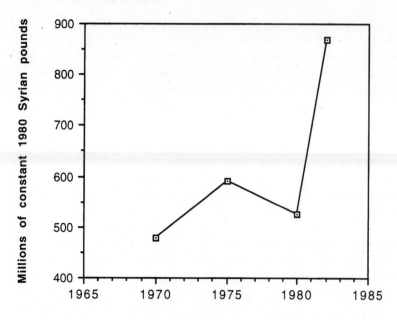

Figure 15. Gross fixed capital formation in agriculture, 1970–1982

First, the new agrarian capitalists posed a direct challenge to the state-run agricultural collectives that had been set up in the north-central provinces during the late 1960s. Although the newer private farms and the established state enterprises were given equal access to subsidized inputs and agricultural machinery, the latter found themselves saddled with covering the costs of the high dam at Tabqa and its associated network of irrigation channels and reclaimed lands. The spiraling costs of this project led government officials to shift their attention to the development of dry-land farming; Damascus finally implementated a long-delayed Ford Foundation plan to increase production on the north-central plains by agreeing to allow the establishment of the International Center for Agricultural Research in the Dry Areas just south of Aleppo. At the same time, the government invited the United Nations Development Program to undertake a comprehensive survey of range management and forage crop production in the comparatively arid districts around Hamah.[19] Finally, Robert Springborg reports that the state planning organization "virtually threw open the entirety of its agricultural sector to scrutiny by the US Agency for International

Development, which with a team of 37 American agronomists scoured the countryside in 1978 in an effort to pinpoint those bottlenecks impeding the rapid growth of the agricultural sector."[20]

In line with the recommendations of the U.S. Agency for International Development, the regime began dismantling existing state farms and redistributing the lands to their employees in the form of independent holdings loosely organized into cooperatives. Springborg observes that as of 1980 "there are fewer than ten state farms in Syria and several of these might more accurately be thought of as research stations than as production units."[21] This move left the members of the General Federation of Farm Laborers and other state-affiliated agricultural associations vulnerable to the vagaries of the market, alienating them from other forces inside the dominant social coalition and greatly reducing the regime's capacity to control developments in the countryside.

Second, the rise of the nouveaux riches farmers created rivalry between members of this class and influential scions of the old landowning elite, particularly in the north-central provinces. The land reforms of the 1960s dispossessed the most prominent large landlords of Aleppo, Hamah, Idlib, Homs, and Damascus; nevertheless, through a variety of legal technicalities and irregularities in the implementation of the reform laws, some families managed to retain control of, if not actual title to, significant portions of their former estates.[22] In the years after 1970, these families stepped up their efforts to reclaim their old lands, while at the same time attempting to regain their former position as moneylenders and patrons in the countryside.[23] They encountered three primary obstacles as the decade passed: resistance on the part of smaller farmers or landless laborers organized into state cooperatives, particularly ones linked to the General Organization for the Development of the Ghab and Asharnah; a shortage of skilled agricultural laborers to work their lands, resulting from the proliferation of small and medium-sized landholdings; and severe competition from the newer large landholders for subsidized inputs, credit, labor, and influence in rural districts.[24] Such difficulties prompted some prominent families to supply dissident urban forces with funds and weapons to use in fighting the regime, as they had during the mid-1960s.[25]

Faced with growing challenges both in the cities and in the countryside, the forces that constituted the al-Asad regime adopted a variety of measures intended to shore up their collective political position around the turn of the decade. State officials introduced a system of bonuses for public sector employees in early 1979 to reward those whose performance exceeded prescribed production levels; this program was supplemented by a general pay raise at state-run firms, as well as by new policies designed to enhance the autonomy of local-level management from central supervision.[26] These measures boosted output and productivity in public sector enterprises. And they accompanied both the imposition of higher tax rates on private manufacturing firms and a concerted effort—focused particularly on the north-central provinces—to pull domestically produced raw materials away from smaller independent enterprises and into public sector companies.[27] The following spring, party leaders convened a series of emergency congresses of the workers', students', and farm laborers' federations. President al-Asad himself appealed for the continued support of each of these organizations; each responded by forming a paramilitary brigade to assist in what it termed "the defense of the Revolution." These units received basic training and small arms and were reported by Radio Monte Carlo "to have taken part in massive search operations launched in Aleppo and Hamah by the army and the internal security services" in April 1980.[28]

While buttressing the regime's ties to public sector workers, government officials reintroduced a substantial degree of state control over the commercial and financial sectors of the Syrian economy as a way of regulating the activities of the urban petite bourgeoisie. In January 1981, state budgetary authorities began shifting government monies away from long- and short-term investment in heavy industrial projects and into current spending to prop up public sector manufacturing. Three months later, the Ministry of Supply and Internal Trade introduced new price controls on a wide range of household appliances, and the prime minister ordered a ban on further truck imports.[29] The cabinet issued Laws 181 and 182 at the end of April, which required private importers both to obtain the credit they needed from state institutions such as the Commercial Bank of Syria and to take out import licenses from the Ministry of the Economy and Foreign Trade. These measures were adopted in an attempt to increase the level of financial resources in government hands, reduce the flow of imports coming into Syrian markets, and diminish the influence of what Deputy Prime Minister for Economic Affairs 'Abd al-Qadir Qaddurah called "parasitic groups in and around the public sector."[30] Merchants who sidestepped the new regulations were arrested on charges of smuggling and tax evasion.[31] Such measures produced a marked increase in the country's gross domestic product at the turn of the decade.

At the same time, state officials stepped up their use of Syria's security forces to suppress the urban-based Islamist movement. In March 1980, for instance, commandos belonging to the Special Units (*al-wahdat al-khassah*) headed by 'Ali Haidar surrounded the northern town of Jisr al-Shughur, forcibly suppressing a series of demonstrations directed against the local headquarters of the Ba'th party and the Popular Defense Army. Five months later, the Special Units intervened to break up a cell of suspected Islamist militants in the al-Masharaqah district of Aleppo; helicopter-borne paratroopers from the Special Units moved into western and northern neighborhoods of Hamah in late April 1981, hunting for a team of fighters (*mujahidin*) that had ambushed a check-point on the outskirts of the city.[32] To carry out these operations, the Special Units were doubled in size during the early 1980s, reaching a peak strength of almost eight thousand in 1982–1983.

Other internal security forces expanded in size and importance after 1979 as well. The Defense Brigades (*sarayat al-difa' 'an al-thawrah*), commanded by the president's brother, Rif'at al-Asad, mushroomed to some twenty-five thousand troops, organized into three armored and one mechanized infantry formations. Sometime after 1980 one of Rif'at al-Asad's more powerful lieutenants, 'Adnan Makhluf, was put in command of a newly formed Presidential Guard consisting of around ten thousand elite troops stationed in several districts of central Damascus. In addition, such clandestine organizations as Military Intelligence (*al-mukhabarat al-'askariyyah*) headed by 'Ali Duba, Air Force Intelligence (*mukhabarat al-quwwah al-jawiyyah*) led by Muhammad al-Khawli, and Internal Security (*al-'amn al-siyassi*) headed by Muhammad Nassif enlarged the scope of their operations. Military Intelligence took a leading role in infiltrating political associations banned by the regime, along with monitoring professional associations such as those of physicians and engineers.[33] As one longtime observer of Syrian affairs has remarked, by the early 1980s, "Intelligence agencies, much used in the Middle East as instruments of state power by Arab regimes, by Israel, and by interested foreign states, loomed larger than ever. . . . The big expansion occurred with the struggle against the Muslim Brothers."[34]

As this struggle started to take the form of repeated assassinations and reprisals during 1981–1982, members of Syria's governing elite assigned themselves formations of bodyguards. In the words of Michael Seurat, "A good measure of the power of each member of the [ruling] clan is the size of their personal guard. The president has a guard of 12,000. The three generals who head the state security services have 60 each. Only four are assigned to such personalities as Faysal Dayyub, Dean of the Dental School, or Asad ʿAli, Professor of Arab Literature at Damascus University and one of the regime's most zealous apologists."[35] At the same time, Black Shirt units sprang up throughout predominantly ʿAlawi regions of Tartus and Latakia provinces; these units formed the basis of the ʿAli al-Murtadah association directed by President al-Asad's younger brother Jamil from 1981 to late 1983.[36]

The Domestic Crisis of 1981–1982

Mounting conflict between the dominant social coalition and its most powerful political challengers accompanied a slowdown in the agricultural, manufacturing, and commercial sectors of the local economy (see Figure 12). Total value added in agriculture—after rising 40 percent from 1979 to 1980—remained virtually stagnant during the subsequent two years. Low levels of sugar beet production proved particularly disruptive, delaying the opening of a network of new refineries in the north and northeast. Cotton production, though sufficient to keep up with growing domestic demand, provided only modest surpluses for export at the end of the 1981–1982 season.[37] Partly because of shortages of raw materials, manufacturing value added also stagnated between 1980 and 1981, resulting in severe limits on the amount of goods available for sale overseas; the authorities attempted to offset these shortages by allowing the sales of some industrial products to be financed through the parallel foreign exchange market.[38] "Furthermore," Eliyahu Kanovsky observes, "between the end of 1979 and the end of 1982 the money supply (including quasi-money) rose by 23 per cent per annum, suggesting higher rates of inflation than officially acknowledged, and lower rates of economic growth than officially claimed. This would lead to the conclusion that 1981–83 were years of stagnation at best, if not absolute decline."[39] Syrian commentators tended to focus instead on stagnant agricultural and industrial output: reports of "difficulties" and "problems" confronting both public and private enterprises appeared regularly in the local press as the year went by.[40]

It was under these circumstances that the government drew up Syria's fifth Five-Year Plan, scheduled to run from 1981 to 1985. At the heart of this plan lay a wide range of projects designed to make the country's agriculture not only more efficient but also more productive. For the most part, these projects were located in districts outside the heavily cultivated central plains: al-Qunaytirah, Dir'a, al-Hasakah, and Tartus were targeted for new agrarian investments in the initial stages of the plan.[41] As a complement to higher output objectives in agriculture, public sector canning plants were constructed or modernized throughout the northeast, as well as around Idlib and Dir'a. In addition, rural electrification and irrigation schemes received high priority, as did the expansion of pesticide, phosphate, and fertilizer production. Gross fixed capital formation in the public sector, which had dipped in 1981, recovered the following year (see Figure 14).

More important, the fifth Five-Year Plan mandated major changes in fiscal policy intended to reduce the government's recurrent budget deficits and boost domestic savings. Subsidies on diesel oil, bottled gas, and gasoline were drastically cut at the beginning of September; prices for grain, onions, potatoes, and other foodstuffs were raised a month later as part of a move by the Ministry of Agriculture and Agrarian Reform to "increase the market element in pricing, and to phase out or reduce commodity subsidies."[42] At about the same time, state officials altered the country's tax system to include a gradual but significant increase in the rate at which taxes were assessed. These measures accompanied additional restrictions on manufactured imports aimed at protecting public sector industry.[43] Toward the end of the year, the finance minister announced that the regime would reevaluate its decision to set up free trading areas at Damascus, Aleppo, Tartus, and Latakia because "they have not brought tax benefits for the economy and have failed to attract foreign investment."[44]

Such policies reinforced the position of Syria's party-affiliated farm laborers' and workers' organizations in their struggles against larger farmers and private manufacturers for control over the local market. The General Federation of Farm Laborers gained a considerable advantage relative to its members' wealthier opponents in the countryside when the leadership of the Ba'th appointed prominent federation officials to the central committee of the parliamentary National Progressive Front, while at the same time putting the associations of larger farmers—the Chambers of Agriculture—under tighter government control.[45] Activists within the farm laborers' federation used their newfound strength to push a bill through the National Assembly that granted substantial increases in compensation to small farmers whose tenancy contracts were abrogated by private landowners or state agencies.[46]

Encouraged by these successes, the General Federation of Farm Laborers joined the left wing of the Ba'th party in overseeing the implementation of new ceilings on the size of agricultural landholdings and changes in the allocation of agricultural investment monies. Throughout late 1981 and early 1982, larger private farmers were refused access to the foreign exchange necessary to maintain production using the relatively capital-intensive methods they had introduced on their lands in the late 1970s; smaller farmers and other members of the state-run cooperatives, on the other hand, enjoyed unprecedented access to a wide range of credit instruments.[47] Output of cotton, sugar beets, apricots, apples, and tomatoes grown on public and mixed-sector land consequently rose, while the amount of wheat, barley, lentils, watermelons, chickpeas, okra, and eggplants produced by private landholders contracted (see Table 1).

Members of the farm laborers' federation passed a series of resolutions at their 1981 congress designed to roll back the advance of market mechanisms in the agricultural sector of the Syrian economy. One of these, according to Raymond Hinnebusch, "called for the complete nationalization of the agricultural wholesale trade and for establishment of a public marketing agency for animal products"; a second petitioned the state-controlled Agricultural and Cooperative Bank "to regard land reform holdings as equivalent to private title for the purposes of longer term loans"; a third protested the sale of cooperative land to a newly formed mixed-sector Saudi-Syrian company.[48] In addition, the congress called on the Ministry of the Economy and Foreign Trade to take over the importation of agricultural machinery and spare parts and condemned private merchants who manipulated the supply of such goods for personal profit.[49]

Table 1. Crop production by sector, 1980–1982 (in thousands of tons)

Crop	1980	1981	1982
Cotton			
Cooperative	112	120	147
Other	213	235	275
Sugar beets			
Cooperative	209	300	340
Other	317	264	520
Wheat			
Cooperative	714	678	555
Other	1512	1409	1001
Barley			
Cooperative	311	289	193
Other	1276	1117	468
Tomatoes			
Cooperative	327	334	446
Other	317	389	344
Apples			
Cooperative	43	52	73
Other	46	52	66
Lentils			
Cooperative	32	26	24
Other	51	35	29
Apricots	48	49	81
Watermelons	906	969	869
Chickpeas	73	64	37
Okra	32	31	27
Eggplant	184	188	170

SOURCE: Syrian Arab Republic, *Statistical Abstract 1983* (Damascus: Central Bureau of Statistics, August 1983), pp. 126, 129, 132, and 142.

These moves put the General Federation of Farm Laborers at odds with Syria's public sector industrial workers on two related fronts. First, the urban proletariat, as direct consumers of foodstuffs and other items produced in the countryside, suffered when farmers used their growing influence within the ruling coalition to restructure the country's agriculture so as to increase or secure growers' profits at the expense of purchasers. By late 1981, conflicts over prices became evident in the deliberations of the Higher Agricultural Council, as representatives of the farm laborers' federation wrestled with officials from the Ministries

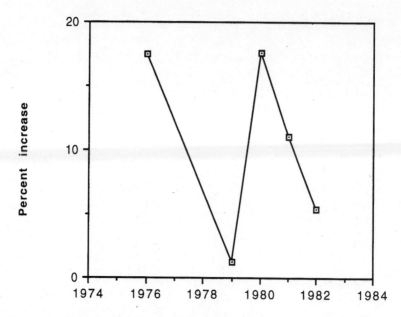

Figure 16. Industrial production index, 1976–1982

of Supply and Industry over proposed changes in the ceilings imposed on the prices of a wide range of agricultural goods on local markets.[50]

Second, the regime's evident willingness to accommodate the interests of smaller-scale agriculturalists led to greater competition between the farm laborers' federation and the trade unions for control over the diminishing resources at the disposal of the central administration. Hinnebusch reports that in 1981, members of the General Federation of Farm Laborers successfully blocked the expropriation of farmland on the outskirts of Hamah for the construction of an industrial park, despite the expressed support of provincial party leaders and local trade union officials for the project.[51] At about the same time, the government proposed extending health and disability insurance, eligibility for sick leave, protection from arbitrary dismissal, and other social benefits to agricultural workers, putting them on a par with the employees of public sector industry.[52] And it appears that the funds earmarked for agricultural expansion in the fifth Five-Year Plan, though not hurting such "transformation industries" as cloth production, sugar refining, and glass making, did reduce the state's overall commitment to heavy industry: plans to modernize the ironworks at Hamah received no more than approval in principle from state planners, and a more ambitious project to build an integrated steel mill adjacent to the plant was put on indefinite hold.[53]

Such conflicts dampened activity in virtually every sector of the Syrian economy. Agricultural production stagnated, industrial output sagged (see Figure 16), and the country's balance of trade plunged deeply into the red.[54] Revenues coming into the local economy from outside sources dried up as well. According to Volker Perthes, "Foreign assistance, transit fees, and remittances from Syrians working abroad tended to drop, and from 1981 onward the country was left with a negative balance of payment."[55] In no region was the impact of the accumulation crisis of 1981–1982 more severe than in Hamah province.

POLITICAL-ECONOMIC CRISIS AND PROVINCIAL REVOLT

Hamah had long been a center for both small-scale manufacturing and the processing of agricultural goods. Cotton ginning, cloth weaving, leather working, tobacco processing, and sugar refining were the major economic activities carried on within the city in the early 1980s. Twenty percent of Syria's cotton gins and butter factories were located in Hamah province, as were ten of Syria's fifty-two cheese factories.[56] These industrial concerns were relatively small compared to those in Damascus, Aleppo, and Latakia. In 1965, there were 4,603 unionized workers in Hamah, divided among twenty-two separate trade unions. By contrast, Damascus had 23,827 workers among thirty trade unions, while Aleppo was home to 23,899 workers spread among twenty-eight unions.[57] The persistence of small-scale units within the official trade union organizations of Hamah indicates the degree to which independent artisanal operations remained predominant within the city's economy. As late as the 1970 census, 31.5 percent of the province's urban workers were classified as self-employed. This figure compared with 26 percent of the urban workers in Aleppo, 24.6 percent of those in Homs, and 20.5 percent of those in Damascus.[58]

Throughout the 1970s, however, the regime's program of promoting heavy industrialization fostered the emergence of a number of large-scale, capital-intensive factories in and around Hamah. Such factories included the state's iron and steel works, a cement factory opened at the end of 1976, and a plant to produce automobile and truck tires. The Arab Company for Ceramic Wall Tiles and Sanitary Wares opened its main porcelain factory on the outskirts of the city in August 1977 and began operating a nearby pipe and bathroom fixture plant that December.[59] The state constructed modern textile mills in the adjacent cities of Idlib and Homs between 1977 and 1979.[60] A large government shoe factory was set up at Masyaf, just outside the city of Hamah.[61] This wave of industrial expansion significantly altered the character of manufacturing in the region; it also increased the importance of the construction sector in the provincial economy, as roads, railways, and public utilities in north-central Syria were improved and extended to support the new factories.

Regime-sponsored heavy industrialization hurt Hamah's small-scale manufacturers in several interrelated ways. By the end of the 1970s, artisans and shopkeepers in the city found themselves increasingly less well-off relative to the employees of public sector enterprises. The government periodically raised salaries in state industries during these years in an attempt to offset inflation. The raises did not extend to workers outside the public sector, although the regime did make an effort to establish minimum wages in both public and private firms. Paradoxically, these regulations exacerbated the economic difficulties of smaller manufacturers, who were forced to pay their own employees the mandated wage scale. Thanks to these policies, the incomes of Hamah's independent artisans and traders deteriorated markedly after 1980 relative to those of public sector workers engaged in similar activities.[62]

This wage differential widened as inflation pushed the cost of living to higher and higher levels (see Figure 17). Skyrocketing prices made it harder for Hamah's artisans to make a profit on their operations because higher raw materials costs could be passed on only at the risk of encouraging local consumers to buy cheaper factory-made articles instead.[63] And the regime's steady opening up of the Syrian market to imported goods brought indigenous artisanal manufacturers into growing competition with foreign producers as well.

At the same time, underemployed rural laborers throughout Hamah province increasingly found work in constructing and maintaining the

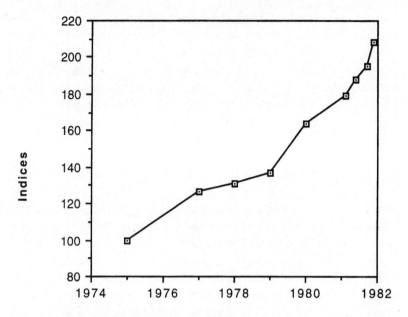

Figure 17. Cost of living indices, 1975–1981

new state-sponsored industrial and infrastructural projects. According to Syrian government reports, 48 percent of the country's labor force was engaged in agriculture in 1970, with 12.2 percent in industry and 7.3 percent in construction. By 1979, these proportions were 31.8 percent, 17.1 percent, and 13.7 percent, respectively.[64] Construction jobs provided rural workers with a comparatively steady income and relieved them from the seasonal unemployment that had previously been a fact of life for agricultural laborers in Syria's north-central plains. Consequently, these workers became less dependent upon moneylending and advance purchases, which had constituted lucrative sources of additional income for Hamah's traders and shopkeepers in earlier years. Instead, the growing ranks of construction workers around the city raised demand for the comparatively inexpensive goods produced in the province's state-run factories, along with that for certain luxury imports. Thus the expanding state-controlled construction sector seriously undercut several of the most important ways in which Hamah's tradespeople maintained their political and economic predominance over the surrounding countryside.

After 1979, large-scale industrialization within the province accelerated and began to involve industries that had traditionally formed the
foundation of the Hamawi economy. Chinese, British, and Libyan capital invested in a cluster of very large spinning and weaving mills, and the
French firm Sonice contracted to build a modern blanket factory in
northern Syria, no doubt associated with the new wool spinning and
dyeing factory that opened in Hamah in late 1981. Massive new industrial complexes were constructed not only around Hamah but also in
the areas around Idlib, Aleppo, Homs, and Latakia.[65] As these plants
began to come on line toward the end of 1982, the market for the
comparatively expensive items produced by Hamah's smaller-scale
manufacturers could be expected to shrink yet again.

Hamah's independent artisans and tradespeople found their position weakened even further as a result of changes in the structure of
agricultural production in the surrounding countryside. The province's
smaller farmers, who had been the primary beneficiaries of the government's land reform programs of the 1960s and 1970s, faced growing
challenges not only from the larger landholding families residing in the
city but also from the province's remaining landless agricultural laborers who previously had shifted between seasonal agricultural work
and unskilled day work in the towns. As the latter found steady employment in the expanding construction sector, the price of day labor for
medium-sized landholders rose correspondingly. Moreover, the former
landless laborers, now construction laborers—whose numbers were
greater in Hamah province than in any other part of the country[66]—
constituted a reservoir of potential opposition to the provincial status
quo. This threat was particularly salient because of Hamah's long history of rural radicalism and rebellion.[67] Finally, small farmers who produced cotton, sugar beets, and livestock came into perpetual conflict
with urban artisans over the prices and allocation of the goods used in
smaller workshops. Whenever the output of industrial crops diminished
or the state's centralized distribution network proved inadequate or
faulty, Hamah province's small-scale landholders became both targets
of hostility from urban craftspeople and victims of the government's
system of price controls, which prevented them from profiting propor-
tionately when the goods they produced fell into short supply.

These tensions were exacerbated by the actions of Hamah's older,
large estate–owning families, who attempted to reassert their control

over provincial agriculture as the 1980s began. During the first years of the decade, a variety of larger landholdings began to reappear in the area between Homs and Aleppo. Some of these were in the hands of former small farmers who started to hire significant numbers of wage laborers to assist them in working their lands and whose ability to provide capital and credit in the countryside put them in direct competition with urban forces based in Hamah. Others were connected to the region's traditional landowning elite, whose holdings had been the target of earlier land reform measures. The resurgent grandees, whose fortunes had for the most part been made in the decades before to the Ba'thi era, played a vital if inconspicuous role in political struggles within Hamah province during 1981–1982 by supplying dissident city dwellers with funds and weaponry, as well as by undermining the position of the regime's supporters in the countryside.[68]

Given these circumstances, a pair of state programs implemented in late 1981 and early 1982 sparked widespread disaffection throughout Hamah province. First, the Supreme Agricultural Board began paying substantially higher prices for cotton produced during the 1981–1982 crop year as a means of encouraging higher output to offset the decline of petroleum prices on world markets. This move was also intended to increase the amount of cotton available for use in the government's newly constructed processing and weaving mills, whose capacity had largely outstripped domestic production by mid-1981.[69] As a result of the new pricing structure, an even higher proportion of the province's cotton crop was pulled away from local workshops and channeled either toward the larger state-run factories or into overseas markets.

The new subsidies signaled a significant shift in the central administration's agricultural development program, which became evident at the end of 1981. Up to that time, the regime had placed primary emphasis on large-scale, capital-intensive projects such as the land reclamation schemes situated in the districts around Dayr al-Zur.[70] But during the first weeks of 1982, the new prime minister, 'Abd al-Rauf al-Kasm, implemented a package of agricultural policies specifically designed to benefit middle and smaller farmers.[71] It remained unclear as January passed precisely what local-level projects these policies would entail. But it was immediately apparent which forces would be expected to pay for the new program: the provincial tradespeople, whose tax rates were substantially raised at the close of 1981, who bore the brunt of the government's simultaneous decision to cut fuel subsidies, and whose commercial establishments were hurt most severely by the more restrictive trading regulations that were introduced in conjunction with the revised tax code.[72]

The incendiary nature of the political situation in the province became evident when, in the first week of February 1982, troops belonging to the Defense Brigades and Special Units raided buildings in an older section of Hamah suspected of serving as hideouts for local cells of the Muslim Brotherhood.[73] Ikhwani militants repulsed the raid using small arms and grenade launchers. The mujahidin then attacked a variety of government installations, including the headquarters of the police, the local branch offices of the Ba'th party, and the military airfield on the edge of town. By the second day of the fighting, mosques in some neighborhoods had begun broadcasting calls for a general uprising against the al-Asad regime. Whole districts, particularly the popular quarter of Hadrah in the center of the city, joined the rebellion in response to these appeals. Umar Abd-Allah reports that under the supervision of the mujahidin, "arms seized from armories, barracks, and police stations were distributed among the people, and about fifty persons directly responsible for Asad regime atrocities were put to death."[74] The rebels then barricaded themselves in the labyrinthine alleyways of the old city.

Broadsheets circulated in Syria's other major cities calling on the populace to initiate a nationwide uprising to "liberate" itself from the "tyranny" of the al-Asad regime. But these appeals fell on deaf ears.[75] Simultaneous pleas broadcast on Iraqi-sponsored Voice of the Mujahidin radio by the leadership of the ikhwan urging shopkeepers in the capital to close their businesses and students and factory workers to take part in a nationwide general strike went largely unheeded as well, although isolated skirmishes between Islamist militants and police were reported to have occurred in Aleppo and Latakia.[76] The isolated character of the Hamah rebellion leads Thomas Mayer to conclude that "the Hamma revolt, for all its fierceness and brutality, demonstrated that the Islamic revolutionaries did not enjoy the support of the entire Sunni community in Syria."[77] Hamid Algar adds that "inadequate countrywide planning on the part of the Islamic Front," combined with "old divisions within the Islamic movement [that] had not been fully surmounted," may have contributed to the absence of a general uprising in solidarity with the activists of Hamah.[78] The leadership of the ikhwan, more perceptively, pointed to the nature of the regime's reaction to the revolt to explain this outcome.

CONTRADICTORY REGIME RESPONSES

Syria's ruling social coalition responded to the Islamist uprising in Hamah by pursuing a particularly potent admixture of disparate policies. Military commanders deployed overwhelming firepower against the rebels, while President Hafiz al-Asad himself is reported to have threatened "to hang [the merchants and tradespeople of Damascus and Aleppo] in front of their shops" if they joined the revolt.[79] State planners moved to institute "a more liberal and capital-oriented economy" by implementing measures that effectively "loosened state controls on the private economy, shifting weight from the public to the private sector, while inside the private sector the role of the larger enterprises and merchants was strengthened."[80] And officials in the party apparatus and Ba'thi popular front organizations initiated a comprehensive "campaign to increase production" in public sector enterprises.[81]

As soon as fighting flared between the Defense Brigades and the mujahidin, several of the Syrian army's best-equipped and most experienced formations rushed to Hamah. These forces proved unable to secure a foothold in the old city for two days but then steadily "gained the initiative" by "blast[ing] the city with helicopter-launched bombs and rockets, artillery, and tank fire."[82] House-to-house fighting went on for three days and nights thereafter, followed by what Middle East Watch has called another three days of "fierce collective punishment," in which "troops pillaged stores and homes and fired weapons indiscriminately, treating all citizens as responsible for the insurrection."[83] In the end, somewhere between five and ten thousand of Hamah's residents died in the fighting, and the homes of more than sixty thousand were destroyed.

Use of the armed forces to crush the Hamah rebellion succeeded in crippling Syria's Islamist opposition but at the cost of heightening tensions between senior commanders in the military-security apparatus and other forces within the dominant social coalition. Hanna Batatu noted that even before the rebellion, the president's "reliance on the

'Alawis generally is clear from other significant military appointments. Thus Yunis Yunis, commander of the Ninth Armored Divison, is from the tribe of al-Haddadin. Again, Tawfiq al-Jahani, who headed the First Armored Division from 1971 to 1978, is from the Raslan section of al-Kalbiyyah. Moreover, 'Ali Umran, who commanded until recently one unit of the Special Forces, is from al-Khayyatin."[84] It would be a mistake to conclude from this list that the Syrian armed forces had become a sectarian institution by early 1982. As Yahya Sadowski argues, the regime's appointments to high command were on the whole "confessional, not sectarian. [President al-Asad] has placed Alawis in command of the military, but has never permitted them—or any sect—to threaten his personal rule. Nor has he confined this strategy to the Alawis: he also curried the favor of several Christian communities. Christian villages where the regime was popular contributed many volunteers to the General Intelligence Service (al-Mukhabarat al-'Amna). Armenian troops became popular as bodyguards for the Ba'thist elite." Moreover, "many members of the president's inner circle, his *jama'a* or 'gang,' are actually Sunnis, including 'Abd al-Halim Khaddam (foreign minister and vice president), Mustafa al-Tallas (minister of defense), 'Abdallah al-Ahmar (assistant secretary general of the Ba'th), and Hikmat Shihabi (army chief of staff)." Nevertheless, it remained the case that "confessionalism as practiced by the Assad regime often blends into outright nepotism. Hafiz's brother-in-law, Shafiq Fayyad, commanded the Third Army Division; his cousin, Ghazi Kan'an, is chief of military intelligence for Lebanon; and Rif'at al-Assad's son-in-law, Mu'in Nassif, was appointed director of internal security" in March 1984.[85]

Consequently, the prominence accorded to the armed forces in defending the regime during the course of the Hamah revolt reinforced widely held perceptions that Syria's governing elite represented little more than "a close kinship group which draws strength simultaneously, but in decreasing intensity, from a tribe, a sect-class, and an ecologic-cultural division of the people."[86] Islamist militants had published a manifesto in November 1980 accusing the Ba'th of creating a "sectarian fascist" order in the country, buttressed by the 'Alawi-dominated armed forces and pervasive corruption.[87] Central to the Muslim Brotherhood's program for reforming the Syrian state was a wholesale purge of the military establishment: in an Islamic state, the ikhwan claimed "the army would not become involved in internal politics or sectarian struggles; rather, it would concentrate on training, organization, and military discipline."[88]

After February 1982, richer urban merchants displayed some sympathy for the newly formed Islamic Front's vision of the future. Hinnebusch remarks that "the return of calm to Syria's cities hardly signifies acceptance of Ba'th rule. Political Islam is deeply rooted in the suq and the families that carry on its age-old mercantile traditions and in the pervasive religious sensibility nurtured by the 'ulama—interests too durable, sentiments too diffuse to be eradicated by coercion alone."[89] In a desperate attempt to tap these sentiments, more moderate Islamist organizations joined Nasirists, Hawranists, dissident Ba'this, and other leftists in forming a National Alliance for the Liberation of Syria (*al-tahaluf al-watani li-tahrir suriyah*) at the beginning of March 1982. The manifesto published by the alliance the following month committed its members to a set of remarkably liberal political objectives.[90] Overreliance on the state's "communal" armed forces thus opened up the possibility of widespread disaffection on the part of Syria's richer merchants, potentially alienating them from other forces within the ruling coalition.

Syria's central administration appealed to large-scale private capital for help in resurrecting the country's economy in the immediate aftermath of the Hamah rebellion. According to Perthes, "With diminishing public resources and austerity budgets, the government tried to mobilize private capital and skim off some of its profits, thus hoping to uphold the state's sphere of action and to save both the public sector and the public administration from bankruptcy. The private sector's role thereby increased."[91] This trend was most clearly apparent in agriculture, where loans from the state-run Agricultural Cooperative Bank shifted away from the public sector and toward the private and cooperative sectors beginning in 1982 (see Table 2).

Conciliating private interests ran the risk of further undermining Syria's already shaky public sector enterprises. The government's annual budget for 1982, announced in the days immediately preceding the Hamah rebellion, increased public sector investment by just over 14 percent from the level for 1981, but this increase barely matched the rate of inflation.[92] The budget envisaged no new large-scale enterprises, although the 1981–1985 Five-Year Plan allocated some $300 million for expanding the state-owned iron and steel works.[93] As the fighting in

Table 2. Agricultural cooperative bank loans, 1982–1986 (in thousands of Syrian pounds)

	Public sector	Cooperative sector	Private sector
1982	38,241	309,434	355,113
1983	30,828	407,285	438,361
1984	820	567,392	559,211
1985	1,794	649,412	602,113
1986	2,593	672,105	692,686

SOURCE: Syrian Arab Republic, *Statistical Abstract 1987* (Damascus: Central Bureau of Statistics, August 1987), p. 160.

Hamah drew to a close, Deputy Prime Minister Qaddurah told the country's construction companies that they would have to reduce their consumption of concrete because state-run factories could not keep up with current demand.[94] Early March brought clear indications that the country's existing oil fields were "past their prime and that the government is maintaining production at modest levels to promote conservation," at the very time that expensive public sector refinery complexes had just started to come on line. The minister of oil and mineral resources met with Soviet and North Korean representatives to discuss the possibility of increasing phosphates exports to cover the anticipated shortfall in revenues from petroleum production.[95] In an attempt to reduce spending on staples, government officials hinted toward the end of the month that total imports of wheat flour would be slashed almost in half during 1982; informed observers noted that whatever savings might be achieved by this move would almost certainly be spent on imports of corn to support the country's burgeoning livestock industry.[96] Under these circumstances, the outlook for the fifth Five-Year Plan appeared increasingly gloomy and state planners were forced to adopt a much more "realistic" position regarding the prospects for public sector expansion over the short run.[97]

Workers employed in state-run enterprises expressed deep dissatisfaction with the regime's concerted efforts to encourage private enterprise during the first quarter of 1982.[98] In an attempt to pacify these employees, government officials redoubled their commitment to implement the system of individual incentives for productivity in public sector firms that had been introduced five years earlier. This program aimed at "giving employees in highly productive establishments reasonable wages and, therefore, help[ing] stabilize [both] the work force and production."[99] It complemented a well-publicized campaign to promote national economic self-reliance by stepping up local production of the spare parts and other industrial inputs necessary to keep state-owned factories operating efficiently. Perthes reports that "the campaign met with some success in traditional light industries where some spare parts for imported machinery were manufactured locally." But paradoxically, the primary beneficiaries of the program appear to have been private entrepreneurs, who moved into import substitution as a way of "replacing the importation of goods which had been prohibited because of the production of similar products (which were being manufactured under foreign license and were completely dependent upon imported machinery and material)."[100]

Taken together, the divergent programs implemented by the forces that made up Syria's dominant social coalition in response to the Hamah revolt made continued collaboration among them increasingly problematic. Deploying the armed forces to suppress challengers to the regime proved not only disruptive to the transportation and manufacturing sectors of the local economy but also inordinately expensive. Damage to the city of Hamah during the ten days of the uprising was estimated at around $500 million.[101] The potential cost to the regime of losing the confidence of Syria's commercial elite was even greater. And stepping up efforts to appease private interests in the wake of the rebellion threatened to alienate trade unionists, farm laborers, and other public sector forces. Initiating a confrontation with Iraq provided a way to paper over the spreading cracks inside the ruling coalition before they turned into gaping fissures, while at the same time boosting internal and external support for the country's military establishment, which had captured a more central role within the regime in the course of suppressing the Islamist challenge.

EXTERNAL CONFRONTATION AND REGIME CONSOLIDATION

Syria's leaders lost little time in accusing the rival Ba'thi regime in Baghdad of instigating the Hamah revolt. President al-Asad told a rally commemorating the nineteenth anniversary of the March 1963 revolution that despite persistent attempts by the United States to undermine the "corrective movement," "the one who has the biggest share this time is a very generous person. It is the ruler of fraternal Iraq. It is the ruler of fraternal Iraq who honored us with this big quantity of weapons. . . . It is obvious that the hangman of Iraq is not content to only kill tens of thousands of the fraternal Iraqi people. He came to Syria to carry out further of his favorite hobbies: killing, assassination and sabotage." A month later, Damascus television broadcast the confession of a Syrian citizen alleged to be an Iraqi agent; about the same time, Ba'th party members suspected of harboring pro-Iraqi sympathies were rounded up in several cities.[102] Not all of these accusations were totally fanciful. Eberhard Kienle records that "at least partly in conjunction with the Islamic opposition, pro-Iraqi officers had planned a coup that was to coincide with the rising in Hama. In this most serious and best prepared conspiracy during the Asad period, an air strike was planned on the building in which the Ba'th party Central Committee convened, and possibly also on the residences of Hafiz and Rif'at al-Asad. It was foiled at the last minute and a great number of officers, particularly in the air force, were arrested and executed."[103] Linking the Hamah rebellion to Syria's long-standing rivalry with Iraq was an intuitively obvious, if perhaps somewhat disingenuous, move on the regime's part.

More concretely, confrontation with Baghdad provided an opportunity for state officials to discipline the party-affiliated popular front organizations, thereby restoring the regime's damaged credibility with richer private interests. Persistent demands by workers, farm laborers, and students that the Syrian state maintain its commitment to the socialist programs of the mid-1960s posed a major obstacle to the central administration's efforts to court private capital two decades later. Tensions between radicals and liberals inside the dominant coalition heightened immediately after the uprising in Hamah: workers' and farm laborers' militias—which had taken an active part in suppressing the rebels[104]—expected the government to recommit itself to Ba'thi socialism in gratitude for their assistance, even as private merchants and manufacturers in the cities worried that the regime had assumed a more sectarian cast. Minister of Defense Mustafa Talas's rationale for escalating the confrontation with Iraq, that Baghdad had scuttled the 1978 proposal to unify the two countries,[105] pointedly hinted at the dangers of adhering too single-mindedly to doctrinaire Ba'thism. Saddam Husain's purported lack of moderation and reasonableness made him unfit to lead a Ba'thi regime, the daily *Tishrin* asserted at the height of the confrontation, providing legitimate grounds for the Iraqi people to take steps to overthrow him.[106]

Calls for the ouster of Saddam Husain accompanied moves on the part of the authorities in Damascus to restructure the Syrian economy that significantly weakened the position of public sector workers. In mid-April, the Agricultural Cooperative Bank announced plans to cooperate with the World Bank and United Nations Development Program to encourage the expansion of small-scale, rain-fed agriculture in the southern provinces of Dir'a and al-Suwayda; cash crops for export were to make up a substantial proportion of the produce generated by this scheme.[107] A month later, Prime Minister al-Kasm informed state agencies that they would be required to reduce current spending by 10 percent across the board.[108] Three months after that, the government cut subsidies on fuel oil, kerosene, and certain staple foodstuffs, raising prices by 10 percent.[109] Such measures nudged public sector workers and agricultural laborers onto the fringes of the regime's overall economic program, while at the same time decimating the state-sponsored social welfare programs that had been put in place in the mid-1960s.

To offset the weakening of its radical wing, the al-Asad regime solicited greater external economic and technical assistance, particularly from the Communist bloc. State officials sought foreign aid to finance the expansion of the oil refinery at Homs, the modernization of the cement factory at Tartus, and the construction of the proposed Nahr al-Kabir dam and irrigation network, along with the ongoing high dam project at Tabqa.[110] Syrian strategic cooperation with Iran was rewarded with substantial increases in the supply of low-cost Iranian crude oil and other economic concessions on Tehran's part as the spring went by.[111] But by far the largest increase in external assistance to Damascus came from Bucharest. Following an official visit to Syria by Romania's President Nicolae Ceauscescu in late May, new joint economic committees were formed to promote further collaboration between Romanian construction, engineering, and industrial enterprises and their Syrian counterparts.[112] In partial payment for this assistance, officials in Damascus more than doubled the value of Syria's exports to Romania during the course of 1982.[113] These developments catapulted Romania into first place among Syria's East European trading partners.

Assistance to the Syrian armed forces jumped beginning in 1982 as well, although it did so more in response to the Israeli invasion of Lebanon that June than as a result of the confrontation with Iraq. Pedro Ramet notes that during the ten months after the invasion, "the Soviets shipped some 800 T-72 tanks, 200 armored personnel carriers, 600–800 trucks, 160 fighter aircraft including 20–30 more MiG fighters and Su-22 fighter bombers, 50–100 self-propelled 122 mm. and 152 mm. howitzers, 100 BM-21 multiple rocket launchers, as well as SAM-5, SAM-6, SAM-9, and SS-21 missile systems."[114] The new weaponry, reportedly worth some $2.8 billion, was complemented by substantially greater numbers of Soviet military technicians, along with direct access to the Soviets' worldwide radar and satellite reconnaissance network. By the end of the year, two SAM-5 battalions operated by Soviet personnel were defending installations around Damascus and Homs from Israeli air strikes—"the first time that such missiles had been deployed outside the Soviet Union."[115]

Increased military assistance from outside reinforced the massive buildup of Syria's armed forces that had been under way since the signing of the Camp David accords between Egypt and Israel. This trend saw the size of the regular army grow from some 200,000 troops in 1979 to around 300,000 at the end of 1984, while the active reserves jumped from about 100,000 soldiers to almost 270,000 during the same period. The number of main battle tanks in the regular armored divisions almost doubled in these same years, rising from 2,300 to 4,050, and the total number of military helicopters grew from 56 to 148.[116] Increases in personnel and weaponry were matched by a consistently high level of government expenditure on the armed forces and a rising share of Syria's gross domestic product devoted to military spending. In 1979, Damascus spent some $4.7 billion on its military forces, which represented 16.0 percent of the country's gross domestic product. Three years later, Syrian military spending totaled just under $5.1 billion; this figure remained virtually constant over the following two years, pushing the proportion of gross domestic product devoted to military spending to 16.7 percent in 1984.[117]

By 1983–1984, the expansion of the regular armed forces and the mushrooming of the state security services combined to make the military establishment the most dynamic, if not the largest, sector of the Syrian economy. Some 24 billion Syrian pounds were being used for military purposes in 1984, a figure equaling the total value of the country's gross domestic product for 1980.[118] Such resources provided the paramilitary construction and supply companies, most notably the Military Housing Company (*sharikah al-iskan al-'askariyyah*), with immense capital reserves to use in purchasing modern equipment and materials in bulk. At the height of the military boom, this company, according to Patrick Seale, "was the largest firm in the country—in fact a conglomerate of sixty-six companies—employing a good half of the 150,000 workers in the Syrian construction industry and responsible for some of the best buildings in the country: the new international airport, the Asad library, the president's official banqueting hall elaborately decorated in oriental style, the Aleppo Meridien, the sports city in Latakia used for the Mediterranean Games of 1987, numerous schools and university faculties, and the 5,000 houses of the Asad Villages," to name only a few.[119] Through projects such as these, the Military Housing Company soon eclipsed the remaining dozen or so state construction companies and began diversifying its operations into livestock agriculture and the manufacture of construction materials and furniture at factories in Aleppo and Damascus.

Programs adopted by the members of the al-Asad regime in conjunction with the April–May 1982 confrontation with Iraq, unlike those implemented in response to the Hamah rebellion two months earlier, thus provided a foundation for largely complementary relations within the dominant social coalition. Mobilizing the party-affiliated popular front organizations to resist an external threat, particularly one originating from a "fraternal" radical Ba'thi regime, made it much more difficult for the leaders of these organizations to resist subordination to the state. Restructuring the local economy to facilitate the expansion of private capital, while at the same time augmenting the state's armed forces, could be accomplished with much less friction in the name of strengthening the country vis-à-vis foreign adversaries. And the flow of economic and military assistance to the al-Asad regime from the Eastern bloc accelerated as a result of Syria's patrons' growing worries about the strategic instability of the region.

Syria's brief but intense military confrontation with Iraq in the spring of 1982 dropped the keystone into the regime's efforts to parry the persistent threat emanating from the country's Islamist movement.

During the late 1970s, Islamist militants took advantage of festering contradictions among the forces that made up the dominant social coalition to launch a campaign to overthrow the al-Asad regime and replace it with one reflecting the interests and values of the country's urban petite bourgeoisie.[120] The forcible suppression of the Hamah rebellion at the beginning of February 1982 blunted this campaign. But the means adopted to combat the Islamists by each of the forces inside the ruling coalition exacerbated conflicts of interest among these forces, making continued collaboration among them increasingly problematic. It was only in the context of limited military confrontation with Baghdad that the most salient intraregime dissonances were at last harmonized, enabling the al-Asad coalition to survive the internal and external challenges of the mid-1980s.[121]

CHAPTER FIVE

Abjuring Confrontation
with Turkey, 1994

As the 1980s drew to a close, the delicate rapprochement that had blossomed between Syria and Turkey during the middle years of the decade withered.[1] Turkish officials expressed growing irritation over Damascus's persistent failure to interdict attacks by Kurdish and Armenian militants against Turkish facilities; Ankara even threatened to order Turkey's armed forces to raid Kurdish guerrilla bases in central Lebanon if Syrian authorities continued to turn a blind eye to the activities of the Kurdistan Workers' party (PKK). At the beginning of 1988, the Turkish government initiated a two-pronged strategic offensive to undermine Syria's position in regional affairs: Prime Minister Turgut Ozal led a high-ranking delegation to Tehran that February to discuss new areas of Turkish-Iranian economic cooperation; Ozal then traveled to Cairo, where he and the army chief of staff, General Necip Torumtay, arranged for a series of joint Turkish-Egyptian naval exercises and drew up plans for the coproduction of military helicopters, light armored vehicles, and other weapons systems. The latter visit opened the door to closer defense collaboration between Turkey and Saudi Arabia, the primary financial backer of Egypt's indigenous armaments industry.[2]

Overtures to the Islamic Republic disrupted Ozal's concurrent effort to serve as honest broker between Iran and Iraq, prompting Baghdad to announce that it could no longer afford to pay for the consumer goods Iraqi merchants had been importing from Turkey.[3] Turkish-Iraqi relations further deteriorated that fall, when some sixty thousand Kurdish refugees flooded into southeast Turkey in the wake of a concerted campaign on the part of the Iraqi armed forces to uproot Kurdish militias operating inside Iraq.[4] Ankara's relations with Tehran almost immediately followed suit, as Turkish officials openly encouraged displaced Kurds to emigrate into northwestern Iran.[5]

By mid-1989, the influx of Kurdish refugees into southeastern Turkey precipitated a revival of the long-running, PKK-led insurrection against the Turkish government. When fighting escalated that fall between Kurdish guerrillas and Turkish troops, the authorities in Ankara publicly accused Iran, not Syria, of sponsoring the rebellion.[6] Nevertheless, Damascus stepped up military activities along its northern border, heightening tensions between the two countries. On 21 October, a pair of Syrian MiG-21 interceptors crossed into Turkish airspace east of Iskandarun and shot down a Turkish surveying plane, killing five civilians.[7] The attack prompted not only sharp denunciations on Ankara's part but also an announcement that Turkish engineers intended to interrupt the southward flow of the Euphrates River for an entire month, purportedly to fill the massive reservoir behind the newly completed Ataturk Dam.[8]

Instead of taking steps that might have further escalated the crisis, Damascus dispatched Deputy Foreign Minister Yusuf Sakkar to Ankara with instructions to defuse the situation. Sakkar's visit set the stage for the appointment of a joint committee composed of Turkish and Syrian air force officers to investigate the circumstances surrounding the October incident. This course of action succeeded in dampening hostility between the two governments, although as one well-informed observer noted at the time, "Turkish suspicion of the Syrians remains almost ineradicable, which is hardly surprising given the Damascus regime's almost overt support of the Kurdish terrorists/guerrillas in the past."[9]

Four years later, Ankara suddenly resumed its campaign to eradicate the PKK presence in southeastern Turkey. Damascus's continuing, albeit tacit, support for the more radical wing of the Kurdish national movement prompted Turkish Prime Minister Tansu Ciller at the end of October 1993 to accuse Syria of collaborating with Iraq, Iran, and Armenia to undermine her country's security.[10] At the same time, the chief of the General Staff warned that Turkish forces were planning to launch a series of "deadly strikes" against the leadership of the PKK, several of whose members were known to reside in Damascus.[11] Accusations of Syrian complicity in PKK operations were reiterated when Foreign Minister Hikmet Cetin visited Israel a month later: Cetin encouraged the Israeli government to join Ankara in resisting what he called "Syrian-supported terrorism."[12] Damascus riposted by ordering its navy to carry out exercises in which missile frigates based at Latakia practiced repelling an attack from the sea; these exercises accompanied large-scale maneuvers by ground forces intended, in the words of the deputy commander in chief, General Mustafa Talas, to ensure that the Syrian armed forces "would remain the Arab nation's army that defended its rights, safeguarded its land and sanctities and worked for its objectives of unity, freedom and socialism."[13] In the wake of these exercises, Syrian radio broadcast a statement criticizing Ankara for having issued threats against its neighbors; the statement further reported that the League of Arab States had recently "affirmed" that "Turkish control of [the Euphrates and Tigris rivers] had gravely harmed Syrian and Iraqi Arab vital interests and threatened the lives of people in both countries."[14]

Syria's persistent refusal to cut its links to the PKK leadership provided Turkish commanders with an excuse to order their troops to pursue Kurdish guerrillas into Syrian territory on more than one occasion during the first weeks of 1994.[15] Following the incursions, Turkey's foreign minister asked Tehran to help persuade Damascus to stop harboring Kurdish militants. As an added incentive to convince the Syrian authorities to assist in suppressing the PKK, Turkish officials opened the floodgates of the Ataturk Dam, temporarily raising the level of the Euphrates River and thus substantially increasing the amount of water entering Syria.[16] Nevertheless, Prime Minister Ciller told a television audience that although her government would not intentionally manipulate the flow of the Euphrates for political reasons, neighboring countries could count on receiving an unhindered supply of water only so long as they maintained amicable relations with Ankara.[17] At the same time, Turkey took steps to upgrade relations with both Egypt and Israel. Turkish representatives negotiated mutual security protocols with Egyptian and Israeli officials in February.[18] These moves set the stage for a notable thaw in the chilly relations between Ankara and Baghdad.[19]

Confronted with growing Turkish belligerence throughout the winter of 1993–1994, Syria's leadership adopted an even more accommodative posture than it had four years earlier. Foreign Minister Faruq al-Shar' received a high-level Turkish delegation in Damascus at the height of the confrontation in early November, remarking to his guests that "neither of the two countries benefited from the exchange of hostile statements and media campaigns."[20] The delegation then met with President Hafiz al-Asad, who personally approved the implementation of a new set of "cooperation mechanisms between [the two countries'] respective interior ministries."[21] Foreign Minister al-Shar' traveled to Istanbul the first week of February 1994 to discuss the future of Iraq with his Turkish and Iranian counterparts. He used the occasion to offer a conciliatory reply to Prime Minister Ciller's thinly veiled threat to withhold Euphrates water from any state that acted against Turkish interests: al-Shar' told reporters that his government harbored fewer concerns regarding "the quantity of water" flowing downstream than it did about "the lack of a comprehensive agreement" regulating the distribution of water throughout the region.[22] In an equally accommodative vein, President al-Asad responded to Ankara's subsequent overtures to Egypt and Israel by inviting the Turkish minister of the interior to come to the Syrian capital to discuss a wide range of security-related matters.[23]

Damascus's unwillingness to escalate the 1993–1994 confrontation with Turkey can be seen as part of a turn toward moderation in the al-Asad regime's overall posture toward regional affairs. Measures to defuse the crisis accompanied Syrian participation in U.S.-sponsored negotiations with Israel, moves to improve relations with both Cairo and Amman, and even tentative steps toward reconciliation with Iraq.[24] This general shift in strategy occurred in the context of marked improvements in the Syrian economy, along with a dramatic reduction in the level of threat posed to the dominant social coalition by forces opposed to the al-Asad regime and its program of controlled economic liberalization.

THE ECONOMIC TURNAROUND OF 1989–1990

Throughout the 1980s, Syria's economy suffered from a variety of debilitating structural weaknesses.[25] Shortages of imported machinery and spare parts resulted in persistent underproduction and quality

control problems in the country's larger public and private sector factories. The State Planning Commission reported in 1986 that "production costs in all sectors of converting industries—refineries excluded—
have been increasing more than the value of production. . . . Large and
increasing losses were a common characteristic. . . . Losses in all years of
the fifth five-year plan [1981–1985] surmounted capital consumption,
thus the surplus generated was negative."[26] Volker Perthes reports that
"production at the Hama iron and steel plant stopped completely for
about two years [around 1987], and partial or complete stoppages
occurred in the production of fertilizer, synthetic fibers, cement pipes,
paper, refrigerators, shoes, aluminium shapes, batteries, and mineral
water."[27] External indebtedness rose to some $4.9 billion by 1988; pay-
ments on foreign loans fell more than $100 million into arrears by early
1989 and around $210 million behind by the winter of 1989–1990.[28]
Foreign exchange became so scarce in the spring of 1989 that the
central administration started rationing its meager stockpile of hard
currency, giving priority to those enterprises most likely to generate
export earnings, particularly through the production of agricultural
commodities or the assembly of light manufactures.[29]

At the same time, depressed prices on world oil markets severely
limited the flow of new revenues into the state treasury, despite dramatically higher production levels at Syria's main oil fields. Petroleum
exports earned an estimated $814 million in 1989, an increase of some
16 percent over total oil revenues for 1987. But in the same two years,
crude oil production jumped more than 56 percent as a result of the
exploitation of new producing sites in the northeast and southeast.[30]
Stagnating international petroleum prices hurt the local economy in an
indirect way as well by sharply reducing the amount of remittances from
Syrian nationals working in other oil-producing states.[31]

Moreover, bilateral and multilateral economic assistance to Syria
from the richer Arab states virtually disappeared as the decade came to
an end. Total annual aid disbursements to Damascus from these states
averaged almost $500 million during the years from 1982 to 1987, but
in 1988 the total plummeted to less than $80 million. The Organization
for Economic Cooperation and Development calculated that Syrian
repayments to outside lenders exceeded the value of new loans by some
$9 million.[32] Sharp increases in aid commitments from the European
Community and West Germany in 1989 resulted in a substantially

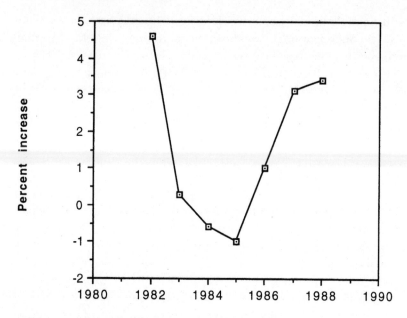

Figure 18. Gross domestic product, 1982–1988

higher level of available resources that year. When these two entities cut back on their pledges for 1990, however, the total amount of external assistance available to the Syrian government fell by almost 50 percent.[33] Partly as a result of these trends, the government's draft sixth Five-Year Plan, scheduled to run from 1986 to 1990, was abandoned even before it could be formally adopted.[34]

Despite such worrisome trends, the situation facing the regime at the close of the decade was not totally bleak. Syria's gross domestic product rose at an increasing rate from 1985 to 1987 before leveling off in 1988 (see Figure 18). Gross fixed capital formation in the public sector, which had been characterized by negative rates of increase after 1984, picked up again in 1988 (see Figure 19). Minister of the Economy and Foreign Trade Muhammad al-Imadi reported at the end of 1989 that aggregate domestic capital formation had risen by almost 15 percent compared to the figure for 1988.[35] During the final quarter of 1989, a sharp rise in sales of raw and processed cotton and cotton goods to the Soviet Union and Eastern Europe helped to relieve the country's peren-

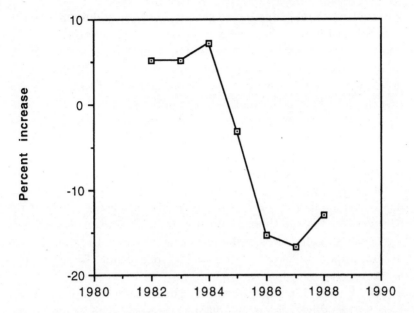

Figure 19. Gross fixed capital formation, public sector, 1982–1988

nially weak balance-of-trade and balance-of-payments positions. Much of this trade took the form of barter arrangements, whereby the value of shipments of Syrian raw materials and manufactured goods to former Eastern bloc countries was counted against Damascus's massive military debt to Warsaw Pact governments, estimated at some $10 to $18 billion.[36]

In early 1990, Syrian officials reported that the country's balance of trade had moved into the black for the first time in more than three decades. The Ministry of the Economy and Foreign Trade attributed this surplus to a 60 percent rise in nonpetroleum exports during 1989, the largest share of which consisted of private sector manufactures and private and mixed-sector agricultural produce.[37] Much of the surplus resulted from a sharp increase in the value of goods shipped to the Soviet Union, which jumped to just over $1 billion for the year. Skeptics in the local press and the People's Assembly speculated that the improved figures were no more than a statistical illusion because trade with the USSR was automatically calculated at the most favorable of the government's three different exchange rates. In addition, observers noted that official commercial statistics completely ignored Syria's lucrative but unlicensed trade through Lebanon.[38]

Nevertheless, the remainder of 1990 brought the al-Asad regime good economic news. Syria's gross domestic product rose by some 6 percent in real terms during the course of the year; inflation fell to an annual rate of around 40 percent, a notable drop from the 70 percent registered for 1989.[39] During the first six months of 1990, the value of Syrian exports reached almost $1.3 billion, a jump of some 62 percent over the figure recorded for the corresponding period in 1989. Approximately one-third of the total consisted of cotton goods, virtually all of which—along with sizable quantities of phosphates—went to the Soviet Union.[40] Meanwhile, production at the oil fields around Dayr al-Zur achieved record levels as the year came to an end, largely as a result of improved methods of extracting petroleum from existing wellheads.[41]

Syria's economic prospects continued to brighten in 1991. The European Community rescinded its 1986 freeze on economic assistance and immediately released a package of concessionary loans worth almost $200 million. In June, the Japanese government announced a new set of grants totaling some $466 million.[42] Gulf regimes supplemented these monies with low-interest loans targeted at specific investment programs: the Kuwait Fund for Arab Economic Development (KFAED) extended more than $100 million in credits for infrastructural projects in December 1990, while the Arab Fund for Economic and Social Development took over financing the extensive irrigation project in the eastern Khabur River valley. KFAED officials hinted in January 1991 that they intended to provide funding for improvements to Syria's telecommunications network.[43] Additional KFAED monies were earmarked at the end of March for small-scale manufacturing and services companies.[44]

Developments inside Syria complemented these windfalls from abroad. Preliminary estimates for wheat production during the 1991 crop year projected an increase of more than 20 percent over the previous year's total output.[45] Minister of Finance Muhammad Khalid Mahaini reported in early 1992 that profits derived from the sale of locally raised vegetables and animals during the preceding year more than offset the cost of agricultural imports.[46] The French oil company

Elf Aquitaine began production at two new wells around Dayr al-Zur in January 1991, then discovered an additional pool of light crude in the same concession that summer.[47] In March 1991, burgeoning bilateral trade between Syria and Egypt set the stage for a formal agreement between their respective Ministries of Industry aimed at promoting joint ventures in the manufacturing and transportation sectors.[48] A prominent Syrian entrepreneur told reporters in August that the private sector was growing at an annual rate of some 20 percent.[49] And in what should surely be seen as a reliable indicator of Syria's recovering economic health, the World Bank and International Monetary Fund both dispatched high-level missions to Damascus during the spring of 1991 in an attempt to convince the authorities to begin repaying their outstanding external debt.[50]

Syria's domestic economic crisis therefore appears to have dissipated as the 1990s opened. But more important than such purely economic considerations is a fundamental political point: trends in the Syrian economy at the turn of the decade reinforced the collective political position of the social forces that made up the al-Asad coalition, leaving them better able both to resolve conflicts of interest among themselves and to fend off actual or potential challenges from their primary opponents.

ECONOMIC IMPROVEMENT AND INTRAREGIME RIVALRY

Four powerful social forces constituted Syria's dominant coalition when the 1990s began. The first was the collection of senior commanders who controlled the state's extensive military and security apparatuses. The second was the cadre of state-affiliated managers who supervised the operations of the extensive network of public sector enterprises that had been created at the height of Ba'thi socialism in the mid- to late 1960s. The third consisted of large-scale commercial interests, based primarily in Damascus, who enjoyed intimate connections to the central administration. And the fourth was the richer agriculturalists whose members reemerged as powerful actors in the Syrian countryside during the course of the mid-1980s.[51]

Of these four forces, the latter pair profited handsomely from the controlled liberalization of the Syrian economy after 1985.[52] Despite the general economic crisis gripping the country, private capital managed to consolidate its position in the local economy: private interests represented some 40 percent of total fixed capital formation throughout the second half of the decade.[53] Agriculture and construction accounted for the largest share of the overall increase in capital formation. Mixed-sector farm companies producing cash crops for export and commercial real estate projects proved particularly profitable at the end of the 1980s. In addition, poorer quality foodstuffs found ready markets in Eastern Europe during the winter of 1990–1991; simultaneous increases in domestic cereals production permitted the regime sharply to reduce the amount of hard currency earmarked for overseas food purchases.[54]

Meanwhile, the share of Syria's total trade moving through the private sector rose from 10 percent in the early 1980s to over 20 percent in 1986. This proportion jumped to more than 30 percent by 1988.[55] Greater private sector involvement in internal and external commerce accompanied a marked resurgence on the part of large-scale, mixed-sector and private industry. Perthes reports that the second half of the 1980s saw "a significant real increase in the number of bigger industrial establishments" operating in the country, particularly ones having "comparatively large capital investments" and employing more than fifty workers each.[56] The most profitable of these enterprises were the larger clothing factories, which produced underwear, shirts, and socks for both domestic and foreign markets; firms specializing in the manufacture of cosmetics, fabrics, and tobacco products also earned healthy profits throughout most of the decade. All of these companies carried on a booming trade with the USSR and Eastern Europe, whose value was estimated to average some $200–300 million annually.[57] During the late 1980s, Syrian firms contracted with Soviet trading companies to supply increasing quantities of moderate-quality goods at premium prices, generating returns that greatly exceeded any that locally manufactured items could command on the open market.

As the decade ended, Soviet authorities slashed the prices they were willing to offer for goods manufactured in Syria. Moscow also began to insist upon a greater number of countertrading arrangements, whereby specified quantities of Syrian products would be shipped to Soviet buyers as a means of retiring Damascus's outstanding military debts. In response to shifts in the terms of Soviet-Syrian trade, officials in

Damascus moved to subsidize commercial exchanges between the two countries by granting greater access to the state's limited hard currency reserves to those companies that supplied manufactured goods to Eastern bloc governments. Largely as a result of this policy change, Syrian exports to the Soviet Union rebounded in 1989–1990.[58] At the same time, greater incentives to produce consumer goods for the Soviet market precipitated the proliferation of a host of smaller-scale textile and food processing factories in the suburbs surrounding the north-central city of Aleppo.

Private sector gains steadily altered the distribution of power inside Syria's ruling social coalition. The shift was most evident in the role of the country's Chambers of Commerce in the formulation of state economic policies. Between 1963 and 1981, these institutions had exercised little if any influence over government decision making. Steven Heydemann reports that in 1974 "a Syrian economist noted in a semi-official study that the chambers of commerce no longer had a meaningful place in the country's political economy, and were badly in need of reform in keeping with the new realities of Syrian socialism."[59] But by the end of the 1980s, prominent members of the Damascus chamber had assumed positions in several key government agencies, most notably the Committee for the Guidance of Import, Export, and Consumption, which had been created in 1981. Such positions enabled the rich merchants of the capital to voice their opinions at the highest levels of the central administration. As one senior member of the Damascus chamber told Heydemann in August 1991, "Whether we agree or disagree with its decisions, we are there in the room and they consult us on every step."[60]

Military commanders and public sector managers grew increasingly concerned about the burgeoning wealth and influence of their rich merchant allies as the new decade began. In his March 1990 Revolution Day address, President al-Asad himself hinted at the political fissures that might arise from the regime's program of controlled liberalization. He observed that "restricting freedom tarnishes it, but regulating its practice makes it brighter. Restricting freedom means dwarfing it, but regulating its practice means developing it and making it healthy. . . . Like everything else in this universe, freedom needs order."[61] His remarks accompanied a campaign by the Ba'th to reinvigorate its institutional links to the General Federation of Workers' Unions, the farm laborers' union, and the youth federation.[62] The presidents of the first two of these party-affiliated organizations were appointed to the newly reconstituted Committee for the Guidance of Import, Export and Consumption, which was charged with coordinating the week-to-week activities of public and private enterprises.[63]

At the same time, the regime increased the number of seats in the People's Assembly from 195 to 250 to encourage a greater number of non-Ba'thi candidates to run for parliamentary seats. The elections of 22–23 May 1990 resulted in victories for a number of richer merchants who had campaigned on platforms advocating further economic reform and greater efforts to stimulate private enterprise.[64] Confronted with a strong showing by liberal candidates, the two wings of the Syrian Communist party announced on 22 July that they would merge to "bolster national identity, back efforts to raise Syria's defense capabilities . . . and enhance the role and implement the charter of the [Ba'th-dominated] National Progressive Front."[65] The front had, in fact, won two-thirds of the seats contested in the parliamentary elections.[66] Nevertheless, the success of the liberals in capturing a broad range of popular support—not to mention the victory of four religious notables from districts in Aleppo and Idlib provinces—signaled an escalation in the nascent struggle among forces inside the dominant coalition for control over economic policy making.

Private interests were clearly in the ascendant during the months immediately following the 1991 Gulf War. In May 1991, the government promulgated a revised investment law codifying major components of the al-Asad regime's economic strategy for the 1990s. According to the terms of the new code, any projects that increased the number of jobs within the country, reduced imports, and augmented exports were awarded three distinct benefits. First, the machinery necessary to construct and operate such plants could be brought into the country duty-free. Second, the products of such plants were exempted from all taxes for seven years if the factory were part of the mixed sector—that is, if it had at least 25 percent state participation—and for five years if it were completely private; the grace period could be extended for an additional two years if half the plant's total output were exported. Third, investors were permitted to repatriate their entire investment capital after five years and to repatriate profits annually.[67] The new law set up a Higher Council for Investment, headed by Prime

Minister Mahmud al-Zu'bi, to issue licenses to companies eligible to operate under its terms.

The Higher Council immediately set about implementing the terms of the new investment code. In early June 1991, it created special industrial zones in several provinces to provide attractive locations for modern private and mixed-sector plants; a month later, the People's Assembly substantially lowered the rates charged in the highest personal and corporate tax brackets as a further stimulus to private investment.[68] More than 250 companies received licenses to operate under the terms of the revised law during its first year in force; the majority of these companies was engaged in transportation, automobile renting and leasing, or the processing of locally produced foodstuffs.[69] The government's evident interest in expediting the approval of new enterprises generated renewed interest in manufacturing among some of Syria's richest private entrepreneurs. One prominent expatriate announced at the end of August 1991 that he intended to invest in a pharmaceuticals plant, an infant formula bottling plant, a chemicals factory, and a surgical yarn factory during the fall and winter of 1991–1992.[70]

Encouraged by a generally positive response from overseas, state officials amended the investment law in early October to permit Syrian nationals residing within the country to invest hard currency on the same terms as non-nationals and expatriates.[71] This step led to the authorization of some 150 additional projects by the Higher Council for Investment during the first half of 1992. In contrast, in a bid to prevent new private enterprises from expanding too rapidly, the authorities in August 1991 revoked virtually all export licenses to the Soviet Union on the grounds that the annual quota for funds subsidizing these commercial transactions was exhausted.[72]

Government efforts to promote foreign and domestic private investment carried the potential to consolidate the alliance between Syria's richer commercial interests on the one hand and the country's resurgent larger landholders on the other. Relations between these two forces had deteriorated during the late 1970s, when the former acquiesced in the state's program of large-scale, capital-intensive industrialization, while the latter offered covert assistance to the Islamist movement challenging that program.[73] A combination of policy shifts and underlying economic dynamics laid the basis for a gradual reconciliation between the two forces in the late 1980s.[74] Any steps that might have enhanced the complementarity of their respective activities only augmented the stability of the ruling coalition as a whole. At the same time, however, providing greater encouragement to private investment threatened to alienate public sector managers from other forces inside the dominant coalition.

Public sector workers grumbled throughout the late 1980s that the central administration was courting foreign and indigenous private capital at the direct expense of Syria's existing state-run enterprises. The economic report circulated among delegates to the November 1986 annual conference of the General Federation of Workers' Unions accused state officials of encouraging private merchants to import products into the country, which sharply diminished local demand for the goods produced in public sector factories.[75] The lack of dynamism shown by state-run companies was reflected in a steady reduction in the number of workers employed by these firms: between 1985 and 1988 total employment at public industrial establishments fell from 141,000 to 139,000. Analogous reductions took place in public sector construction firms.[76]

More important, the state-dominated sectors of the Syrian economy—most notably mining, manufacturing, and transportation— evidenced precipitate drops in capital formation. Public sector managers attempted to reverse the trend by modernizing their deteriorating plants. At the end of 1990, the General Organization for Textile Industries put out a tender for offers to construct a new cotton spinning mill at Idlib, and the General Fertilizer Company (GFC) solicited bids for the construction of a state-of-the-art triple superphosphate fertilizer factory.[77] In January 1991, Minister of Planning Sabah Baqjaji told al-Hayat of London that the state's fiscal 1992 budget would include a larger allocation for investment in public sector industry, including funds for a new iron and steel complex at al-Zara outside Hamah and the renovation of the problem-plagued paper mill at Dayr al-Zur.[78] The General Organization for Cement and Building Materials asked for bids on a project to renovate and expand its cement factory at Hamah in early May, and the GFC tendered a proposal to do the same for its ammonia/urea plant at Homs a month later.[79]

Public sector managers hoped that such projects would attract the attention of Western investors, but firms based in the United States proved particularly reluctant to involve themselves outside the petroleum sector of the Syrian economy. West European capital evidenced a somewhat greater willingness to take advantage of investment opportunities in the country as the 1990s began: German, French, and Spanish consortia bid for the contract on the GFC's fertilizer factory; Italian and German firms made offers to build the Idlib spinning mill; and Austrian, Italian, Japanese, and German corporations tendered bids for the al-Zara iron and steel complex. But Western investment came nowhere near being sufficient to replace the funding and technical support that had previously been provided by the former Eastern bloc states. Instead, Arab Gulf governments stepped in to finance the modernization of Syria's public sector enterprises. The Kuwait Fund for Arab Economic Development agreed in July 1991 to provide the $60.5 million needed to build the cotton mill at Idlib; the iron and steel complex at al-Zara was to be funded by Saudi Arabia at a cost of approximately $500 million.[80] European and Gulf financing, paradoxically, provided the regime with the resources it needed to maintain its longstanding ties to the rapidly disintegrating Communist bloc.

CONTINUING TIES TO EASTERN EUROPE

Technicians from Russia, Czechoslovakia, Bulgaria, and Hungary provided vital expertise in several key sectors of the Syrian economy as the 1990s began. East European specialists remained prominent in supervising the construction of power plants, urban water and sewage facilities, and agricultural irrigation projects centered in the far northeastern provinces. Such operations continued to be virtually monopolized by the public sector, in spite of the government's efforts to promote liberalization in the local economy as a whole.

As Kuwait and Riyad restored the flow of economic assistance to Damascus from the Gulf, the new monies were used at least in part to finance existing projects involving skilled personnel from the former Eastern bloc. The eastern Khabur River valley irrigation scheme, whose funding was taken over by the Arab Fund for Economic and Social Development at the end of 1990, was contracted to a group of Bulgarian companies. A $102 million KFAED project to improve the water and sewage system of Damascus drew bids from Eastern European firms with past experience working on urban development projects in the country, and a similar project in Hamah elicited bids from several Polish and Bulgarian companies.[81] Syrian authorities attempted to earmark an even larger proportion of Gulf aid for the rehabilitation of ailing state-run industrial enterprises. But KFAED officials insisted upon promoting smaller, presumably private, manufacturing and services companies instead. At the end of March 1991, the Fund set up a $25 million account to support the creation and expansion of such enterprises.[82]

Despite this setback, Syria's public sector managers persisted in working to maintain the country's links to the economies of the former Communist bloc as a way of counterbalancing pressure from the Arab Gulf states to promote an internal economic order dominated by private enterprise and market relations. Damascus solicited greater levels of economic assistance from the People's Republic of China during 1991 as one means of offsetting the flow of funds from the Gulf.[83] April 1992 saw the signing of a bilateral accord between Damascus and Beijing that committed the Chinese government to assisting in the completion of a number of irrigation schemes in al-Hasakah province.[84] In May, Syria obtained from North Korea further financial and technical assistance for agricultural projects located in the far northeastern areas of the country.[85] Minister of Industry Ahmad Nizam al-Din initialed a wide-ranging industrial cooperation agreement with the Republic of Armenia in mid-July. The General Organization for Foreign Trade in Raw Materials and Chemicals received authorization to import 13,000 tons of Cuban sugar in October.[86]

Maintaining close ties to the former Eastern bloc not only suited Syria's public sector managers but also served the interests of the commanders of the country's military and security services, who persisted in cultivating strategic connections with Moscow even after the momentous winter of 1989–1990. Minister of Defense Mustafa Talas traveled to the Soviet capital in early February 1991 to discuss developments in the Gulf and to lay the groundwork for a formal request for new equipment. The Syrian delegation argued that accelerated shipments of military assistance were necessary to offset the advanced armaments and other war matériel that had been dispatched to Israel by the United States in the fall and winter of 1990–1991.[87] Syrian foreign minister Faruq al-Shar' visited Moscow two months later on a similar mission; he was told by Soviet President Mikhail Gorbachev that the USSR remained determined "to develop relations of friendly cooperation with Syria in all areas, including the defense sphere—with due consideration, of course, for the new international situation and capabilities that are limited by the current state of the Soviet economy."[88] As soon as al-Shar‛ returned home, however, Soviet officials announced that they would not resume military assistance to Syria, partly out of concern for regional stability in the wake of the 1991 Gulf War and partly because Soviet industry found itself incapable of producing the goods that the Syrians were requesting.[89]

Not even this announcement severed Damascus's long-standing ties to the former Eastern bloc. The Czech government agreed in May 1991 to provide the Syrian armed forces with one hundred T-72 main battle tanks as a way of ensuring that Damascus would repay its outstanding military debt to Prague, estimated to be worth some $1 billion.[90] Two months later, it was rumored that Beijing had at last begun shipping a consignment of M-9 short-range missiles that the Syrian government had ordered in the late 1980s; the *Wall Street Journal* reported the delivery of one hundred Scud-C missiles to the Syrian armed forces from North Korea a month later.[91] At the start of 1992, *al-Hayat* released details of a deal whereby Russia would sell Syria some $2 billion worth of MiG-29 fighters, Su-24 ground support aircraft, and SAM-10s and 11s. The newspaper also reported that Damascus had initiated serious negotiations with Moscow over the resumption of shipments of T-72 tanks to the Syrian armed forces.[92] Although the Slovakian government reneged on Prague's May 1991 tank deal in July 1992, Russian cargo aircraft delivered a number of North Korean–made chassis for Scud missile launchers to Damascus early the next month.[93]

SYRIA'S "EASTERN CONNECTION" AND REGIME CONSOLIDATION

Thanks to their links to the former Eastern bloc, Syria's public sector managers and elite military commanders gained the resources they needed to protect their position in local society in the face of the growing wealth and political influence of the country's private commercial and industrial entrepreneurs. The al-Asad regime's "Eastern connection" was facilitated not only by the revenues flowing directly into the state treasury from increased oil production, estimated at $2 billion annually as of late 1991, but also by the profits and kickbacks generated by the illicit trade in narcotics originating in Lebanon, also valued at around \$2 billion per year.[94] These resources enabled the Syrian high command to court China, North Korea, and Russia in pursuit of its increasingly chimerical goal of "strategic parity" with Israel, even as state officials contracted with Bulgarian, Czech, and Yugoslavian companies for desperately needed industrial and agricultural machinery and expertise.[95]

Simmering tensions between public sector managers on the one hand and influential private interests on the other became apparent in the regime's attempt to modernize Syria's extensive system of public transportation. In March 1991, state officials contracted with the Serbian firm Fap-Famos to provide more than one thousand buses to municipalities throughout the country, reportedly transferring some \$9 million in scarce hard currency to a Swiss bank account as a down payment for the sale.[96] A month later, the Ministry of the Economy and Foreign Trade revised the regulations governing the importation of mass transportation vehicles into the country, opening the trade in trucks and buses to private import-export houses.[97] The new regulations dramatically raised the cost of the Fap-Famos buses compared to vehicles supplied through the private sector, leading the government to negotiate a barter arrangement with India's Minerals and Metals Trading Corporation (MMTC) whereby some 700,000 tons of rock phosphate would be exchanged for eleven hundred Tata vehicles.[98] These negotiations collapsed in November 1991, when MMTC announced that Japanese automobile manufacturers had intervened to quash the deal, although MMTC reiterated its intention to purchase Syrian phosphate from third parties.[99] At some point in the midst of these talks, the state-sponsored private investment office approved the creation of Syria's first private bus company.[100] To complicate matters even further, the spring and summer of 1992 saw an influx of privately owned shared taxis into Syria's larger cities and towns. These vehicles competed directly with the municipal bus services not only for passengers but also for loading space at the main terminals.

Other public utilities generated similar tensions. Output by the state-run electricity company proved less and less able to keep up with spiraling demand as 1992 went by. The increasing incidence and length of power cuts to residential and industrial neighborhoods made it increasingly difficult for new manufacturers to keep production lines operating at a profit. Rising discontent over the state's inability to guarantee steady supplies of electricity precipitated a flurry of activity on the part of government officials aimed at renovating the country's deteriorating network of power generating stations. In late December, the General Establishment for Electricity solicited bids from several Western firms to upgrade facilities around Damascus.[101] To cover the costs of these contracts, the company raised electricity rates for all domestic users at the start of March 1993.[102]

Steady increases in electricity consumption, particularly on the part of private factories using state-of-the-art machinery, exacerbated the difficulties confronting Syria's network of state-run power stations throughout 1993. Finally, in a desperate attempt to placate residential and industrial consumers, the municipality of Aleppo announced in mid-August that it had granted a pair of private companies permission to set up neighborhood generating stations in two of the city's wealthier districts. At the same time, government officials issued a formal request to all factory owners to install diesel-powered generators so that more electricity could be earmarked for residential users. Meanwhile, a cabinet-level commission convened to discuss possible solutions to the country's burgeoning electricity problem.[103] These episodes illustrate not only the technical pitfalls that accompanied the regime's program of controlled liberalization but also the potential for intraregime conflict inherent in this fundamentally bifurcated economic policy.

OPPOSITION TO ECONOMIC LIBERALIZATION

Moves to construct market-driven commercial and industrial sectors at the heart of the Syrian economy precipitated muted opposition on the part of forces lacking the capacity to take advantage of the lucrative opportunities created by the new order. As early as 1987, the General Federation of Workers' Unions issued a conference report criticizing the government for its neglect of public sector enterprises. The report urged state officials to devote greater attention and resources to improving the equipment and the management of these firms so that the public sector could continue to play its historic role in promoting industrial self-sufficiency.[104] Representatives of the Syrian Communist party spoke against the adoption of the revised 1991 investment law when it was debated in the People's Assembly that March, charging that the code represented "a retreat from the nationalist and populist principles that have guided the Syrian economy" throughout the Ba'thi era.[105]

Left-wing Ba'thi and Communist deputies expressed considerable displeasure over the government's draft annual budget when it was submitted to the People's Assembly for consideration at the end of April 1992. Planned reductions in social welfare spending and the generally low tax rates levied on private enterprise elicited particularly strong criticism from representatives of the workers' and farm laborers' federations.[106] Rank-and-file discontent within the latter organization rose once again toward the end of August, when Prime Minister al-Zu'bi told a convention of the executive officers of the country's Chambers of Commerce that the government planned to increase its support for export-oriented projects in the private agricultural sector.[107] Similarly, the president of the Damascus Chamber of Industry, Yahya Hindi, complained during a radio interview on 2 December that the pivotal May 1991 investment law had enriched the country's merchants at the direct expense of both state-supported and some privately owned manufacturing companies.[108] His comments reflected festering resentment among less fortunate and less well-connected businesspeople over the evident success enjoyed by a relatively small number of entrepreneurs, even as many established manufacturing enterprises found it harder and harder to operate at a profit in the new market-oriented domestic economy. Meanwhile, the directors of the Damascus Chamber of Commerce found themselves subjected to growing criticism for moving too cautiously to take advantage of the opportunities created by the government's economic policies. General elections for seats on the chamber's governing council were fiercely contested throughout late November and early December.[109]

In preparation for its December 1992 congress, the General Federation of Workers' Unions compiled a lengthy list of grievances concerning the adverse impact of the state's program of economic liberalization on the general public. Skilled industrial workers were deserting the public sector in growing numbers to take higher-paying jobs in private manufacturing companies; price increases on staples continued to outpace wage increases for government employees; private schools and hospitals had become clearly better equipped and better administered than those operated by the state; and the gap between the ostentatious rich and the struggling poor appeared to be widening at an alarming rate. An influential grouping within the federation was even prepared to propose that the organization's long-standing ties to the Ba'th be relaxed so that workers' demands could be expressed outside the party's existing channels.[110] The potential for widespread worker disaffection continued to escalate during early 1993, as managers of public sector industrial enterprises began laying off more experienced, higher-paid employees and replacing them with younger laborers in an effort to cut production costs.[111] The spring of 1993 even saw the state-run Military Housing Company delay wage payments to its workers because of severe cash flow difficulties.[112]

Faced with widespread grumbling inside the Ba'thi popular front organizations, the regime allocated additional resources to revitalize Syria's public sector enterprises. The board of directors of the al-Furat tractor factory, for example, announced in August 1992 that it would reopen its assembly line on the outskirts of Aleppo using diesel engines imported from the United Kingdom.[113] Between mid-1992 and mid-1993, the government contracted with the Military Housing Company to build twenty-eight large grain silos throughout the country.[114] At the same time, however, state officials took steps to consolidate their ties with nouveaux riches entrepreneurs. Reports were leaked in September that the Ministry of the Economy and Foreign Trade was prepared to revise its regulations so as to permit private companies to keep 100 percent of their export earnings to purchase imports necessary for maintaining or expanding their operations. In addition, the ministry began granting six-month lines of credit to private import firms, and the Higher Council for Investment awarded operating licenses to an additional twenty private sector projects under the terms of the May 1991 investment law.[115]

State officials acted to head off disaffection on the part of those who favored preserving the extent and role of the public sector within the Syrian economy by creating an extraordinary commission to study various means of restructuring government-run companies. The panel announced in November 1992 that it planned to explore such options as granting managers of public enterprises greater autonomy in setting day-to-day policy and permitting state companies to keep any hard currency they earned.[116] At the same time, though, the Ministry of the

Economy and Foreign Trade reaffirmed its intention to set up a new bank to provide investment funds to the private and mixed-sector firms that had received operating licenses under the terms of the May 1991 law. A year later, and over the strenuous objections of a number of leftist delegates to the People's Assembly, Minister of the Economy and Foreign Trade al-Imadi took steps to increase Syria's borrowing rights in the International Monetary Fund. Meanwhile, Prime Minister al-Zu'bi publicly rejected proposed salary raises for public sector workers on the grounds that they might upset wage and price stability.[117]

Growing pressure to resolve the coordination problems plaguing Syria's economy provided state officials with strong incentives to rely on the military establishment as a policy-implementing instrument. When a group of prominent private entrepreneurs announced plans in the spring of 1993 to construct a new cigarette factory outside Damascus, army units led by the president's son were ordered to suppress the widespread smuggling of tobacco products into the country from Lebanon.[118] More predictably, when fighting broke out in a poorer district of Aleppo in July 1993, following a dispute over the distribution of interrupted public water supplies, regular army troops were sent into the neighborhood to restore order. In this fashion, the government's twin policies of deregulating the local economy and promoting private enterprise provided opportunities for Syria's senior military and security commanders to reassert their prerogatives. This eventuality heightened the importance of the al-Asad regime's maintaining its ties to its primary source of sophisticated weaponry, the former Eastern bloc.

DOMESTIC POLITICS OF MODERATION TOWARD TURKEY

Renegotiating intraregime relations at the start of the 1990s gave the forces that made up Syria's dominant social coalition little incentive to adopt a hard line in response to Turkish strategic initiatives. On the contrary, steady improvement in the Syrian economy led state officials, public sector managers, richer farmers, and private merchants and manufacturers alike to collaborate in an effort further to expand the domestic pie. At the end of 1991, for instance, the state-run Commercial Bank of Syria announced that it would set up at least one branch in

the capital whose exclusive function would be to promote private investment.[119] Government officials subsequently moved to consolidate the
gains that had been achieved by the country's private farmers in both
total output and aggregate capital formation by exempting all 1992
agricultural profits from taxation.[120]

Accommodation, or what could perhaps be called a form of benign
isolationism, vis-à-vis surrounding states provided the regime with additional resources that it could use to resolve coordination problems
within the local economy. The most obvious of these resources were the
grants and loans that surged into Syria from the Arab Gulf states in the
wake of the 1991 war in the Gulf. The availability of investment capital,
combined with the provisions of the revised investment law, spurred
some $2 billion in industrial and infrastructural projects throughout
Syria during the summer and fall of 1991.[121] Furthermore, officials of
the Kuwait Fund for Arab Economic Development insisted on rigorous
feasibility studies before the organization would authorize funding for
any new projects. The fiscal and administrative discipline imposed
upon the Syrian economy as a result of KFAED guidelines improved the
level of coordination not only between private and public enterprises
but also within the public sector itself. Given the conjunction of greater
complementarity within the domestic economy and sufficient resources
both to fund new projects and to rehabilitate existing installations,
none of the forces that made up the dominant social coalition was
willing to risk being excluded from the postwar bonanza by adopting
programs that might enhance its own political-economic position by
jeopardizing the interests of its partners. And no force within the regime found itself in need of additional resources that could be secured
only through mobilizing the country for war.

Damascus's evident rapprochement with Turkey thus complemented
the ascendance of richer private commercial and agricultural interests
inside the ruling coalition. These two forces stood opposed to moves
that might, for instance, have diverted scarce resources away from investment at home to support a permanent Syrian military presence in
the Gulf under the terms of the 1992 Damascus Declaration. By the
same token, the country's nouveaux riches entrepreneurs feared that
stationing Syrian troops in the Gulf on a long-term basis would eventually alienate the richer Arab oil-producing states, whose governments
had become vital providers of new capital to the local economy.

Syria's public sector managers acquiesced in the shift away from a more active role in the Gulf in the hope that the funds which had begun to arrive from the Arab Gulf governments might be used to reinvigorate their own flagging enterprises. At the same time, they joined senior military commanders in resisting steps that might completely disarm Iraq, on the grounds that the collapse of the Iraqi armed forces would leave Syrian industrial facilities and infrastructure more vulnerable to Israeli attack. Moreover, by offering Baghdad an outlet for its petroleum exports, managers of public sector enterprises expected to reinforce the centrality of the state-run oil sector within the Syrian economy. Reinforcing the role of oil might not only create more jobs for hard-pressed public sector workers but also lend greater weight to petroleum-related projects in the government's ongoing deliberations concerning Syria's future development priorities.[122]

DOMESTIC POLITICS AND THE MIDDLE EAST PEACE TALKS

Paradoxically, during the two years immediately following the end of the 1991 Gulf War, sporadic eruptions of domestic discontent precipitated greater accommodation and flexibility, rather than greater intransigence, in the al-Asad regime's stance toward the State of Israel. Damascus adopted an evidently acquiescent posture regarding the Middle East peace talks on three distinct occasions from the spring of 1991 to the spring of 1993. The first coincided with the outset of the August 1992 round of negotiations; the second involved President al-Asad's highly publicized November 1992 interview with reporters from *Time* magazine; and the third was evident in the president's keynote address to the December 1992 annual convention of the General Federation of Workers' Unions. In each of these cases, political developments inside Syria played a primary role in shaping Damascus's strategy vis-à-vis Jerusalem.

There can be little doubt that the momentary relaxation in Syria's overall intransigence that was evident in the summer of 1992 represented an overture to Israel's newly elected Labor government and was consequently driven in part by the exigencies of interstate diplomacy. Nevertheless, a pair of developments in the domestic political-economic arena during the spring and summer of that year provided the broader context within which Syrian negotiators undertook this particular accommodative move. In the first place, it appears that popular disaffection over the effects of the regime's economic liberalization program intensified during these months. In April leftist deputies in the People's Assembly criticized the planned reductions in social welfare spending and low tax rates on private enterprises contained in the draft 1992–1993 budget. Two months later, members of the farm laborers' federation expressed discontent over the government's plans to increase support for private agricultural exports.[123]

Second, new resources were flowing into the central treasury at an exceptionally high rate. It became clear by late summer that Syria's cotton producers were going to harvest a record crop during the 1992 season. Projections estimated an increase in total output of almost 20 percent over the level achieved the previous year.[124] This increase complemented a notable rise in phosphates exports. Bumper crops of foodstuffs, however, proved somewhat less profitable. The Federation of Syrian Chambers of Agriculture set up a commission at the end of August to coordinate the output and marketing of such produce as tomatoes, potatoes, apples, and raisins in an effort to avoid a recurrence of the sharp drops in the prices of these items that had occurred in mid-1992.[125]

The regime had responded to widespread grumbling within the ranks of the Ba'thi popular front organizations by earmarking additional resources to revitalize Syria's public sector. At the same time, however, state officials took steps to consolidate their links to nouveaux riches private entrepreneurs. Squaring the circle of placating disaffected members of the popular front organizations while at the same time buttressing the burgeoning private sector—itself the very focus of left-wing discontent—could best be accomplished in an atmosphere of heightened national concern regarding the peace talks. And although many members of the Ba'th party and its affiliated popular front organizations no doubt favored the hard line that the leadership was already pursuing in its dealings with Israel, and thus might have been expected to object to the specific content of the diplomatic initiative undertaken at the beginning of August 1992, the unmistakable shift in strategy captured the public's attention long enough for simmering discontent over the economic situation at home to dissipate. The comparative weakness of the political challenge confronting the dominant social coalition made it possible for the initiative to take the form of accommodation rather than mobilization for war.

Thus when representatives of the General Federation of Workers' Unions grew restive the first week of December, the Syrian leadership undertook a pair of highly visible initiatives in the external arena.[126] President al-Asad's accommodative interview with *Time* was accorded extensive coverage in the local media, eclipsing debate over whether the government should permit international firms to reenter the country to assist in setting up large-scale private industrial plants.[127] By the same token, whatever proposals might have been put forward by the workers' federation for revising the organization's relations with the Ba'th were not only completely overshadowed but also severely undercut by the president's keynote speech. In light of the gravity of the external security issues addressed by President al-Asad, it would have been trifling, if not seditious, to raise the more mundane matter of restructuring trade union–party relations.

This message was driven home in the rhetoric that pervaded the address.[128] President al-Asad began by praising the delegates for their many accomplishments in the areas of factory construction, dam building, and technical training. He then asserted that "great as those achievements are, the greatest is our national unity, which is our pride." The honor of the nation, he went on to say, lay in the fact "that the achievement was accomplished within the framework of a coherent and strong national unity that achieved security and consolidated both stability and progress." Finally, the president expressed his gratitude that the trade unionists "understood freedom within the framework of responsibility and distinguished between interacting in the context of integration to reach a goal [on one hand] and contradiction and fragmentation which lead to wasted effort and crumbling power [on the other]." The necessity of forging internal unity as a means of ensuring external security could not have been stated more clearly. The assembled trade unionists undoubtedly got the message.

Domestic political-economic trends militated heavily against Damascus's provoking confrontations with neighboring governments in the early 1990s, as well as against a reversal of the al-Asad regime's longstanding orientation toward the Arab-Israeli conflict in the months following the 1991 Gulf War. Freeing up hard-won financial resources for domestic investment lay at the heart not only of Damascus's decision to cooperate with Washington and Riyad during the Iraq-Kuwait crisis but also of its unwillingness to escalate simmering conflicts with Ankara in the aftermath of the war.

At the same time, state officials adopted a consistently firm stance in the U.S.-sponsored talks with Israel as a way both of mobilizing members of the popular front organizations to sacrifice in defense of the nation and of reassuring public sector workers that their contribution to the nation's well-being continued to be of the utmost importance. The regime's refusal to compromise with the historical enemy of the Syrian and Palestinian people was explicitly associated with the diligence and self-sacrifice with which the country's factory and farm laborers were expected to carry out their duties. As President al-Asad told the workers' federation, "You were, and you still are, dear workers, the substance of economic and social changes. In addition, each gain of the Correctionist Movement's achievements was basically aiming at achieving the people's prosperity, security and stability; and you are in the front."[129] Inflexibility in the peace talks therefore complemented the unwavering discipline that the regime demanded from industrial workers and farm laborers.

By the same token, an unwaveringly hard line vis-à-vis Israel helped to prevent Syria's private entrepreneurs from becoming overly complacent about their role in the country's economic future. In the first place, the possibility that negotiations might break down and Syrian-Israeli relations revert to outright belligerence put a damper on moves by local businesspeople to collaborate with foreign corporations, as well as on unbridled investment by indigenous and expatriate capitalists. Recognizing the disruptions that had accompanied wholesale liberalization in Egypt and Iraq, state officials appreciated the necessity of imposing firm limits upon speculative or nonproductive private investment. But they then confronted the puzzle of how to regulate the activities of private entrepreneurs without reintroducing direct state intervention into the local economy, a step that would have frightened potential investors away from Syria. Raising the specter of renewed external conflict thus kept the expansion of the private sector within comparatively circumscribed—even manageable—bounds.

Second, the possibility that the forty-five-year state of war with Israel might persist entailed the potential that the Syrian economy might on short notice be recentralized for military purposes. Such a step could be expected to work to the direct benefit of the public sector, much of whose raison d'être was "for the realization of economic autonomy" and national defense.[130] In this way, the state's continued purchases of sophisticated weaponry from the former Eastern bloc effectively buttressed the position of the public sector relative to that of private enterprise.[131]

Yet a softer line toward Israel carried with it the distinct likelihood that Syria's private entrepreneurs would step up their activities, further undercutting the collective position of the country's military officers, party-state officials, and public sector managers. It may therefore not have been a coincidence that plans for both a major joint venture pharmaceuticals project and a path-breaking private aluminum fabrication mill were finalized during the brief period of accommodation that occurred at the end of November 1992.[132] More important, a comparatively flexible posture in the peace talks could be expected to prompt even greater numbers of workers to abandon the state-run enterprises and seek jobs in privately owned companies. Such a trend would make it virtually impossible for the already weakened public sector to survive, dramatically raising the level of unemployment throughout the country.

Equally dangerous, from the standpoint of those advocating a continuation of state supervision over the local economy, a general exodus of skilled employees away from the public sector might provide the basis for a political alliance between private capitalists and industrial labor that could prove potent enough to threaten the preeminence of the ruling coalition of military officers, party and state officials, and public sector managers. So long as workers and farm laborers remained distanced from—if not actually opposed to—private interests, they represented a heavy counterweight to the wholesale liberalization of the Syrian economy.[133] But to the extent that the labor movement forged a common front with private capital, the distribution of power within Syria could be expected to shift profoundly. Mobilizing industrial workers and farm laborers to carry on the struggle against Israel thus did more than distract these forces' attention from their rapidly accumulating domestic grievances; it also provided the al-Asad coalition with the resources necessary to win their continued allegiance to the regime.

CHAPTER SIX

Domestic Conflict and Crisis Escalation in a Liberal-Democratic Syria

It might be argued that the connection proposed here between accumulation crises, high levels of domestic political conflict, and contradictory regime responses on the one hand and belligerent foreign policies on the other may well be present in an authoritarian Syria but would disappear were the country to be governed along liberal-democratic lines. A growing body of literature claims that the combination of a possessive-individualist ideology, an elected parliament, and formal guarantees on the freedom of public expression mitigates against aggressive policies toward the outside world.[1] Successive episodes of foreign belligerence could thus be attributed to the absence of such features from Syria's political order during the Ba'thi era.

Michael Hudson sketches an elegant refutation of this chain of reasoning. He observes that Syria possessed a "limited liberal parliamentary system" during both the last three years of French rule and the first three years following the country's de jure independence in April 1946. The system included rival political parties, regular competitive elections to choose delgates to parliament, an orderly replacement of successive cabinets by their opponents, and a virtually free press, all minimal but definitive features of liberal-democratic polities.[2] Far from promoting moderation and accommodation toward its neighbors, however, this liberal-democratic order amplified widespread public "support for the Palestinians against Zionist encroachment," eventuating in "powerful domestic backing for Syria's military involvement in the 1948 war."[3] It is not entirely clear from Hudson's abbreviated account why or how popular sentiment forced the government of President Shukri al-Quwwatli to escalate the first Arab-Israeli crisis. But given the argument offered here, it is possible to construct a compelling explanation for liberal-democratic Syria's puzzlingly aggressive policy toward the newly emergent, social-democratic State of Israel.[4]

THE ACCUMULATION CRISIS OF 1947

At independence in April 1946, Syria's economy displayed distinctly contradictory trends. On one hand, the abrupt release into the labor market of some thirty thousand Syrian nationals who had been employed by the Allied armies during the years of the Second World War pushed unemployment to unprecedented levels.[5] Massive unemployment came hard on the heels of a prolonged bout of severe inflation, sparked by wartime scarcities of foodstuffs and other basic commodities. Deteriorating wages and living conditions among the country's industrial laborers precipitated a wave of strikes in Syria's larger cities during the spring of 1946. Increases in the incidence and severity of industrial actions coincided with a well-organized campaign on the part of the Syrian Communist party to promote workers' rights.[6]

In response to rising proletarian militance, the General Federation of Workers' Unions drafted a comprehensive labor code at its May 1946 congress. Trade union leaders presented the federation's proposal to the National Assembly the following month, where it was quickly passed into law.[7] The new regulations officially recognized labor's right to strike but prohibited workers from engaging in a broad range of "political activities." Exhilaration over retaining government approval of the right to strike, combined with simmering discontent over the relatively tight restrictions that the law imposed upon other activities by the labor movement, prompted a continuation of trade union activism throughout the remainder of the year.

Wartime restrictions on foreign trade, combined with substantial Allied military purchases of locally manfactured products, however, laid the foundations for a dramatic expansion of Syrian industry in 1945–1946. Aggregate capital formation soared as the flow of goods into the country suffered repeated disruptions, effectively preventing well-to-do consumers from spending a sizable proportion of their income.[8]

Forced savings created a sizable pool of capital, which was readily available for industrial investment as the war drew to a close.[9] Large-scale, mechanized cloth factories proliferated around Aleppo during late 1945 and early 1946, driving down fabric and clothing prices on local markets.[10] The great majority of the new enterprises was owned by Syrian entrepreneurs because foreign firms generally preferred to ship goods into the country with the help of trading companies based in Lebanon, rather than invest in local plants.[11] Small-scale textile manufacturers prospered during the months immediately after the war as well. Tabitha Petran reports that when larger firms replaced obsolescent weaving machines with newer models, the older looms were purchased by the owners of smaller workshops, who then hired displaced textile workers to produce rayon cloth for sale across the border in Turkey, Iraq, and Jordan.[12]

Meanwhile, mechanized commercial farming spread across the northeastern plains, largely as a result of the wartime activities of the Middle East Supply Center (MESC). This agency distributed motorized farming equipment throughout the Syrian countryside in an effort to ensure that Allied troops stationed in the region could be provisioned locally.[13] Rich merchants based in Aleppo took advantage of the opportunities created by the MESC by purchasing large tracts of previously uncultivated land along the Euphrates and Khabur rivers, then bringing these fields into production using machinery provided by the center at subsidized prices.[14] Smaller farmers in the mountainous western region of the country, where introducing mechanized agriculture proved to be considerably more difficult, found themselves unable to keep up with the newfound prosperity of the agrarian entrepreneurs of al-Jazirah.[15]

Postwar growth in the industrial and agricultural sectors of the Syrian economy coincided with a substantial expansion in both the size and scope of the country's central administration. According to Petran, "The number of civil servants had by 1947 increased more than three times over the 1939 level; their salaries now consumed more than half the state budget."[16] Government officials assumed responsibility for overseeing the implementation of the revised labor law, as well as the imposition and collection of a variety of new taxes. The cabinet's March 1946 decision to require citizens to pay an income tax prompted a succession of strikes by urban tradespeople, who, according to Gordon

Torrey, "claimed that it should be imposed on the big merchants who benefited from the import quota and from the government's allocations of dollars."[17] During the first year after independence, the state also extended its control over Syria's foreign commerce. In April 1947, for instance, the Ministry of National Economy temporarily prohibited the exportation of locally grown cereals to Lebanon.[18] This measure's success in moderating wildly fluctuating grain prices on domestic markets encouraged state officials to begin issuing import licenses as a means of regulating the flow of goods coming into the country. Allegations of favoritism in the awarding of such licenses became more and more frequent as the year went by.[19]

More important, government officials took a more active part in determining what forms of political activity were considered legitimate and what behaviors were proscribed. In November 1946, the cabinet proposed a series of emergency measures limiting the range of activities open to political organizations and the press; liberals in the National Assembly objected strenuously to the proposed decrees on the grounds that they directly contravened constitutional guarantees regarding freedom of expression.[20] In the wake of this row, members of parliament who voiced criticisms of the cabinet found themselves subject to surveillance by the security services, while antigovernment newspapers were repeatedly shut down by order of the Ministry of the Interior.[21]

Growing government involvement in the Syrian economy proved a mixed blessing for local manufacturers. On one hand, the state-sponsored customs union with Lebanon greatly facilitated the importation of industrial machinery and other inputs from outside suppliers. On the other, membership in the customs union enriched the local merchant community at the direct expense of owners of new manufacturing firms, who generally favored higher tariffs as a means of protecting their fledgling operations. Furthermore, the central administration assumed a key role in enforcing the 1946 labor code, whose terms mandated the establishment of a network of arbitration committees charged with resolving disputes between labor and management in an unbiased manner.[22] Displeasure with the central administration's increasing intervention in the labor market led larger manufacturers to scale back their investments beginning in mid-1947.[23]

Tensions among Syria's industrial entrepreneurs, richer commercial farmers, and government bureaucrats opened the door to rising levels of agitation against the regime, particularly in the countryside. Long-standing peasant hostility toward the large landowners of Hamah province had already provided the impetus for the emergence of a nascent Arab Socialist party (*al-hizb al-ishtiraki al-'arabi*) in the spring of 1945 under the leadership of Akram Hawrani.[24] This organization pressed for political and social reforms and criticized the pervasive nepotism of the regime. In the spring of 1947, the party orchestrated a campaign to force the government to change the voting laws so as to allow direct elections to the National Assembly. Party leaders even urged the peasantry to sabotage production on the larger private estates as a way of gaining leverage over the agrarian elite.[25]

At virtually the same time, the Arab Ba'th party (*hizb al-ba'th al-'arabi*) convened its first congress in Damascus. This organization had its roots in the anti-French movement of the 1930s but gained strength by mobilizing popular sentiment in support of pan-Arabism at the time of France's withdrawal from Syria in the spring of 1946.[26] By early 1947, the party had opened branches in Damascus, Aleppo, Dayr al-Zur, Homs, Latakia, and Banyas. Its leaders, Michel 'Aflaq, Salah al-Din Bitar, and Jalal al-Sayyid, at this point "realized the time had come to put the organization on a more formal basis."[27] From 4 to 7 April, they presided over a meeting in a Damascus coffee house during the course of which an executive committee was elected and a constitution adopted. The new party immediately entered a slate of candidates into the running for seats in the National Assembly, campaigning on a platform that advocated extensive reforms in the electoral process and an end to administrative corruption. Despite its failure to win representation in parliament, the party continued to denounce the government, which it claimed consisted exclusively of "feudalists, reactionaries and exploiters." In this way, the Ba'th played a major role in "contributing to the general turmoil that characterized Syria in 1947 and 1948."[28]

Deep-seated conflicts of interest among industrial and agricultural workers, factory owners, large-scale importers, commercial farmers, and state officials intensified in the months surrounding the 1947 National Assembly elections. In May 1946, the cabinet ordered the police to arrest the leadership of the Liberal Union (*ittihad al-ahrar*), an informal grouping of prominent individuals who had expressed criticism of the government, and to close its main office in Damascus.[29] Eight months later, the country's governing elite, the National Bloc (*al-kutlah al-*

wataniyyah), "embarked on a campaign of intimidation, purges, and arrests in an attempt to silence its critics and destroy all political opposition."[30] The evident self-interestedness and blatant corruption that permeated the regime were epitomized by President Shukri al-Quwwatli: during the first year after independence, al-Quwwatli's "rule was comparable to the rule of the Turkish vali [governor-general] who made no accounting to anyone for his actions."[31] The immorality of the political establishment fueled the country's radical Islamist movement, the Muslim Brotherhood (*ikhwan al-muslimin*), which won new adherents in virtually all parts of the country during the winter of 1946–1947.[32]

In the end, the electoral campaign of June–July 1947 exacerbated fissures inside the dominant social coalition. As Torrey remarks, "The election discredited the Nationalists."[33] Prominent liberal candidates opposed to President al-Quwwatli prevailed in Aleppo; representatives of the ikhwan won the balloting in a number of key constituencies in Damascus; and pro-regime notables were routed in the predominantly Druze districts of al-Suwayda.[34] When the independent but former National Bloc leader Jamil Mardam was asked to form a cabinet in the aftermath of the voting, seventeen liberal notables from Aleppo, Homs, and Damascus met in Ba'albak to forge a People's party (*hizb al-sha'b*) to challenge the new government. The party's initial manifesto called for an end to autocratic rule, as well as for the implementation of a wide range of economic and social reforms. It also announced that it would not support the new cabinet unless its members received at least four ministerial positions.[35]

When Prime Minister Mardam found himself unable to meet the People's party's demands for representation in the government, he tendered his resignation to President al-Quwwatli. But the president urged him to try once again to form a cabinet, and this time Mardam succeeded in persuading two leading figures from the People's party—Ahmad al-Rifa'i and Wahbi al-Hariri—to accept ministerial posts.[36] The appointment of the latter proved particularly divisive because the al-Hariri family owned a large cotton mill in Aleppo whose primary competition came from a factory owned by the al-Mudarris family, which had sponsored the National Bloc's list in the July elections.[37] The first item on the new government's agenda, amending the constitution to permit President al-Quwwatli to run for a second term in office, not only provoked further dissension within the National Assembly but also sparked popular protest, orchestrated by the Ba'th party newspaper in Damascus.[38]

The political-economic difficulties associated with such intraregime splits were compounded by shortages of foodstuffs on Syrian markets, which resulted from a shortfall in local grain production during the 1947 crop year.[39] The lack of adequate supplies of wheat, maize, and barley sent prices soaring in virtually all parts of the country. At the beginning of November, a mob attacked government offices in Dayr al-Zur after state-run warehouses in the town ran out of wheat. Some thirty rioters were killed or injured in the melee.[40]

As popular disaffection spread, state officials found themselves increasingly unable to guarantee public order. The national police force, which had grown haphazardly out of the preindependence gendarmerie, continued to be severely understaffed and poorly disciplined.[41] Officers stationed in the provinces regularly extorted money and supplies from the local citizenry, while virtually all police and military vehicles, along with most of the country's meager stockpiles of weaponry and military matériel, had been diverted onto the black market. The regular armed forces, which emerged from the French-era Troupes Spéciales, fared no better. Salaries generally failed to arrive as promised; equipment and training proved woefully inadequate; senior officers openly bridled at civilian attempts to supervise military affairs; prominent members of parliament, including President al-Quwwatli, proposed radical reductions in the size of the army, even as opposition representatives argued that the military establishment should be enlarged to meet internal and external threats. Joshua Landis reports that under these circumstances, "Syrian officers quickly learned to fend for themselves. Abandoned by their political leaders in the squalid military outposts that ringed Syria's borders, military units turned to graft, smuggling, the narcotics trade, and petty bribery in order to keep their bellies full and barracks warm during the cold winter months." Throughout 1947 rumors persisted that the armed forces were planning to overthrow the regime by force, and a number of influential commanders established close ties to the British-supported government of al-Amir 'Abdullah in Jordan as a signal to the authorities in Damascus that they had other options besides acquiescing in the status quo.

CONTRADICTORY REGIME RESPONSES

Forces inside the dominant coalition responded to the accumulation crisis of 1947 by carrying out a number of programs, each of which threatened the interests of their political partners. Rich merchants attempted to weaken the labor movement by increasing the flow of imported goods into the Syrian market. Meanwhile, government officials pulled out of the customs union with Lebanon, effectively raising the cost of such imports. Finally, the country's manufacturers postponed new investments, diverting their savings into gold instead. The conjunction of these trends severely undermined not only the health of the Syrian economy but also the ability of the forces that made up the ruling coalition to continue cooperating with one another to their mutual advantage.

As the labor movement grew in size and influence, Syria's commercial elite stepped up the importation of manufactured goods into the country.[42] The jump in imports occurred despite the fact that trends in the international financial system created a situation in which "long-standing orders for merchandise could now be filled only at prices considerably higher than when placed."[43] The steep rise in imports during the first quarter of 1948 therefore put a severe strain on the state's already inadequate stockpile of foreign currency.

Raising the amount of imports entering the country became even more costly beginning in January 1948, when the authorities in Damascus backed out of a provisional agreement that would have devalued the Syrian pound against the French franc.[44] On 10 February, Lebanese and Syrian officials stopped the circulation of Syrian pounds inside Lebanon; this step effectively terminated the monetary union between the two countries. [45] The Syrian government then erected a strict system of controls over the holding and exchange of foreign currency. As a result of these measures, the value of the Syrian pound plummeted relative to that of its Lebanese counterpart. Moreover, Syrian traders found themselves forced to negotiate with the Exchange Office in Beirut to obtain the convertible Lebanese pounds they needed to deal with the outside world.[46]

Large-scale manufacturers responded to growing restiveness among urban workers by delaying new plant construction and canceling orders for capital goods. Instead of investing in local industry, Syrian capitalists converted their funds into holdings of precious metals.[47] Consequently, aggregate industrial investment stalled beginning in early 1948. Only one new manufacturing corporation was formed during the course of the year.[48] Chronic labor militance, combined with the flood of foreign goods entering the Syrian market, made manufacturing much less attractive for the emergent industrial bourgeoisie than either investment in real estate or speculation in gold and overseas stock offerings.

Taken together, these three strategies made it virtually impossible for the al-Quwwatli–Mardam regime to pull Syria out of the accumulation crisis of 1947. The activities of merchants and manufacturers particularly exacerbated Syria's persistent balance-of-payments difficulties. More important, the costs of each of the measures adopted by the members of the dominant coalition were borne directly by other forces inside the regime. Under these circumstances, continued collaboration among the country's large-scale industrialists, rich merchants, and state officials became increasingly problematic. Syria's leadership thus turned to programs associated with an escalation of the crisis in Palestine in a desperate attempt to resolve burgeoning contradictions within the dominant social coalition.

INTERVENTION IN PALESTINE AND REGIME CONSOLIDATION

During the fall and the winter of 1947–1948, political conflict at home merged with popular outrage over Zionist activities in Palestine. Leaders of the Muslim Brotherhood accompanied representatives of the Mufti of Jerusalem, al-Hajj Amin al-Husaini, in traveling from city to city to call for the creation of a popular army to defend the rights of Palestinians against Jewish and British depredations.[49] Tradespeople in Damascus carried out a spontaneous general strike when they learned that the United Nations General Assembly had on 27 November 1947 voted to partition Palestine into separate Jewish and Arab states. The strike sparked two days of rioting in the capital, during which a crowd of some ten thousand vandalized the embassies of the United States, France, and Belgium. Demonstrators also attacked the Soviet cultural center and the headquarters of the Syrian Communist party, killing ten party workers. Simultaneous rioting in Aleppo resulted in the death of some seventy-five Syrian Jews, along with the destruction of several ancient synagogues.[50]

In the wake of this wave of popular protest, prominent critics of the regime, most notably Akram Hawrani and leaders of the Ba'th party, announced that they and their followers intended to volunteer to fight alongside guerrilla forces preparing to resist the emergence of a Jewish state in Palestine. They were accompanied by a collection of ambitious mid-level army officers, who saw service in the newly formed Arab Liberation Army as a way to gain both battlefield experience and public recognition. One of these officers, Colonel Adib Shishakli, joined Hawrani's ragtag brigade of volunteers from Hamah in raiding Jewish settlements along the Syria-Palestine border during the first weeks of 1948.[51] Meanwhile, broadsheets issued by the Ba'th party urged the government to distribute arms to the Syrian citizenry so that the general population could take part in the struggle against Zionism.[52]

The Mardam government manipulated growing popular belligerence over Palestine in three ways. First, it incorporated proponents of greater Syrian intervention in the conflict into regime-sponsored institutions. In December 1947, the cabinet appointed a blue-ribbon committee to solicit monetary contributions to support the war effort. Prime Minister Mardam himself served on the committee.[53] Beduin leaders, Druze chieftains, and large landowners immediately enlisted their retainers for active duty in guerrilla units organized by the committee. Others who volunteered to fight the Zionists were funneled into training camps run by regular army officers who integrated the new recruits into understaffed units throughout the southeastern provinces.[54] At the same time, the government persuaded the National Assembly to ratify a law requiring all male citizens over nineteen years of age to serve a twelve-month tour of duty in the regular armed forces during peacetime and authorizing compulsory military service for all men over seventeen if war were declared.[55] These regulations effectively co-opted militant supporters of the Palestinian cause, pulling them away from the autonomous formations organized by the Arab Socialist and Ba'th parties.

Second, state officials suppressed political organizations having close ties to the workers' and farm laborers' movements. Most severely hurt by the anti-labor offensive was the Syrian Communist party, which had been the most active advocate of workers' rights in the months following the French evacuation. In mid-December 1947, the authorities declared membership in the party to be illegal; state officials then ordered the police to confiscate its posters and leaflets and to close its district offices throughout the country. The following March, the government banned distribution of the Ba'th party's daily newspaper and shut down its branches inside Syria as well, on the grounds that Ba'this were undermining the war effort by inciting popular disorder.[56] Such steps culminated in the cabinet's declaration of a national state of emergency on 15 May.[57]

Finally, the government in early January 1948 persuaded the National Assembly to impose a number of surtaxes on imports. The new taxes were justified as a way to raise revenue to finance new arms purchases and increase pay for soldiers. The surcharges totaled 5 percent for goods coming from the United States and 2.5 percent for those from the sterling area.[58] They provided the state not only with a means of regulating the flow of manufactured goods coming into the country but also with additional revenues to improve its precarious balance-of-payments position.

Increasingly belligerent moves against Zionist forces in Palestine legitimated these measures. In mid-November 1947, two divisions of Syrian troops staged maneuvers in the area north of al-Qunaitirah.[59] Three months later, Prime Minister Mardam, acting in his capacity as foreign minister, signed the military protocols included in the charter of the League of Arab States, creating a unified command for the armed forces of Syria, Jordan, Lebanon, and Egypt.[60] Several prominent figures in the National party announced immediately following the massacre of Palestinian noncombatants at Dayr Yasin in April 1948 that they intended to volunteer to serve in the Arab Liberation Army.[61] It was thus in an atmosphere of general euphoria, largely orchestrated by the al-Quwwatli–Mardam regime, that units of the Syrian army intervened in Palestine on 16 May.

LIBERAL DEMOCRACY AND AGGRESSION

Liberal-democratic polities may indeed find their capacity to implement aggressive or escalatory foreign policies narrowly circumscribed, particularly when they confront countries with similar governmental systems. But the case of parliamentary Syria should warn against making such sweeping generalizations as Jack Levy's widely cited observation that "the absence of war between democratic states comes as close as anything we have to an empirical law in international relations."[62] Or perhaps it should instead remind us that even a regularity as well founded as the absence of war between liberal-democratic states is unlikely to be universal. Puzzling exceptions to the rule, such as Syria in the late 1940s, demand unorthodox explanations. Situating episodes of aggressive foreign policy in the context of contradictory responses to domestic crises of accumulation by the social forces that make up a country's dominant coalition offers a promising alternative to the current orthodoxy that liberal democracy ensures peace.

CONCLUSION

Implications for Further Research

Syrian foreign policy took a variety of shapes during the three decades after 1963. On several occasions, Damascus initiated armed confrontations with surrounding states or pursued policies that escalated international crises not of its own making. Furthermore, the Syrian regime at times took steps that entailed the exercise of military force, no matter how its adversary responded to the situation at hand. But on other occasions it made use of the country's armed forces in more measured ways, overtly threatening war but hesitating to follow through when the attendant risks or costs became inordinate.

Existing accounts explain why Syrian leaders opted for escalatory foreign policies at some times and implemented accommodative policies at others on the basis of leaders' idiosyncrasies, the sectarian nature of the regime, or the strategic circumstances in which Damascus found itself. Such accounts are useful insofar as they integrate Middle Eastern cases into the mainstream of writings on international security.[1] But they remain inadequate to the extent that they ignore political-economic factors as primary determinants of the policies that governments adopt in crisis situations.[2] The six episodes presented here offer an alternative explanation for why Syria has initiated or escalated external crises at some times and refrained from doing so at others, one informed by current literature on political economy.

Syrian foreign policy during the Ba'thi era provides three pieces of evidence that bear directly on recent attempts to link domestic political conflict to foreign aggressiveness. In the first place, Damascus initiated external crises in its dealings with Israel in 1967 and with Iraq in 1982 at times when powerful forces outside the regime raised major challenges to the dominant social coalition. Severe internal conflicts did not preclude the implementation of an aggressive foreign policy.[3] Instead, growing conflict at home prompted the regime to carry out a variety of programs, many of which greatly enhanced the role of the state, including the regular armed forces.[4] Mobilizing Syria's military establishment to suppress internal challenges lay a large part of the foundation for the deployment of the armed forces against outside adversaries.

By the same token, much lower levels of domestic conflict accompanied Damascus's responses to ongoing external crises such as those involving Jordan in 1970 and Lebanon in 1976. On neither of these occasions was internal opposition to the regime completely absent. The social forces that made up Syria's dominant coalition therefore manipulated the international situation to their own political advantage. But faced with less threatening challenges at home, state officials had little incentive to manufacture crises outside. Similarly, Syrian policy toward Turkey moderated during the early 1990s, when domestic conflict once again diminished. Nevertheless, the al-Asad regime adopted a riskier policy toward Lebanon than did the Salah Jadid regime toward Jordan, primarily because the former confronted a greater internal challenge in 1976 than had the latter six years earlier. High levels of domestic conflict thus prompted successive Syrian governments to escalate foreign crises throughout the Ba'thi era.

Second, Syrian regimes have tended to escalate crisis situations, no matter how their adversary responded, whenever the social forces that made up the dominant coalition met internal challenges in mutually contradictory ways. Deep divisions inside the regime disposed state officials to pursue belligerent foreign policies, even when such policies entailed substantial risks. Conflicts of interest associated with divergent political-economic programs adopted by members of the dominant coalition persuaded the government in 1967 and 1976 to use foreign policy to ameliorate intraregime tensions. Yet even when Damascus initiated a military confrontation with Iraq in 1982, the al-Asad regime defused the crisis before it spiraled out of control, primarily because of the basic complementarity of the programs implemented by the forces that constituted the ruling coalition.

Finally, periodic domestic crises of accumulation lay at the root of successive episodes of foreign aggressiveness in Baʻthi Syria. Arguably the most severe of these accumulation crises preceded the most aggressive episode: Syria's provocation of war with Israel in 1967. But notable crises of accumulation also provided the backdrop for Damascus's 1976 intervention in the Lebanese civil war and the 1982 confrontation with Iraq. A domestic accumulation crisis even provided the context within which the Salah Jadid regime ordered Syrian troops to move into Jordan in 1970. And when the long string of accumulation crises unraveled in the early 1990s, Damascus assumed a comparatively accommodative posture toward its adversaries.

COMPARABLE CASES

If a conjunction of domestic accumulation crises, severe internal challenges, and contradictory regime responses explains important episodes of external aggressiveness in Baʻthi Syria, then it should be able to shed new light on other instances of crisis escalation as well. Two additional cases drawn from the contemporary Middle East indicate the general utility of the argument proposed here. The first, Algeria in the fall of 1963, concerns a government that escalated a crisis by standing firm in response to demands made by an adversary. The second, Egypt in the fall of 1973, involves a state that launched a preemptive strike against an adversary during the course of an ongoing confrontation.

Algeria, 1963

Algeria's six-year war for independence from France ended in the spring of 1962, precipitating severe conflict among the various components of the umbrella National Liberation Front (FLN).[5] One faction quickly consolidated its hold over the country's western provinces, while an equally powerful wing of the FLN established itself in the Berber-dominated region of Kabylia to the east. Skirmishing between the two factions' militias escalated into virtual civil war in late July; the fighting was terminated only after regular army units under the command of Colonel Houari Boumedienne entered Kabylia at the beginning of September. When Boumedienne, in his new capacity as minister of defense, ordered the militias to disband in January 1963, several guerrilla bands refused to submit and were broken up by force. Domestic conflict then took the form of intense jockeying among the six remaining "historic chiefs" who had led the struggle against the French, accompanied by persistent efforts on the part of state officials to impose their will on the country's powerful trade union federation.[6]

Escalating tensions between President Ahmed Ben Bella and the Kabyle leader Hocine Ait Ahmed sparked renewed skirmishing in the eastern highlands during the first week of September 1963. Ait Ahmed took advantage of the confrontation between Kabyle guerrillas and government forces to announce the formation of a Front of Socialist Forces (FFS) to contest the political hegemony of the FLN. David and Marina Ottaway observe that the belated decision of the provincial military commander, Colonel Mohand ou el-Hadj, to join the movement "seemed to give some teeth to the opposition."[7] But Ben Bella hesitated to unleash the regular armed forces against Kabylia once again, choosing instead to discredit the dissidents by charging that their activities were sponsored by Morocco. When Ait Ahmed flatly refused to negotiate, President Ben Bella asked the National Assembly to grant him extraordinary powers to meet a combination of internal and external threats; he then authorized Boumedienne to pacify Kabylia.

These developments transpired in the context of a severe accumulation crisis, which affected virtually all sectors of the Algerian economy. The crisis had its origins in the wholesale exodus of French capital from the country during the spring and summer of 1962.[8] Abandoned farms and factories were formally sequestered by state officials that September, after the great majority of them had already been occupied by displaced agricultural laborers and members of the trade union federation (UGTA). By late October, government bureaucrats were locked in a fierce struggle with local peasants' and workers' committees for control over agricultural and industrial production.

Burgeoning conflict between farm laborers and the UGTA on one side and the central administration on the other prompted the government to promulgate a set of administrative decrees in March 1963 that established a system of workers' self-management (*autogestion*) throughout the country. The decrees instituted uniform procedures for electing managers, administering day-to-day operations, and distributing income in self-managed enterprises, but, as Ottaway and Ottaway argue, nevertheless "failed to spell out the role of the government agency in charge of the socialist sector."[9] State officials implemented the regulations in ways that increased government supervision over the local economy, punishing enterprises that resisted state supervision by withholding operating and investment monies from them. As a result, "the worker-run factories were forced to turn for loans and credits to private banks, which were naturally hostile to the socialist sector. They also had to compete with private companies, which had the necessary capital, the know-how, and the business contracts that public companies lacked."[10] Consequently, self-managed farms and factories quickly began operating at substantial losses, boosting unemployment and encouraging investors to transfer their capital overseas. Mahfoud Bennoune estimates that some 500 million Algerian dinars fled the country every month during the second half of 1962.[11]

By the following summer, some one hundred manufacturing firms had shut down for lack of operating capital. The value of Algeria's total industrial output dropped to no more than two-thirds of what it had been three years earlier. Activity in the construction sector ground virtually to a halt, and some 70 percent of local building companies declared bankruptcy. Mining and metals production fell to 80 percent and 85 percent, respectively, of what they had been only a year before. Consequently, "the total number of Algerian industrial workers decreased from 110,000 in 1962 to 80,000 in 1963."[12] Even though oil production remained profitable, more than half of the revenues generated in this sector of the economy were immediately repatriated overseas. The treasury faced soaring budget deficits.[13]

Government officials attempted to ameliorate the crisis by further augmenting state control. All agricultural land that had fallen into the hands of private entrepreneurs at the time of the French exodus was transferred to the National Office of Agrarian Reform (ONRA) in the name of extending autogestion, while properties belonging to the country's few remaining French inhabitants were nationalized. Party cadres then began confiscating shops, factories, and even cafes owned by Algerian nationals and incorporating them into the public sector. In early September, the leadership of the FLN purged prominent liberals from the government and organized a plebiscite to approve a permanent constitution. The document declared self-management to be "a major arm in the battle against poverty and economic dependency," confirmed the FLN as Algeria's only political party, and designated

Algeria "a socialist state."[14] Such measures solidified President Ben Bella's dominant position vis-à-vis radicals inside the FLN apparatus but simultaneously exacerbated tensions between doctrinaire socialists and moderates both in the party and in the National Assembly.

More important, the policies adopted in September and October 1963 threatened to fracture the ruling coalition. Extending nationalization to Algerian-owned enterprises alienated the FLN leadership from the small-scale merchants and manufacturers who had been key components of the anti-French coalition.[15] Richer merchants, on the other hand, rapidly gained access to lucrative overseas trading networks that had been abandoned by the French and set themselves up as local representatives of foreign firms. The growth of an indigenous commercial bourgeoisie accompanied the rise of a new class of private industrialists, whose members managed to seize control of a handful of sequestered factories and transform them into profitable concerns.[16] Neither of these two forces stood to gain from the implementation of the March decrees, a policy discrepancy that laid the foundation for a succession of subsequent struggles among the country's most powerful social forces.

It was under these circumstances that the regime mobilized Algeria's armed forces to resist a series of Moroccan incursions into disputed territory along the border separating the two countries. Algerian and Moroccan troops clashed on 8 October. President Ben Bella appealed the following week to all former guerrillas to enlist in the regular army to assist in parrying the external challenge. According to the Ottaways, "The response to the president's call for volunteers was tremendous, with close to 100,000 Algerians signing up to go fight the war against invading Moroccan forces. Even the FFS offered its services in defense of the homeland, and indeed Colonel el-Hadj left for the Sahara frontier with a large contingent of Kabyle troops."[17] The government's campaign to mobilize popular support for the struggle against Morocco contributed greatly to the dissolution of Kabylia-based opposition to the Ben Bella regime.

Furthermore, mobilizing the country for war provided the government with an opportunity to dampen the most glaring contradictions in Algeria's domestic political economy. The initial clash with Moroccan forces coincided with the announcement that a national congress of farm laborers would convene in two weeks. When the congress opened in Algiers on 25 October, state and party officials permitted delegates to air a broad spectrum of complaints, most notably about the continuing lack of operating capital and modern equipment, heavy-handed government supervision, and periodic disruptions in the distribution of both inputs and produce. But when the public hearings ended, organizers presented a set of resolutions for ratification by acclamation. The resolutions called for a 30 percent raise in the minimum wage, the establishment of a unified network of marketing cooperatives, and the formation of a state agricultural bank.[18] Such programs effectively undercut the autonomy of the self-managed farms and facilitated their integration into the expanding system of government agencies clustered around the ONRA. At the same time, new restrictions were imposed on the exchange of Algerian currency and additional duties levied on imports that competed directly with locally manufactured goods.[19] These measures increased private merchants' dependence on the central administration and thus laid the foundation for a series of subsequent nationalizations in the commercial sector. In mid-November, the Algerian-Moroccan border war of 1963 quietly dissipated.

Egypt, 1973

Opposition forces inside Egypt grew steadily bolder and more numerous during the two years following the death of President Gamal 'Abd al-Nasir in November 1970. Discontent with the new regime of Anwar al-Sadat was particularly pronounced on university campuses, where posters denouncing the undemocratic character of the government appeared with increasing frequency throughout late 1971 and early 1972. Student activism fueled the formation of a considerable number of clandestine societies throughout the country, whose members organized repeated public demonstrations to protest the regime's policies regarding a wide range of political, economic, and social issues.[20]

Such activities culminated in a wave of strikes and public meetings that shook the capital in mid-January 1972. Popular disaffection over the apparent political-economic reorientation of the post-Nasir regime intensified when President al-Sadat appointed a notorious scion of the country's pre-1952 agrarian elite to be secretary-general of the Arab

Socialist Union at the same time that, as Ahmed Abdalla reports, "the minister of defence announced that the army was now open to student recruits, and that the military training given to students in institutions of higher education was to be intensified."[21] A delegation of student leaders was allowed to present their followers' demands to the parliament at the end of the month, but immediately after a tentative agreement to publish the government's response was finally negotiated, the minister of the interior "ordered his special forces, the Central Security Forces, to storm the universit[ies] and arrest the students."[22] This move sparked two days of rioting in Cairo, which met with sympathy, if not outright approval, on the part of the teachers', lawyers', engineers', and journalists' unions.[23] In the face of widespread popular support for the students' demands, state officials adopted a more conciliatory posture and attempted to turn popular sentiment against the primary external enemy, the State of Israel.[24] But this tactic failed to placate Egypt's university students and industrial workers, who continued to voice their opposition to the regime over the subsequent fifteen months.[25] Chronic disaffection in the larger cities accompanied rising sectarian tension in the countryside, fueled by a succession of incendiary pronouncements by the new Coptic pope.[26]

Forces inside the dominant coalition adopted wildly divergent positions in response to the activities of the opposition. Abdalla observes that "there were sharply differing attitudes within the government over the issue of student activism."[27] Some senior ministers accused underground Nasirist organizations of orchestrating the violence, while others saw the hand of the outlawed communist movement. President al-Sadat publicly hinted that Israeli intelligence had incited the students to riot, while the Ministry of Defense instead blamed a "minority" of "extremists."[28] Such disagreements reflected not only the idiosyncratic perceptions of particular cabinet ministers but also growing fissures within the regime related to the state's contradictory responses to Egypt's escalating economic crisis.

January 1972 saw the government take a marked turn away from the state-sponsored socialist programs that had characterized the Nasir era. The new prime minister, 'Aziz Sidqi, immediately implemented cuts in subsidies for staples and other welfare expenditures in the name of preparing the economy for the coming confrontation with Israel. But despite the cutbacks, growing foreign indebtedness and generally stagnant local production left the treasury unable to cover the state's out-standing financial obligations by the end of the year. Prime Minister Sidqi thus pared government spending a second time in early 1973.[29] Investment in public sector industry was particularly hard hit by the reductions, although funding for a variety of projects in the agri-cultural, transportation, and utilities sectors was preserved in the 1973 budget. In a bid to mollify public sector workers, the prime minister journeyed to the state-owned iron and steel works at Helwan at the end of January to announce that the plant's employees would receive a bonus "in appreciation of their efforts in carrying out this great project."[30] The money to pay this bonus was to come from a tax levied on "all classes of people [at a rate] commensurate with the level of income."[31] The National Assembly shortly thereafter relinquished to the president its constitutional right to approve any new taxes, with the stipulation that parliamentary oversight would be restored with "the end of the current year or the removal of the traces of the [Israeli] aggression, whichever is earlier."[32]

A significant drop in cotton exports in the first months of 1973 heightened state officials' anxieties concerning the health of the Egyp-tian economy.[33] President al-Sadat took over the office of prime minis-ter from Sidqi at the end of March and promulgated a series of mea-sures intended to facilitate the importation of consumer goods into local markets. This program pushed the government further into the red, even as the newly created Economic Committee of the parliament was advocating a comprehensive rescheduling of the country's bur-geoning foreign debt.[34] Cairo's municipal council eased long-standing restrictions on private construction in an effort to encourage new hous-ing starts, at the same time that state officials restructured the Ministry of Economy, Finance, and Foreign Trade as a means of imposing greater central administrative control over the country's economic af-fairs.[35] At the end of May, officials announced the creation of free trading zones in Cairo and Alexandria in an effort to attract larger amounts of foreign direct investment. Meanwhile, the government con-tinued to allocate increasingly scarce investment capital to increasingly uncompetitive public sector firms.[36]

Such contradictions led President al-Sadat to order the formation of a pair of high-level committees to formulate a coherent plan to guide the economy through the years 1973–1978.[37] The work of these committees was largely preempted at the end of July, when the minister of economy, finance, and foreign trade rearranged exchange rates on the Egyptian pound and authorized the creation of a Higher Ministerial Council for Foreign Trade Planning to supervise what he called the "opening up of the Egyptian economy."[38] The minister subsequently encouraged public sector companies to take advantage of liberalization to expand production for export and curtail long-standing barter arrangements with the Eastern bloc.[39] Even the first secretary of the Arab Socialist Union urged private enterprise to assume a greater role in the local economy.[40] These moves generated intense rivalry between public sector management and labor on the one hand and private capital on the other as the autumn began.[41]

Under these circumstances, Egypt's leadership appears to have made a conscious effort to defuse popular discontent by mobilizing the country for war. According to the editor of the government daily *al-Akhbar,* President al-Sadat argued forcefully in cabinet meetings that a military move against Israel was the only way to prevent student disaffection from spreading throughout the general population.[42] Supporting evidence for this view can be found in al-Sadat's published memoirs and other public statements.[43] Egyptian planners appear at first to have envisaged no more than a limited strike across the Suez Canal, designed to establish a token (or trip-wire) beachhead along the eastern shore.[44] The Egyptian army exhibited notable hesitation in exploiting the tactical advantages it gained during the first days of the fighting.[45] Furthermore, the high command persistently refrained from deploying Egypt's air force either to provide support for its own ground troops or to engage Israeli warplanes in combat.

Nevertheless, the leadership in Cairo abandoned its plans for a limited engagement once the actual fighting got under way.[46] As it became clear that the Egyptian armed forces had launched a major offensive and not just another raid against Israeli positions, radical students and intellectuals lost much of their animosity toward the regime. One group of activists concluded after listening to reports from the front that "Sadat no longer looked like a deal-maker. He looked patriotic, as if he were fighting for the national demands of the Egyptian people." The government had finally responded to the opposition's repeated demand that it "do something" regarding the land occupied in June 1967, and even the most vituperative critics of the president were left dumbfounded. Without quite knowing why "the students remained pessimistic about the future for internal Egyptian politics. They assumed that there would not be a defeat, and that whatever happened Sadat and his group would be strengthened by just having gone to war." Doctrinaire socialists, by contrast, were elated, anticipating that Cairo's strained relations with Moscow would improve as the fighting persisted. But the authorities took no chances that opposition forces might use the war as the occasion to forge links to the general population: only the tamest forms of popular participation in the war effort were permitted, and student leaders who tried to rally enthusiasm for more active measures were quickly taken into custody.[47]

Egypt's unexpected strike across the Suez Canal precipitated an exceptionally dangerous round of nuclear diplomacy between Washington and Moscow.[48] And the eventual rout of the Egyptian army on the battlefield opened the door for Israeli forces to drive deep into Egyptian territory just before the cease-fire came into effect.[49] On balance, however, strategic factors are less important than domestic political-economic dynamics in explaining why the Egyptian-Israeli crisis of October 1973 erupted into war, whereas the Egyptian-Israeli "war of attrition" three years earlier remained restricted to aerial sorties, artillery exchanges, and reciprocal troop movements.[50]

POLITICAL ECONOMY AND CRISIS ESCALATION

Recent scholarship has greatly improved our understanding of the interaction among states in crises. Russell Leng demonstrates that "a crisis is most likely to end in war when one of the parties believes that it can win a war relatively easily, the other side believes that it has at least an even chance, and both parties have vital interests, or other immediate security interests, at stake."[51] Leng concurs with Glenn Snyder and Paul Diesing that international crises are more likely to eventuate in war when one party attempts to coerce the other(s) into capitulating through the use of "aggressive Bullying influence strategies" than when the initiator implements a "reciprocal" or "firm-but-fair" strategy.[52] Janice Gross Stein adds that a state's leaders will "choose preventive war if they are convinced that war is inevitable and their position is deteriorating." This implies that "when two adversaries each consider themselves to be defending the status quo and find themselves in the domain of losses, escalation is especially likely."[53]

Incorporating the domestic political economy into the study of international crises buttresses each of these three lines of argument. Leaders evaluate the costs of adopting escalatory foreign policies not only in terms of the diplomatic and strategic problems such policies may engender but also according to the internal difficulties they create or aggravate. Under a wide range of circumstances, domestic conditions militate against aggressive moves in the external arena. Mobilizing societies for war entails considerable costs, and provoking confrontations with neighbors is almost always inordinately risky. Moreover, regimes usually have the option of selecting from among a number of different policies to achieve their objectives. There are thus few occasions when a government can be expected to take steps that heighten external conflict.

Nevertheless, a regime confronting severe internal challenges, and particularly one whose members have implemented contradictory programs in an attempt to resolve a burgeoning crisis of accumulation, may well decide that external conflicts are less costly than further measures to prop up a crumbling political-economic order at home. It may even stir up popular enthusiasm for war as a means of undermining its domestic opponents or to repair splits inside the ruling coalition. Expectations of a short and victorious war may therefore not be an independent source of belligerence in a crisis but instead result from rulers' efforts to generate unity on the home front.

In addition, the domestic political economy provides important insights into the circumstances under which states adopt comparatively uncompromising bargaining strategies, rather than more reciprocal ones. As the cases presented above indicate, successive Syrian governments initiated coercive policies toward neighboring states whenever powerful forces outside the dominant coalition were gaining strength or political leverage as a result of widening intraregime fissures. There may in fact be leaders who undertake aggressive foreign policies purely by fiat. But it seems more plausible to argue that regimes will risk the potentially dangerous and unpredictable consequences associated with manufacturing or escalating external crises only when they become desperate, not when they consider themselves invulnerable.

Finally, internal political-economic trends play a major role in shap-

ing the frames of reference whereby governments evaluate their prospects for the future. Deteriorating circumstances at home are generally
easier to recognize, and their probable consequences easier to estimate,
than are the possible results of pursuing belligerent foreign policies.
Confronted with deepening splits inside the dominant coalition, which
both strengthen forces challenging the regime and make it more
difficult to resolve domestic accumulation crises, almost any state can
be expected to risk war rather than accept the certainty of internal
collapse. This does not mean that an increasingly desperate regime
necessarily behaves in an irrational fashion. But it does imply that the
decision calculus of governments confronting domestic crises of accumulation can be expected to differ markedly from that of ones enjoying
stable political economies. It is the spread of well-integrated ruling
coalitions capable of resolving domestic accumulation crises, not the
proliferation of liberal-democratic institutions, that will do most to promote peace in the post–Cold War world.

Notes

INTRODUCTION

1. For an early attempt to bridge the gap, see Richard N. Cooper, "Trade Policy Is Foreign Policy," *Foreign Policy* 9 (Winter 1972–1973). See also Charles Lipson, "International Cooperation in Economic and Security Affairs," *World Politics* 37 (October 1984); Beverly Crawford, "The New Security Dilemma under International Economic Interdependence," *Millennium* 23 (Spring 1994).

2. George Bush, "Iraq Invasion of Kuwait," *Vital Speeches of the Day*, 1 September 1990, p. 674.

3. Rudolph Rummell, "Dimensions of Conflict Behavior within and between Nations," *Yearbook of the Society for General Systems* 8 (1963); Dina Zinnes and Jonathan Wilkenfeld, "An Analysis of Foreign Conflict Behavior of Nations," in Wolfram Hanreider, ed., *Comparative Foreign Policy* (New York: McKay, 1971); Michael Stohl, "The Nexus of Civil and International Conflict," in Theodore Gurr, ed., *Handbook of Political Conflict* (New York: Free Press, 1980); Michael Ward and Ulrich Widmaier, "The Domestic-International Conflict Nexus: New Evidence and Old Hypotheses," *International Interactions* 9 (1982).

4. Ernst B. Haas and Allen S. Whiting, *Dynamics of International Relations* (New York: McGraw-Hill, 1956), p. 62; Quincy Wright, *A Study of War* (Chicago: University of Chicago Press, 1965), p. 140; Richard N. Rosecrance, *Action and Reaction in World Politics* (Boston: Little, Brown, 1963), pp. 304–306; Fred H. Lawson, "Domestic Conflict and Foreign Policy: The Contribution of Some Undeservedly Neglected Historical Studies," *Review of International Studies* 21 (October 1985): 275–299; Jack S. Levy, "The Diversionary Theory of War: A Critique," in Manus I. Midlarsky, ed., *Handbook of War Studies* (Boston: Unwin Hyman, 1989).

5. Leo Hazlewood, "Diversion Mechanisms and Encapsulation Processes: The Domestic Conflict–Foreign Conflict Hypothesis Reconsidered," *Sage Inter-*

national Yearbook of Foreign Policy Studies, vol. 3 (Beverly Hills: Sage, 1975).

6. Clifton Morgan and Kenneth Bickers, "Domestic Discontent and the External Use of Force," *Journal of Conflict Resolution* 36 (March 1992): 31; Bruce Russett, "Economic Decline, Electoral Pressure, and the Initiation of International Conflict," in Charles Gochman and Alan Sabrosky, eds., *Prisoners of War?* (Lexington, Mass.: Lexington Books, 1990); Bruce Russett, *Controlling the Sword* (Cambridge: Harvard University Press, 1990), p. 44.

7. Patrick James, *Crisis and War* (Kingston: McGill-Queen's University Press, 1988), pp. 99–104.

8. Notable exceptions are Yaacov Bar-Siman-Tov, *Linkage Politics in the Middle East: Syria between Domestic and External Conflict, 1961–1970* (Boulder, Colo.: Westview Press, 1983); Eberhard Kienle, *Ba'th v Ba'th: The Conflict between Syria and Iraq, 1968–1989* (London: I.B. Tauris, 1990). See also Robert Burrowes and Bertram Spector, "The Strength and Direction of Relationships between Domestic Conflict and External Conflict and Cooperation: Syria, 1961–1967," in Jonathan Wilkenfeld, ed., *Conflict Behavior and Linkage Politics* (New York: McKay, 1973); Robert Burrowes and Gerald DeMaio, "Domestic/External Linkages: Syria, 1961–1967," *Comparative Political Studies* 7 (January 1975).

9. Correctives to the existing literature include Bahgat Korany, Paul Noble, and Rex Brynen, eds., *The Many Faces of National Security in the Arab World* (London: Macmillan, 1993); Peter Pawelka, "Die Politische Ökonomie der Aussenpolitik im Vorderen Orient," *Orient* 35 (September 1994); Laurie A. Brand, *Jordan's Inter-Arab Relations* (New York: Columbia University Press, 1995).

10. See Nikolaos van Dam, "Middle Eastern Political Cliches: 'Takriti' and 'Sunni Rule' in Iraq; 'Alawi Rule' in Syria—A Critical Appraisal," *Orient* 21 (January 1980); Alasdair Drysdale, "The Syrian Armed Forces in National Politics: The Role of the Geographic and Ethnic Periphery," in Roman Kolkowicz and Andrzej Korbonski, eds., *Soldiers, Peasants and Bureaucrats* (London: George Allen & Unwin, 1982); Peter Sluglett and Marion Farouk-Sluglett, "Some Reflections on the Sunni-Shi'i Question in Iraq," *British Society for Middle East Studies Bulletin* 3 (1978).

11. Charles W. Yost, "The Arab-Israeli War: How It Began," *Foreign Affairs* 46 (January 1968): 305.

12. Richard B. Parker, "The June 1967 War: Some Mysteries Explored," *Middle East Journal* 46 (Spring 1992): 178.

13. Walter Laqueur, *The Road to War* (Harmondsworth: Penguin, 1968), p. 54.

14. Ibid., pp. 56–60; Bar-Siman-Tov, *Linkage Politics in the Middle East,* pp. 157–161; Patrick Seale, *Asad: The Struggle for the Middle East* (Berkeley: University of California Press, 1988), pp. 124–125; Bassam Tibi, *Conflict and War in the Middle East, 1967–91* (New York: St. Martin's, 1993), pp. 72–73.

15. Yair Evron, *The Middle East: Nations, Superpowers, Wars* (New York: Praeger, 1973), p. 66.

16. Yost, "The Arab-Israeli War," p. 305.

17. Ibid., p. 308.

18. Ibid., p. 310; Parker, "June 1967 War," pp. 180–182; Nadav Safran, *From War to War: The Arab-Israeli Confrontation, 1948–1967* (New York: Pegasus, 1969), pp. 276–277.

19. Richard B. Parker, "The June War: Whose Conspiracy?" *Journal of Palestine Studies* 21 (Summer 1992): 12–13.

20. Muhammad Hasanain Haikal, *1967: Al-Infijar* (Cairo: Markaz al-Ahram lil-Tarjamah wal-Nashr, 1990).

21. Henry Brandon, "Jordan: The Forgotten Crisis (1)," *Foreign Policy*, no. 10 (Spring 1973): 166.

22. Henry A. Kissinger, *White House Years* (Boston: Little, Brown, 1979), pp. 617–631; William B. Quandt, *Decade of Decisions* (Berkeley: University of California Press, 1977), pp. 115–119; Michael I. Handel, "The Evolution of Israeli Strategy," in Williamson Murray, MacGregor Knox, and Alvin Bernstein, eds., *The Making of Strategy* (Cambridge: Cambridge University Press, 1994), p. 535.

23. Malcolm H. Kerr, *The Arab Cold War* (Oxford: Oxford University Press, 1971), p. 149; Alan Dowty, "The U.S. and the Syria-Jordan Confrontation of 1970," *Jerusalem Journal of International Relations* 3 (Winter–Spring 1978); Yaacov Bar-Siman-Tov, "Crisis Management by Military Cooperation with a Small Ally: American-Israeli Cooperation in the Syrian-Jordanian Crisis, September 1970," *Cooperation and Conflict* 17 (1982).

24. Raymond A. Hinnebusch, "Revisionist Dreams, Realist Strategies: The Foreign Policy of Syria," in Bahgat Korany and Ali E. Hillal Dessouki, eds., *The Foreign Policies of Arab States* (Boulder, Colo.: Westview Press, 1991), p. 392; Moshe Ma'oz, *Asad: The Sphinx of Damascus* (New York: Weidenfeld and Nicolson, 1988), p. 39.

25. Chaim Herzog, *The Arab-Israeli Wars* (London: Arms and Armor Press, 1982), p. 222.

26. Tabitha Petran, *Syria* (New York: Praeger, 1972), p. 247.

27. Stephen Oren, "Syria's Options," *The World Today* 30 (November 1974): 473; Daniel Pipes, *Greater Syria* (New York: Oxford University Press, 1990).

28. R. D. McLaurin, Don Peretz, and Lewis W. Snider, *Middle East Foreign Policy: Issues and Processes* (New York: Praeger, 1982), p. 299 n. 159.

29. Yosef Olmert, "Domestic Crisis and Foreign Policy in Syria: The Assad Regime," *Middle East Review* 20 (Spring 1988): 18–19.

30. Bar-Siman-Tov, *Linkage Politics in the Middle East*, p. 164; McLaurin, Peretz, and Snider, *Middle East Foreign Policy*, p. 276.

31. Seale, *Asad*, chap. 11; Petran, *Syria*, pp. 247–248; Hinnebusch, "Revisionist Dreams, Realist Strategies," p. 305; Aryeh Yodfat, "The End of Syrian Isolation?" *The World Today* 27 (August 1971): 334; David Roberts, *The Ba'th and the Creation of Modern Syria* (New York: St. Martin's, 1987), p. 93; David Roberts, "The USSR in Syrian Perspective," in Moshe Efrat and Jacob Bercovitch, eds.,

Superpowers and Client States in the Middle East (London: Routledge, 1991), p. 211; Martha Neff Kessler, *Syria: Fragile Mosaic of Power* (Washington, D.C.: National Defense University Press, 1987), p. 98; Afaf Sabeh McGowan, "Historical Setting," in Thomas Collelo, ed., *Syria: A Country Study* (Washington, D.C.: Department of the Army, 1988), p. 39. More circumspect are Nikolaos van Dam, *The Struggle for Power in Syria* (New York: St. Martin's, 1979), p. 88; John Devlin, *Syria* (Boulder, Colo.: Westview Press, 1983), p. 101.

32. Adam M. Garfinkle, "U.S. Decision Making in the Jordan Crisis: Correcting the Record," *Political Science Quarterly* 100 (Spring 1985): 130–132.

33. Ibid., p. 135.

34. Adeed I. Dawisha, "Syria's Intervention in Lebanon, 1975–1976," *Jerusalem Journal of International Relations* 3 (Winter–Spring 1978): 245–263; Adeed I. Dawisha, "The Motives of Syria's Involvement in Lebanon," *Middle East Journal* 38 (Spring 1984): 229. See also Adeed I. Dawisha, *Syria and the Lebanese Crisis* (New York: St. Martin's, 1980).

35. R. D. Tschirgi with George Irani, "The United States, Syria, and the Lebanese Crisis," UCLA Center for International and Strategic Affairs Research Note 8, Los Angeles, January 1982; R. D. McLaurin, Mohammed Mughisuddin, and Abraham R. Wagner, *Foreign Policy Making in the Middle East* (New York: Praeger, 1977), pp. 260–261.

36. Asad AbuKhalil, "Syria and the Shiites: Al-Asad's Policy in Lebanon," *Third World Quarterly* 12 (April 1990): 7.

37. Moshe Ma'oz, *Syria and Israel: From War to Peace-making* (Oxford: Clarendon Press, 1995), p. 165.

38. Marius Deeb, *The Lebanese Civil War* (New York: Praeger, 1980), p. 134; Ma'oz, *Asad,* chap. 10.

39. Eyal Zisser, "Asad of Syria: The Leader and the Image," *Orient* 35 (June 1994): 254.

40. Ibid., p. 255.

41. Reuven Avi-Ran, *The Syrian Involvement in Lebanon since 1975* (Boulder, Colo.: Westview Press, 1991), p. 51.

42. Olmert, "Domestic Crisis and Foreign Policy," p. 22.

43. Itamar Rabinovich, "The Limits of Military Power: Syria's Role," in P. Edward Haley and Louis W. Snider, eds., *Lebanon in Crisis* (Syracuse: Syracuse University Press, 1979), p. 60. See also Itamar Rabinovich, *The War for Lebanon, 1970–1983* (Ithaca: Cornell University Press, 1984).

44. Malcolm H. Kerr, "Lebanon: The Risks for Syria," *Los Angeles Times,* 13 June 1976.

45. Kienle, *Ba'th v Ba'th,* chap. 1; Amatzia Baram, "Ideology and Power Politics in Syrian-Iraqi Relations, 1968–1984," in Moshe Ma'oz and Avner Yaniv, eds., *Syria under Assad* (New York: St. Martin's, 1986), pp. 126–128; Kamal S. Shehadi, "Trading Places: The Balance of Power and Prospects for Iraqi-Syrian Rapprochement in the 1990's," *Beirut Review* 1 (Fall 1991): 5–6.

46. Alasdair Drysdale and Raymond A. Hinnebusch, *Syria and the Middle East Peace Process* (New York: Council on Foreign Relations, 1991), pp. 88–91.

47. Yair Hirschfeld, "The Odd Couple: Ba'athist Syria and Khomeini's Iran," in Ma'oz and Yaniv, eds., *Syria under Assad*, pp. 115–121; Christin Marschall, "Syria-Iran: A Strategic Alliance, 1979–1991," *Orient* 33 (September 1992); Elie Chalala, "Syria's Support of Iran in the Gulf War," *Journal of Arab Affairs* 7 (Fall 1988).

48. Shehadi, "Trading Places," p. 6.

49. Seale, *Asad*, pp. 354–357. Nuanced treatments can be found in Elizabeth Picard, "La rapprochement Syro-Irakien: Vers une nouvelle donne des alliances au Proche-Orient," *Maghreb/Machrek*, no. 83 (January–February 1979); Malik Mufti, *Sovereign Creations: Pan-Arabism and Political Order in Syria and Iraq* (Ithaca: Cornell University Press), pp. 209–220.

50. Kienle, *Ba'th v Ba'th*, pp. 163, 166–167.

51. Shehadi, "Trading Places," p. 12.

52. Pedro Ramet, *The Soviet-Syrian Relationship since 1955* (Boulder, Colo.: Westview Press, 1990), pp. 148–150; Efraim Karsh, *Soviet Policy towards Syria since 1970* (New York: St. Martin's, 1991), pp. 39–41.

53. Kienle, *Ba'th v Ba'th*, pp. 16–25.

54. Ibid., p. 28.

55. Ibid., p. 152.

56. Ibid., pp. 149–151.

57. Ibid., pp. 140–141.

58. Daniel Pipes, "Understanding Asad," *Middle East Quarterly* 1 (December 1994): 57–58.

59. David Kushner, "Conflict and Accommodation in Turkish-Syrian Relations," in MaANoz and Yaniv, eds., *Syria under Assad*, pp. 91–92.

60. Ibid., p. 89.

61. Ibid., p. 102.

62. Drysdale and Hinnebusch, *Syria and the Middle East Peace Process*, p. 174; Muhammad Faour, *The Arab World after Desert Storm* (Washington, D.C.: United States Institute of Peace, 1993), p. 116.

63. Eyal Zisser, "Syria and the Gulf Crisis: Stepping on a New Path," *Orient* 34 (December 1993): 566.

64. Mahmud A. Faksh, "Asad's Westward Turn: Implications for Syria," *Middle East Policy* 2 (1993): 57.

65. Volker Perthes, "Kriegsdividende und Friedensrisiken: Überlegungen zu Rente und Politik in Syrien," *Orient* 35 (September 1994).

66. Ann Mosely Lesch, "Contrasting Reactions to the Persian Gulf Crisis: Egypt, Syria, Jordan and the Palestinians," *Middle East Journal* 45 (Winter 1991); Zisser, "Syria and the Gulf Crisis"; Marschall, "Syria-Iran," pp. 445–446; Yair

Evron, "Gulf Crisis and War: Regional Rules of the Game and Policy and Theoretical Implications," *Security Studies* 4 (Autumn 1994): 133.

67. Raymond A. Hinnebusch, "Asad's Syria and the New World Order," *Middle East Policy*, no. 43 (1993); Eberhard Kienle, "Syria, the Kuwait War and the New World Order," in Tareq Y. Ismael and Jacqueline S. Ismael, eds., *The Gulf War and the New World Order* (Gainesville: University Press of Florida, 1994); Alasdair Drysdale, "Syria since 1988: From Crisis to Opportunity," in Robert O. Freedman, ed., *The Middle East after Iraq's Invasion of Kuwait* (Gainesville: University Press of Florida, 1993); Fred H. Lawson, "Domestic Transformation and Foreign Steadfastness in Contemporary Syria," *Middle East Journal* 38 (Winter 1994).

68. Asad AbuKhalil, "Syria and the Arab-Israeli Conflict," *Current History* 93 (February 1994); Fred H. Lawson, "Domestic Pressures and the Peace Process: Fillip or Hindrance?" in Eberhard Kienle, ed., *Contemporary Syria* (London: British Academic Press, 1994).

69. Fred H. Lawson, *The Social Origins of Egyptian Expansionism during the Muhammad 'Ali Period* (New York: Columbia University Press, 1992), pp. 19–22.

70. Peter Bell and Harry Cleaver, "Marx's Crisis Theory as a Theory of Class Struggle," in P. Zarembka, ed., *Research in Political Economy* (Greenwich, Conn.: JAI Press, 1982), 5: 258; Rod Aya, "Theories of Revolution Reconsidered," *Theory and Society* 8 (July 1979).

71. James O'Connor, *The Meaning of Crises* (Oxford: Blackwell, 1987), p. 59. Other useful overviews of Marxian crisis theory include Roger Alcaly, "The Relevance of Marxian Crisis Theory," in David Mermelstein, ed., *The Economic Crisis Reader* (New York: Vintage Books, 1975); Roger Alcaly, "An Introduction to Marxian Crisis Theory," in Union of Radical Political Economics, *U.S. Capitalism in Crisis* (New York: URPE, 1978); Anwar Shaikh, "An Introduction to the History of Crisis Theories," in ibid.; Anwar Shaikh, "Political Economy and Capitalism: Notes on Dobb's Theory of Crisis," *Cambridge Journal of Economics* 2 (June 1978); Richard D. Wolff, "Marxian Crisis Theory: Structure and Implications," *Review of Radical Political Economics* 10 (Spring 1978); P. N. Junankar, *Marx's Economics* (Oxford: Philip Allan, 1982), chap. 9; David A. Wolfe, "Capitalist Crisis and Marxist Theory," *Labour/Le Travail* 17 (Spring 1986); James N. Devine, "Empirical Studies of Marxian Crisis Theory: Introduction," *Review of Radical Political Economics* 18 (Spring–Summer 1986); P. Kenway, "Crises," in John Eatwell, Murray Milgate, and Peter Newman, eds., *Marxian Economics* (New York: Norton, 1990); Bruce Norton, "Radical Theories of Accumulation and Crisis: Developments and Directions," in Bruce Roberts and Susan Feiner, eds., *Radical Economics* (Boston: Kluwer, 1992); John Milios, "Marx's Theory and the Historic Marxist Controversy on Economic Crisis (1900-1937)," *Science and Society* 58 (Summer 1994).

72. Michael Bleaney, *Underconsumption Theories* (New York: International Publishers, 1976); Raford Boddy and James Crotty, "Class Conflict, Keynesian

Policy, and the Business Cycle," *Monthly Review* 26 (October 1974); Raford Boddy and James Crotty, "Class Conflict and Macro Policy: The Political Business Cycle," *Review of Radical Political Economics* 7 (Spring 1975). Underconsumptionist and profit squeeze arguments are effectively rebutted in Erik Olin Wright, *Class, Crisis, and the State* (London: New Left Books, 1978), chap. 3. See also John Weeks, "The Process of Accumulation and the 'Profit Squeeze' Hypothesis," *Science and Society* 43 (Fall 1979).

73. James O'Connor, *The Fiscal Crisis of the State* (New York: St. Martin's 1973); Jürgen Habermas, *Legitimation Crisis* (Boston: Beacon Press, 1976); Claus Offe, *Contradictions of the Welfare State* (Cambridge: MIT Press, 1984); Cornelius Castoriadis, *Political and Social Writings*, vol. 2 (Minneapolis: University of Minnesota Press, 1988).

74. Patrick Flaherty, "Cycles and Crises in Statist Economies," *Review of Radical Political Economics* 24 (Fall–Winter 1992).

75. James Crotty, "The Centrality of Money, Credit, and Financial Intermediation in Marx's Crisis Theory," in Stephen Resnick and Richard Wolff, eds., *Rethinking Marxism* (New York: Autonomedia, 1985). See also David M. Kotz, "Accumulation, Money, and Credit in the Circuit of Capital," *Rethinking Marxism* 24 (Summer 1991); Duncan K. Foley, *Money, Accumulation, and Crisis* (New York: Harwood Academic, 1986); Charles P. Kindleberger, *Manias, Panics, and Crashes*, rev. ed. (New York: Basic Books, 1989); Hyman P. Minsky, "The Financial-Instability Hypothesis: Capitalist Processes and the Behavior of the Economy," in Charles P. Kindleberger and Jean-Pierre Laffargue, eds., *Financial Crises* (Cambridge: Cambridge University Press, 1982).

76. Crotty, "The Centrality of Money," pp. 52–53.

77. Ibid., p. 54. I owe this formulation to Roger Sparks.

78. Ibid., p. 71; Duncan K. Foley, *Understanding Capital* (Cambridge: Harvard University Press, 1986), p. 142.

79. Crotty, "The Centrality of Money," p. 72.

80. Ibid., p. 73.

81. Ibid., pp. 74–75.

82. Foley, *Money, Accumulation, and Crisis*, pp. 53–54. See also Susan Strange, *Casino Capitalism* (Oxford: Blackwell, 1986).

83. Crotty, "The Role of Money and Finance," p. 80. See also Stephan Haggard and Sylvia Maxfield, "Political Explanations of Financial Policy in Developing Countries," in Stephan Haggard, Chung H. Lee and Sylvia Maxfield, eds., *The Politics of Finance in Developing Countries* (Ithaca: Cornell University Press, 1993); Robert Pollin, "Financial Structures and Egalitarian Economic Policy," *New Left Review*, no. 214 (November–December 1995).

84. John Weeks, "Equilibrium, Uneven Development, and the Tendency of the Rate of Profit to Fall," *Capital and Class*, no. 16 (Spring 1982): 69–70; John Weeks, *Capital and Exploitation* (Princeton: Princeton University Press, 1981), pp. 171–172.

85. Gerard De Bernis, "Propositions for an Analysis of the Crisis," *International Journal of Political Economy* 18 (Summer 1988): 46–47; Foley, *Understanding Capital*, p. 131; Weeks, *Capital and Exploitation*, pp. 208–213.

86. De Bernis, "Propositions for an Analysis of the Crisis," p. 52.

87. Ibid., p. 53. See also James A. Clifton, "Competition and the Evolution of the Capitalist Mode of Production," *Cambridge Journal of Economics* 1 (June 1977).

88. Weeks, "Equilibrium, Uneven Development," p. 70; J. Gough, "Structure, System, and Contradiction in the Capitalist Space Economy," *Environment and Planning D: Society and Space* 9 (December 1991); Michael A. Lebowitz, "Analytical Marxism and the Marxian Theory of Crisis," *Cambridge Journal of Economics* 18 (April 1994): 176–177.

89. Weeks, "Equilibrium, Uneven Development," p. 75.

90. Ibid.

91. Ibid., p. 74; Weeks, *Capital and Exploitation*, pp. 179–180.

92. Weeks, *Capital and Exploitation*, p. 186.

93. James N. Devine, "Underconsumption, Over-Investment, and the Origins of the Great Depression," *Review of Radical Political Economics* 15 (Summer 1983).

94. David Harvey, *The Limits to Capital* (Chicago: University of Chicago Press, 1982), pp. 218–220. See also John Bellamy Foster, *The Theory of Monopoly Capitalism* (New York: Monthly Review Press, 1986).

95. Harvey, *The Limits to Capital*, p. 225.

96. Ibid., p. 390.

97. Ibid., p. 391; Costis Hadjimichalis, "The Geographical Transfer of Value," *Environment and Planning D: Society and Space* 2 (September 1984). Compare John Browett, "On the Necessity and Inevitability of Uneven Spatial Development under Capitalism," *International Journal of Urban and Regional Research* 8 (June 1984).

98. Harvey, *The Limits to Capital*, pp. 391–392; Michael Storper and Richard Walker, *The Capitalist Imperative* (Oxford: Blackwell, 1989), pp. 211–212; Doreen Massey, *Spatial Divisions of Labour* (London: Macmillan, 1984), pp. 53–54; J. Gough, "Workers' Competition, Class Relations, and Space," *Environment and Planning D: Society and Space* 10 (June 1992).

99. Harvey, *The Limits to Capital*, p. 388. For a different view, see Richard A. Walker, "Two Sources of Uneven Development under Advanced Capitalism: Spatial Differentiation and Capital Mobility," *Review of Radical Political Economics* 10 (Fall 1978).

100. Harvey, *The Limits to Capital*, p. 394; Gough, "Structure, System, and Contradiction," pp. 442–443.

101. Harvey, *The Limits to Capital*, pp. 428–429.

102. John E. Roemer, "Technical Change and the Tendency of the Rate of Profit to Fall," *Journal of Economic Theory* 16 (1977); Philippe Van Parijs, "The

Falling-Rate-of-Profit Theory of Crisis: A Rational Reconstruction by Way of Obituary," *Review of Radical Political Economics* 12 (Spring 1980); Jon Elster, *Making Sense of Marx* (Cambridge: Cambridge University Press, 1985). These arguments are effectively countered in Anwar Shaikh, "The Falling Rate of Profit and the Economic Crisis in the U.S.," in Robert Cherry et al., eds., *The Imperiled Economy*, vol. 1 (New York: Union for Radical Political Economics, 1987).

103. Eric Sheppard and Trevor J. Barnes, *The Capitalist Space Economy* (London: Unwin Hyman, 1990), p. 249.

104. Empirical support for this claim can be found in Enzo Nocifora, "Poles of Development and the Southern Question," *International Journal of Urban and Regional Research* 2 (June 1978); Samuel Bowles, David M. Gordon, and Thomas E. Weisskopf, "Power and Profits: The Social Structure of Accumulation and the Profitability of the Postwar U. S. Economy," *Review of Radical Political Economics* 18 (Spring–Summer 1986); Andrew Glyn, Alan Hughes, Alain Lipietz, and Ajit Singh, "The Rise and Fall of the Golden Age," in Stephen A. Marglin and Juliet B. Schor, eds., *The Golden Age of Capitalism* (Oxford: Clarendon Press, 1990); Ann M. Oberhauser, "Social and Spatial Patterns under Fordism and Flexible Accumulation," *Antipode* 22 (December 1990); Costis Hadjimichalis, *Uneven Development and Regionalism* (London: Croom Helm, 1987), chap. 4; Elias Ioakimoglou and John Milios, "Capital Accumulation and Over-Accumulation Crisis: The Case of Greece," *Review of Radical Political Economics* 25 (June 1993).

105. Neil Smith, *Uneven Development* (Oxford: Blackwell, 1990), p. 150; M. J. Webber, "Agglomeration and the Regional Question," *Antipode* 14 (1982).

106. See Volker Perthes, *The Political Economy of Syria under Asad* (London: I. B. Tauris, 1995), chap. 2. This exemplary study appeared too late to be incorporated into the chapters that follow.

1. PROVOKING CONFRONTATION WITH ISRAEL, 1967

1. Avner Yaniv, "Syria and Israel: The Politics of Escalation," in Moshe Ma'oz and Avner Yaniv, eds., *Syria under Assad* (New York: St. Martin's, 1986), pp. 160–162.

2. Malcolm H. Kerr, *The Arab Cold War* (Oxford: Oxford University Press, 1971), chaps. 3–5.

3. Richard B. Parker, *The Politics of Miscalculation in the Middle East* (Bloomington: Indiana University Press, 1993), p. 11; Richard B. Parker, "The June War: Whose Conspiracy?" *Journal of Palestine Studies* 21 (Summer 1992); Richard B. Parker, "The June 1967 War: Some Mysteries Explored," *Middle East Journal* 46 (Spring 1992): 178–179.

4. Parker, *Politics of Miscalculation*, p. 25.

5. Yaniv, "Syria and Israel," p. 166; Patrick Seale, *Asad* (Berkeley: University of California Press, 1988), pp. 118–121 and 126–127.

6. Parker, *Politics of Miscalculation,* chaps. 3–4; David Hirst, *The Gun and the Olive Branch* (New York: Harcourt Brace Jovanovich, 1977), chap. 7.

7. Charles W. Yost, "The Arab-Israeli War: How It Began," *Foreign Affairs* 46 (January 1968): 315.

8. Kerr, *Arab Cold War,* p. 126.

9. Yost, "Arab-Israeli War," p. 307; Parker, "June 1967 War," pp. 178–179.

10. Walter Laqueur, *The Road to War* (Harmondsworth: Penguin, 1968), p. 108.

11. V. V. Vavilov, "The Nature of the Socioeconomic Changes in Syria," in E. S. Yefimov et al., eds., *Problems of the Economy and History of the Countries of the Near and Middle East* (Washington, D.C.: Joint Publications Research Service, 1967), p. 50.

12. Itamar Rabinovich, *Syria under the Ba'th, 1963–66* (New York: Halsted Press, 1972), pp. 64 and 69; Syed Aziz al-Ahsan, "Economic Policy and Class Structure in Syria: 1958–1980," *International Journal of Middle East Studies* 16 (August 1984): 306.

13. al-Ahsan, "Economic Policy," p. 306.

14. Rabinovich, *Syria under the Ba'th,* pp. 124 and 128.

15. Ibid., p. 92.

16. Ibid., p. 64.

17. Vavilov, "Nature of the Socioeconomic Changes," p. 50.

18. Rabinovich, *Syria under the Ba'th,* p. 73.

19. Ibid., p. 73.

20. Ziad Keilany, "Socialism and Economic Change in Syria," *Middle Eastern Studies* 9 (January 1973): 69.

21. Vavilov, "Nature of the Socioeconomic Changes," p. 51.

22. Ibid., p. 52.

23. Rabinovich, *Syria under the Ba'th,* pp. 110–111.

24. Ibid., p. 112.

25. Tabitha Petran, *Syria* (New York: Praeger, 1972), p. 176.

26. Keilany, "Socialism and Economic Change," p. 68.

27. Rabinovich, *Syria under the Ba'th,* p. 122; Vavilov, "Nature of the Socioeconomic Changes," p. 50.

28. Vavilov, "Nature of the Socioeconomic Changes," p. 51; Rabinovich, *Syria under the Ba'th,* pp. 111–112; Petran, *Syria,* p. 177.

29. Vavilov, "Nature of the Socioeconomic Changes," p. 52; Elizabeth Picard, "Une crise syrienne en 1965," *Sou'al,* no. 8 (February 1988): 85–86.

30. Rabinovich, *Syria under the Ba'th,* p. 132.

31. Petran, *Syria,* p. 177.

32. Ibid., p. 178; Rabinovich, *Syria under the Ba'th,* p. 134; Nikolaos van Dam, *The Struggle for Power in Syria* (New York: St. Martin's, 1979), p. 49 n. 51 and p. 84.

33. Vavilov, "Nature of the Socioeconomic Changes," p. 50.

34. Petran, *Syria*, p. 178; Rabinovich, *Syria under the Ba'th*, p. 141 n. 31.

35. Eliyahu Kanovsky, *Economic Development of Syria* (Tel Aviv: University Publishing Projects, 1977), p. 12.

36. Ibid., p. 36.

37. Rabinovich, *Syria under the Ba'th*, pp. 134–135.

38. Ibid., pp. 136–137; van Dam, *Struggle for Power in Syria,* chap. 3.

39. Rabinovich, *Syria under the Ba'th*, pp. 134–135.

40. Ibid., p. 139; Petran, *Syria*, p. 178.

41. Petran, *Syria*, p. 174.

42. Alan W. Horton, "Syrian Stability and the Baath," *American University Field Staff Reports, Southwest Asia Series* 14 (1965): 125.

43. Rabinovich, *Syria under the Ba'th*, p. 141.

44. Ibid., p. 135.

45. Petran, *Syria*, pp. 230–231; Picard, "Crise syrienne," pp. 86–87.

46. Elisabeth Longuenesse, "Travail et rapports de production en Syrie," *Bulletin d'études orientales* 32–33 (1980–1981): 169.

47. See Rabinovich, *Syria under the Ba'th*, pp. 135–139.

48. Ibid., pp. 140–142; Petran, *Syria*, p. 179.

49. Economist Intelligence Unit, *Quarterly Economic Review of Syria (QERS)*, 15 April 1965.

50. Petran, *Syria*, p. 179; chronology entry in *Middle East Journal* 19 (Summer 1965): 350.

51. Vavilov, "Nature of the Socioeconomic Changes," p. 53.

52. Ibid., p. 55.

53. Ibid., p. 54.

54. Keilany, "Socialism and Economic Change," p. 66.

55. Kanovsky, *Economic Development of Syria*, p. 28; United Nations Economic and Social Office in Beirut (UNESOB), *Studies on Selected Development Problems in Various Countries in the Middle East, 1971* (New York: United Nations, 1971), p. 36.

56. Hossein Askari and John T. Cummings, *Middle East Economics in the 1970s* (New York: Praeger, 1976), p. 182.

57. Rabinovich, *Syria under the Ba'th*, p. 140; chronology entry in *Middle East Journal* 19 (Spring 1965): 210.

58. Chronology entry in *Middle East Journal* 19 (Autumn 1965): 510.

59. Ibid.

60. *QERS*, fourth quarter 1965.

61. *Arab Report and Record (ARR)*, 15–28 February 1966, p. 45; chronology entry in *Middle East Journal* 20 (Summer 1966): 379.

62. Rabinovich, *Syria under the Ba'th*, p. 207.

63. Syrian Arab Republic, *Statistical Abstract 1966* (Damascus: Government Printing Office, 1967), pp. 330–331; Ziad Keilany, "Land Reform in Syria," *Middle Eastern Studies* 16 (October 1980): 212.

64. Bichara Khader, "Propriété agricole et réforme agraire en Syrie," *Civilisations* 25 (1975): 72–73; Françoise Metral, "Le monde rural syrien a l'ère des réformes," in André Raymond, ed., *La Syrie d'aujourd'hui* (Paris: CNRS, 1980), p. 300.

65. *Middle East Record 1967*, p. 504.

66. Robert Springborg, "Baathism in Practice: Agriculture, Politics, and Political Culture in Syria and Iraq," *Middle Eastern Studies* 17 (April 1981): 192–193.

67. UNESOB, *Studies on Selected Development Problems in Various Countries in the Middle East, 1969* (New York: United Nations, 1969), pp. 85–86.

68. *ARR*, 16–30 June, 1–15 October, and 16–30 November 1966.

69. Kanovsky, *Economic Development of Syria*, p. 47.

70. Yahya M. Sadowski, "The Knife's Edge: A Study of the Failure of Liberalisation in Syria," unpublished manuscript, p. 30.

71. Chronology entry in *Middle East Journal* 20 (Summer 1966): 380.

72. *ARR*, 16–31 July 1966.

73. Chronology entry in *Middle East Journal* 21 (Spring 1967): 250.

74. *ARR*, 1–15 September 1966.

75. *ARR*, 16–31 October 1966.

76. *ARR*, 16–30 November 1966.

77. Syrian Arab Republic, *Second Five Year Plan, 1966–1970* (Damascus: Office Arabe de Presse et de Documentation, n.d.), p. 65.

78. Keilany, "Socialism and Economic Change," p. 67; *ARR*, 16–31 May 1966.

79. Petran, *Syria*, p. 206.

80. Ibid.

81. *ARR*, 16–30 September 1966.

82. *QERS*, first quarter 1967.

83. *Middle East Record 1967*, p. 505.

84. Ibid., p. 501.

85. *ARR*, 16–31 May 1967.

86. Kanovsky, *Economic Development of Syria*, pp. 12 and 15.

87. *Middle East Record 1967*, p. 506.

88. *al-Hayat*, 5 May 1967; Bernard Lewis, *Islam and the West* (New York: Oxford University Press, 1993), p. 150.

89. *Middle East Record 1967*, p. 500.

90. Ibid., p. 493.

91. Ibid., p. 503.

92. van Dam, *Struggle for Power in Syria*, p. 78.

93. Petran, *Syria*, p. 197; BBC, *Summary of World Broadcasts*, 10 May 1967.

94. *al-Ba'th*, 12 May 1967.

95. *Middle East Record 1967*, p. 490.

96. Ibid., p. 493.

97. Laurie Brand, "Palestinians in Syria: The Politics of Integration," *Middle East Journal* 42 (Autumn 1988): 631.

98. Moshe Ma'oz and Avner Yaniv, "On a Short Leash: Syria and the PLO," in Ma'oz and Yaniv, eds., *Syria under Assad,* pp. 194–195.

99. *ARR,* 16–30 April and 1–15 May 1967.

100. *Middle East Record 1967,* p. 500.

101. Ibid., p. 502.

102. Ibid., p. 492.

103. Ibid., p. 493.

104. Ibid., pp. 497–498.

105. *ARR,* 16–31 May 1967.

106. *ARR,* 1–14 March 1967.

107. *Middle East Record 1967,* p. 494.

108. Ibid., p. 494.

109. Ibid., p. 493.

110. Ibid.

111. Ibid., p. 502.

112. Ibid., p. 492.

113. Ibid., pp. 493–494.

114. Pedro Ramet, *The Soviet-Syrian Relationship since 1955* (Boulder, Colo.: Westview Press, 1990), pp. 35 and 243; George Lenczowski, *Soviet Advances in the Middle East* (Washington, D.C.: American Enterprise Institute, 1971), p. 113.

115. Ramet, *Soviet-Syrian Relationship,* p. 36.

116. Ibid., p. 39.

117. Ibid., p. 41.

118. Ibid.

119. Ibid., p. 46.

120. *Middle East Economic Digest* (*MEED*), 8 July, 2 September, and 9 December 1966.

121. *MEED,* 20 April and 16 November 1967.

122. *MEED,* 27 July 1967.

2. LIMITING INTERVENTION IN JORDAN, 1970

1. Malcolm H. Kerr, *The Arab Cold War* (Oxford: Oxford University Press, 1971), p. 149.

2. Patrick Seale, *Asad* (Berkeley: University of California Press, 1988), pp. 158–159.

3. Ibid., p. 159.

4. Eliyahu Kanovsky, *Economic Development of Syria* (Tel Aviv: University Publishing Projects, 1977), p. 43.

5. Ziad Keilany, "Socialism and Economic Change in Syria," *Middle Eastern Studies* 9 (January 1973): 67.

6. Elisabeth Longuenesse, "The Class Nature of the State in Syria," *MERIP Reports,* no. 77 (May 1979): 7.

7. Ibid., pp. 7–8.

8. *Middle East Record 1969–1970,* p. 1127.

9. *Arab Report and Record (ARR),* 16–30 June 1968 and 1–15 July 1968.

10. *ARR,* 1–15 July 1968.

11. Fred Gottheil, "Iraqi and Syrian Socialism: An Economic Appraisal," *World Development* 9 (September–October 1981): 831; *ARR,* 1–15 July 1968.

12. *Middle East Record 1968,* p. 722.

13. *ARR,* 16–31 October 1968.

14. *ARR,* 1–15 December 1968.

15. *ARR,* 1–14 February 1969.

16. *ARR,* 1–15 December 1968, 16–31 January, and 15–28 February 1969.

17. Yahya M. Sadowski, "The Knife's Edge: A Study of the Failure of Liberalisation in Syria," unpublished manuscript, pp. 18–19 and 29.

18. Alasdair Drysdale, "Center and Periphery in Syria: A Political Geographic Study" (Ph.D. dissertation, University of Michigan, 1977), p. 180.

19. *Middle East Record 1968,* pp. 718–719.

20. *ARR,* 1–15 August and 1–15 October 1969.

21. *ARR,* 1–15 December 1969.

22. Economist Intelligence Unit, *Quarterly Economic Review of Syria (QERS),* first quarter 1970.

23. *Middle East Record 1969–1970,* p. 1182.

24. Ibid.

25. *ARR,* 1–15 April 1970.

26. *ARR,* 16–30 April 1970.

27. Kanovsky, *Economic Development of Syria,* pp. 12 and 45.

28. Longuenesse, "Class Nature of the State," p. 7. On the *salafiyyah,* see John O. Voll, *Islam: Change and Continuity in the Modern World* (Boulder, Colo.: Westview Press, 1982), chap. 3; Malcolm H. Kerr, *Islamic Reform* (Berkeley: University of California Press, 1966); Antonino Pellitteri, *Il riformismo musulmano in Siria* (Naples: Instituto Universitario Orientale, 1987).

29. Umar F. Abd-Allah, *The Islamic Struggle in Syria* (Berkeley: Mizan, 1983), pp. 102–103.

30. Thomas Mayer, "The Islamic Opposition in Syria," *Orient* 24 (1983): 594. See also Itzchak Weismann, "Sa'id Hawwa: The Making of a Radical Muslim Thinker in Modern Syria," *Middle Eastern Studies* 29 (October 1993).

31. Hanna Batatu, "Syria's Muslim Brethren," *MERIP Reports,* no. 110 (November–December 1982): 19.

32. Abd-Allah, *Islamic Struggle in Syria,* p. 106.

33. Ibid., pp. 107–108.

34. *ARR,* 16–30 November 1969.

35. *ARR,* 1–14 February 1969.

36. *Middle East Record 1969–1970*, pp. 1178–1179.

37. Ibid., p. 1179.

38. *ARR*, 1–15 November 1969.

39. *ARR*, 16–31 January 1970.

40. *Middle East Economic Digest (MEED)*, 9 January 1970.

41. *MEED*, 27 February 1970.

42. *MEED*, 6 March 1970.

43. *al-Nahar*, 6 July 1970.

44. *MEED*, 5 June 1970.

45. Raymond A. Hinnebusch, *Authoritarian Power and State Formation in Ba'thist Syria* (Boulder, Colo.: Westview Press, 1990), p. 139.

46. *ARR*, 16–30 June 1970.

47. *MEED*, 17 July 1970.

48. *Commerce du Levant*, 5 August 1970.

49. *ARR*, 16–31 July 1970.

50. *ARR*, 1–15 June 1970.

51. *ARR*, 16–31 July 1970.

52. *Commerce du Levant*, 19 August 1970.

53. *Commerce du Levant*, 15 August 1970.

54. Ibid.

55. *MEED*, 18 September and 9 October 1970.

56. *New York Times*, 28 June 1970.

57. *New York Times*, 21 August 1970; *MEED*, 28 August 1970.

58. *Middle East Record 1969–1970*, p. 1173.

59. *MEED*, 17 July 1970.

60. *Middle East Record 1969–1970*, p. 1150.

61. *ARR*, 16–30 September 1970.

62. *Middle East Record 1969–1970*, p. 1166.

63. Ibid., p. 1173.

64. *ARR*, 1–15 August 1970.

65. *MEED*, 28 August 1970.

66. *MEED*, 11 September and 23 October 1970.

67. *MEED*, 11 September and 6 November 1970; Raymond A. Hinnebusch, *Peasant and Bureaucracy in Ba'thist Syria* (Boulder, Colo.: Westview Press, 1989), pp. 134–135.

68. *MEED*, 7 August and 4 December 1970.

69. *MEED*, 3 and 24 April, 24 May, 12 June, and 7 August 1970.

70. *MEED*, 31 July and 28 August 1970.

71. *MEED*, 4 December 1970.

72. *MEED*, 2 October 1970.

73. *MEED*, 31 July 1970.

74. *MEED*, 14 August 1970.

75. *MEED*, 11 September 1970.

76. Syrian Arab Republic, *Statistical Abstract 1973* (Damascus: Central Bureau of Statistics, 1973), pp. 235 and 777.

77. Kanovsky, *Economic Development of Syria,* p. 12.

78. Volker Perthes, "The Syrian Economy in the 1980s," *Middle East Journal* 46 (Winter 1992): 38.

79. *Middle East Record 1969–1970,* p. 1155.

80. Ibid., pp. 1155–1156.

81. *al-Baʿth,* 13 November 1970.

82. *Middle East Record 1969–1970,* p. 1157.

83. Ibid., p. 1162.

84. *al-Baʿth,* 22 November 1970.

85. *al-Baʿth,* 23, 24, and 25 November 1970.

86. *al-Baʿth,* 25 and 27 November 1970.

87. *Middle East Record 1969–1970,* p. 1163.

88. Hinnebusch, *Authoritarian Power and State Formation,* pp. 139–140.

89. See Henry Brandon, "Jordan: The Forgotten Crisis (1)," *Foreign Policy,* no. 10 (Spring 1973); Raymond A. Hinnebusch, "Revisionist Dreams, Realist Strategies: The Foreign Policy of Syria," in Bahgat Korany and Ali E. Hillal Dessouki, eds., *The Foreign Policies of Arab States* (Boulder, Colo.: Westview Press, 1991), p. 392.

90. *Middle East Record 1969–1970,* pp. 1150–1151.

91. Hinnebusch, *Authoritarian Power and State Formation,* p. 140.

92. Charles Tilly, "State Making and War Making as Organized Crime," in Peter Evans, Dietrich Rueschemeyer, and Theda Skocpol, eds., *Bringing the State Back In* (Cambridge: Cambridge University Press, 1985).

3. EXPANDING INTERVENTION IN LEBANON, 1976

1. Wadi D. Haddad, *Lebanon: The Politics of Revolving Doors* (New York: Praeger, 1985), pp. 49–50.

2. Walid Khalidi, *Conflict and Violence in Lebanon* (Cambridge: Harvard Center for International Affairs, 1979), p. 58.

3. *Middle East Record 1969–1970,* p. 1164.

4. Ibid., p. 1165.

5. Economist Intelligence Unit, *Quarterly Economic Review of Syria* (*QERS*), second quarter 1971.

6. *QERS,* first quarter 1972.

7. Elisabeth Longuenesse, "The Class Nature of the State in Syria," *MERIP Reports,* no. 77 (May 1979): 7.

8. Hossein Askari and John T. Cummings, *Middle East Economics in the 1970s* (New York: Praeger, 1976), p. 461.

9. Elisabeth Longuenesse, "The Syrian Working Class Today," *MERIP Reports,* no. 134 (July–August 1985): 23.

10. *QERS,* second quarter 1971.

11. Eliyahu Kanovsky, *Economic Development of Syria* (Tel Aviv: University Publishing Projects, 1977), p. 125.

12. *QERS,* third quarter 1971.

13. *QERS,* second quarter 1974; *Middle East Economic Digest (MEED)*, 7 June 1974.

14. Syed Aziz al-Ahsan, "Economic Policy and Class Structure in Syria: 1958–1980," *International Journal of Middle East Studies* 16 (August 1984): 311.

15. *MEED,* 12 July 1974.

16. "L'Industrie: Secteur pilote de l'économie," *Syrie et Monde Arabe,* 25 February 1983.

17. Longuenesse, "Class Nature of the State."

18. Bent Hansen, "Economic Development of Syria," in C. A. Cooper and S. S. Alexander, eds., *Economic Development and Population Growth in the Middle East* (New York: Elsevier, 1972), pp. 351–352; Longuenesse, "Class Nature of the State," pp. 4–5; Adeed I. Dawisha, *Syria and the Lebanese Crisis* (New York: St. Martin's, 1980), p. 43.

19. Tabitha Petran, *Syria* (New York: Praeger, 1972), pp. 82–83 and 156–157.

20. Dawisha, *Syria and the Lebanese Crisis,* p. 43; U.S. Department of Agriculture (USDA), *Cotton in Syria,* FAS-M-280 (Washington, D.C.: U.S. Government Printing Office, 1978), p. 27.

21. *MEED,* 20 April 1976; Ziad Keilany, "Land Reform in Syria," *Middle Eastern Studies* 16 (October 1980): 212.

22. *MEED,* 30 April and 7 May 1976; USDA, *Cotton in Syria,* p. 6.

23. David W. Carr, "Capital Flows and Development in Syria," *Middle East Journal* 34 (Autumn 1980): 460.

24. USDA, *Cotton in Syria,* p. 27.

25. Syrian Arab Republic, *Statistical Abstract 1977* (Damascus: Central Bureau of Statistics, 1977), pp. 128 and 144. By contrast, the official rate of unemployment dropped in Damascus and Homs, as well as in Aleppo, during these same years.

26. Petran, *Syria,* p. 211; *MEED,* 19 March 1976; *Wall Street Journal,* 2 March 1981.

27. P. J. Vatikiotis, "The Politics of the Fertile Crescent," in Paul Y. Hammond and S. S. Alexander, eds., *Political Dynamics in the Middle East* (New York: Elsevier, 1972), p. 226.

28. Elisabeth Longuenesse, "L'Industrialisation et sa signification sociale," in André Raymond, ed., *La Syrie d'aujourd'hui* (Paris: CNRS, 1980), p. 338.

29. Ibid., p. 336; Michel Chatelus, "La Croissance économique: Mutations des structures et dynamisme du déséquilibre," in Raymond, ed., *Syrie d'aujourd'hui,* p. 233.

30. *Middle East Contemporary Survey 1976–77,* p. 609; *Arab Report and Record*

(*ARR*), 16–30 April 1976; *Christian Science Monitor,* 26 May 1976, p. 9; *MEED,* 26 March 1976.

31. *MEED,* 19 March 1976.

32. Carr, "Capital Flows," p. 459.

33. *MEED,* 25 August 1975 and 19 March 1976; *ARR,* 1–15 September 1976.

34. *Middle East Contemporary Survey 1976–77,* p. 606; *Los Angeles Times,* 7 April 1980, p. 1.

35. *ARR,* 16–30 June 1976.

36. Carr, "Capital Flows," p. 456. During the first quarter of 1976, there were persistent reports that the level of concessionary aid monies coming into Syria from Arab oil-producing countries was about to be reduced substantially, a move that would have greatly exacerbated the regime's financial difficulties. See Kanovsky, *Economic Development of Syria,* pp. 142–143.

37. *MEED,* 11 June 1976.

38. Fruit production in Syria rose significantly between 1974 and 1975 as apricots and apples were introduced by middle and larger landholders in the southwestern parts of the country for shipment to European markets. See *ARR,* 15–20 February 1976; *Arab Economist* 141 (June 1981): 20.

39. *ARR,* 1–14 and 15–29 February 1976.

40. *New York Times,* 11 March 1976.

41. *New York Times,* 29 April 1976.

42. Umar F. Abd-Allah, *The Islamic Struggle in Syria* (Berkeley: Mizan, 1983), p. 109.

43. *Le Monde,* 26 March 1976.

44. John J. Donahue, "The New Syrian Constitution and the Religious Opposition," *CEMAM Reports* 1 (1972–73): 84 and 94.

45. *ARR,* 16–31 July 1975.

46. *ARR,* 1–14 August 1975; *MEED,* 1 August 1975.

47. Abd-Allah, *Islamic Struggle in Syria,* p. 78.

48. *ARR,* 1–14 and 15–29 February, and 1–14 April 1976.

49. *ARR,* 1–15 July 1976.

50. Ibid.; *ARR,* 16–30 September 1976; Nikolaos van Dam, "Middle Eastern Political Cliches: 'Takriti' and 'Sunni Rule' in Iraq; 'Alawi Rule' in Syria—A Critical Appraisal," *Orient* 21 (January 1980): 56 n. 36; *Middle East Contemporary Survey 1976–77,* p. 609; Itamar Rabinovich, "The Limits of Military Power: Syria's Role," in P. Edward Haley and Lewis W. Snider, eds., *Lebanon in Crisis* (Syracuse: Syracuse University Press, 1979), pp. 64–65.

51. *ARR,* 16–31 August and 1–15 September 1976.

· 52. Don A. Schanche, "Syria's Leader Rules by Arms and Conciliation," *Los Angeles Times,* 7 April 1980; Doyle McManus, "Terrorists Try to Shake Syrian Stability," *Los Angeles Times,* 9 March 1980.

53. *MEED,* 30 April and 19 March 1976; *ARR,* 15–29 February 1976.

54. *MEED,* 19 March 1976.

55. Syrian Arab Republic, *Statistical Abstract 1977,* p. 356.

56. Ibid., pp. 427 and 437.

57. *MEED,* 23 April 1976.

58. During the 1960s, Lebanon became a major exporter of manufactured goods to regional markets. Among the items exported by Lebanese companies that had the most dramatic growth rates between 1967 and 1974 were aluminum, soap, clothing, carpets, electrical equipment, medicines, and furniture. André Chaib calls these years "a consumer-goods-leading period" of Lebanese economic development. During most of this period, the largest markets for these goods were in the oil-producing countries. Thus Chaib observes that "Syria's share of these exports fell from around 25 percent to around seven percent" between 1951 and 1973. But light manufactured goods imported from Lebanon continued to enter Syria at a steady rate throughout these years. See Chaib, "Analysis of Lebanon's Merchandise Exports, 1951–1974," *Middle East Journal* 34 (Autumn 1980): 442–446.

59. Kanovsky, *Economic Development of Syria,* pp. 145–146.

60. *MEED,* 13 February 1976.

61. *MEED,* 9 April 1976.

62. Carr, "Capital Flows," passim.

63. Syria's foreign public debt increased by almost one-third to $661 million in 1975. After 1974, a growing proportion of these funds was being borrowed from private lenders at market rates. See United Nations Department of Economic and Social Affairs, *Supplement to World Economic Survey 1976* (New York: United Nations, 1978), p. 189; International Monetary Fund (IMF), *World Debt Tables: External Public Debt of Developing Countries,* EC-167/77 (Washington, D.C.: IMF, 1977), 1:79, 91, 175, 177, and 238; Thomas M. Klein, "The External Debt Situation of Developing Countries," *Finance and Development* 13 (December 1976).

64. *MEED,* 26 March 1976.

65. *ARR,* 1–15 May 1976; IMF, *World Debt Tables,* 1:79 and 81.

66. IMF, *International Financial Statistics* 32 (December 1979): 372–373, lines 26g and 6o.

67. "Lebanon Benefits from Role as a Center for Trading and Finance in the Middle East," *IMF Survey,* 14 April 1975, p. 102; *MEED,* 16 August 1974; *QERS,* second quarter 1974, p. 8.

68. *QERS,* third quarter 1975, p. 12; Salim Nasr, "The Crisis of Lebanese Capitalism," *MERIP Reports,* no. 73 (December 1978); Clement H. Moore, "Le Système bancaire libanais," *Maghreb/Machrek,* no. 99 (January–March 1983).

69. Hossein Askari and John Cummings, *Middle East Economics in the 1970s* (New York: Praeger, 1976), pp. 344 and 352–353; *MEED,* 18 July 1975, p. 8.

70. *ARR,* 15–29 February 1976.

71. Kanovsky, *Economic Development of Syria,* p. 144.

72. Daniel Pipes, *Greater Syria: The History of an Ambition* (New York: Oxford University Press, 1990), p. 121; Reuven Avi-Ran, "The Syrian Military-Strategic Interest in Lebanon," *Jerusalem Quarterly*, no. 46 (Spring 1988): 141.

4. DEFUSING CONFRONTATION WITH IRAQ, 1982

1. Eberhard Kienle, *Ba'th v Ba'th: The Conflict between Syria and Iraq 1968–1989* (London: I. B. Tauris, 1990), chap. 2; Amatzia Baram, "Ideology and Power Politics in Syrian-Iraqi Relations," in Moshe Ma'oz and Avner Yaniv, eds., *Syria under Assad* (New York: St. Martin's, 1986), p. 128.

2. Baram, "Ideology and Power Politics," p. 132; Kienle, *Ba'th v Ba'th*, pp. 97–101.

3. Bruce Stanley, "Drawing from the Well: Syria in the Persian Gulf," *Journal of South Asian and Middle Eastern Studies* 14 (Winter 1990): 53.

4. Kienle, *Ba'th v Ba'th*, p. 159; Christin Marschall, "Syria-Iran: A Strategic Alliance, 1979–1991," *Orient* 33 (September 1992): 437.

5. Kienle, *Ba'th v Ba'th*, pp. 160–161.

6. Baram, "Ideology and Power Politics," p. 136.

7. *Middle East Contemporary Survey 1981–82*, p. 866.

8. Damascus adopted a similarly accommodative posture toward Israel's invasion of Lebanon that June. See Itamar Rabinovich, "The Changing Prism: Syrian Policy in Lebanon as a Mirror, an Issue and an Instrument," in Ma'oz and Yaniv, eds.,4 *Syria under Assad*, pp. 185–186; Itamar Rabinovich, "Controlled Conflict in the Middle East: The Syrian-Israeli Rivalry in Lebanon," in Gabriel Ben-Dor and David B. Dewitt, eds., *Conflict Management in the Middle East* (Lexington, Mass.: Lexington Books, 1987), p. 105.

9. Kienle, *Ba'th v Ba'th*, pp. 166–167.

10. Syrian Arab Republic, *Statistical Abstract 1987* (Damascus: Central Bureau of Statistics, August 1987), pp. 528–529.

11. Elisabeth Longuenesse, "The Class Nature of the State in Syria," *MERIP Reports*, no. 77 (May 1979): 9–10.

12. Volker Perthes, "The Syrian Private Industrial and Commercial Sectors and the State," *International Journal of Middle East Studies* 24 (May 1992): 213–217.

13. Interviews, Aleppo, July 1993; Perthes, "The Syrian Private Industrial and Commercial Sectors," pp. 212–213.

14. See Hanna Batatu, "Syria's Muslim Brethren," *MERIP Reports*, no. 110 (November–December 1982); Raymond A. Hinnebusch, "The Islamic Movement in Syria," in Ali E. Hillal Dessouki, ed., *Islamic Resurgence in the Arab World* (New York: Praeger, 1982), pp. 154–156; Raymond A. Hinnebusch, "Syria," in Shireen T. Hunter, ed., *The Politics of Islamic Revivalism* (Bloomington: Indiana University Press, 1988), pp. 50–51.

15. *Rapport 1977–1978 sur l'économie syrienne* (Damascus: Office Arabe de Presse et de Documentation, n.d.), pp. B-21–B-48.

16. See Bichara Khader, "Structures et réforme agraires en Syrie," *Maghreb/ Mashrek,* no. 65 (September–October 1974); Ziad Keilany, "Land Reform in Syria," *Middle Eastern Studies* 16 (October 1980).

17. Françoise Metral, "State and Peasants in Syria: A Local View of a Government Irrigation Project," *Peasant Studies* 11 (Winter 1984): 78.

18. Ibid., pp. 85–86.

19. Robert Springborg, "Baathism in Practice: Agriculture, Politics, and Political Culture in Syria and Iraq," *Middle Eastern Studies* 17 (April 1981): 193.

20. Ibid., p. 194.

21. Ibid., p. 197.

22. See Raymond A. Hinnebusch, *Peasant and Bureaucracy in Ba'thist Syria* (Boulder, Colo.: Westview Press, 1989), p. 97.

23. Tabitha Petran, *Syria* (New York: Praeger, 1972), pp. 206–209; P. J. Vatikiotis, "The Politics of the Fertile Crescent," in Paul Y. Hammond and Sidney S. Alexander, eds., *Political Dynamics in the Middle East* (New York: Elsevier, 1972), p. 226.

24. Hinnebusch, *Peasant and Bureaucracy in Ba'thist Syria,* chap. 5.

25. Petran, *Syria,* pp. 175–176.

26. David W. Carr, "Capital Flows and Development in Syria," *Middle East Journal* 34 (Autumn 1980): 465.

27. Fred H. Lawson, "Social Bases for the Hamah Revolt," *MERIP Reports,* no. 110 (November–December 1982): 27.

28. *Middle East Contemporary Survey 1979–80,* pp. 767–768.

29. *Middle East Economic Digest (MEED),* 17 and 24 April 1981.

30. John Roberts, "Syria: Taking a Long, Hard Look at the Economy," *MEED,* 22 May 1981.

31. Economist Intelligence Unit, *Quarterly Economic Review of Syria (QERS),* second quarter and fourth quarter 1981; *Wall Street Journal,* 23 July 1981.

32. Amnesty International, *Report to the Government of the Syrian Arab Republic* (London: Amnesty International, 1983), pp. 34–36; Patrick Seale, *Asad* (Berkeley: University of California Press, 1988), pp. 327–328.

33. Amnesty International, *Report,* pp. 12–14; Middle East Watch, *Syria Unmasked* (New Haven: Yale University Press, 1991), chap. 6.

34. Seale, *Asad,* p. 338.

35. Gerard Michaud, "The Importance of Bodyguards," *MERIP Reports,* no. 110 (November–December 1982): 29.

36. Seale, *Asad,* p. 427.

37. *MEED,* 10 July and 21 August 1981.

38. *MEED,* 7 August 1981.

39. Eliyahu Kanovsky, *Economic Development of Syria* (Tel Aviv: University Publishing Projects, 1977), p. 285.

40. *MEED*, 22 May 1981.

41. "Les Transformations économiques et les perspectives de développement agricole," *Syrie et Monde Arabe*, no. 349 (25 March 1983).

42. *MEED*, 11 September and 9 October 1981.

43. *QERS*, third quarter 1981.

44. *MEED*, 20 November 1981.

45. Raymond A. Hinnebusch, *Authoritarian Power and State Formation in Ba'thist Syria* (Boulder, Colo.: Westview Press, 1990), p. 202.

46. Ibid., p. 210.

47. Hinnebusch, *Peasant and Bureaucracy in Ba'thist Syria*, pp. 46–47 and 133.

48. Ibid., pp. 71–75.

49. Hinnebusch, *Authoritarian Power and State Formation*, pp. 209 and 214.

50. Ibid., p. 207.

51. Ibid., p. 210.

52. Hinnebusch, *Peasant and Bureaucracy in Ba'thist Syria*, p. 106.

53. *MEED*, 14 May 1982.

54. Volker Perthes, "The Syrian Economy in the 1980s," *Middle East Journal* 46 (Winter 1992): 41–43.

55. Ibid., p. 42.

56. Syrian Arab Republic, *Statistical Abstract 1965* (Damascus: Government Press, 1966), p. 240; U.S. Department of Agriculture (USDA), *Cotton in Syria*, FAS-M-280 (Washington, D.C.: U.S. Government Printing Office, 1978), p. 22.

57. Syrian Arab Republic, *Statistical Abstract 1965*, p. 114.

58. Syrian Arab Republic, *Population Census in Syrian Arab Republic 1970* (Damascus: Government Press, n.d.), 1:36–37.

59. Petran, *Syria*, p. 211; *Rapport 1977–1978 sur l'économie syrienne* (Damascus: Office Arabe de Presse et de Documentation, n.d.), p. B-63; *QERS*, third quarter 1981, p. 9; *QERS*, second quarter 1981, p. 8.

60. *Rapport 1977–1978*, p. B-63; USDA, *Cotton in Syria*, p. 27; *QERS*, second quarter 1981, p. 8; *QERS*, third quarter 1981, p. 9.

61. *QERS*, third quarter 1980, p. 6.

62. See Bureau International du Travail, *Rapport au gouvernement de la République arabe syrienne sur la règlement des salaires dans l'industrie* (Geneva: Bureau International du Travail, 1971); *QERS*, second quarter 1980, p. 5; Salim Nasr, "Les Travailleurs de l'industrie manufacturière au Machrek," *Maghreb/Machrek*, no. 92 (April–May 1981): 18–20.

63. For some representative prices on industrial raw materials and finished goods in Syria's provinces, see *Rapport 1977–1978*, especially the section of tables entitled "Annual Average of Wholesale Prices in Centers of Mohafazat 1963, 1970–1977."

64. "Les Caractéristiques générales de la force ouvrière en Syrie," *Syrie et Monde Arabe*, no. 324 (25 February 1981): 6–7.

65. *QERS*, first quarter 1980, p. 12; *QERS*, second quarter 1981, pp. 8–9; *QERS*, third quarter 1981, p. 9; *QERS*, fourth quarter 1981, p. 10; *MEED*, 19 March and 30 April 1976.

66. Ziad Keilany, "Land Reform in Syria," *Middle Eastern Studies* 16 (October 1980): 212; International Bank for Reconstruction and Development, *The Economic Development of Syria* (Baltimore: Johns Hopkins University Press, 1955), pp. 36–37.

67. Petran, *Syria*, pp. 87–89, 175–176, and 229.

68. Lawson, "Social Bases for the Hamah Revolt," p. 27; Petran, *Syria*, pp. 175–176.

69. *QERS*, second quarter 1981, p. 10; *QERS*, third quarter 1981, p. 10.

70. Springborg, "Baathism in Practice," passim.

71. *QERS*, fourth quarter 1981, pp. 8 and 11.

72. *QERS*, second quarter 1981, p. 8; *QERS*, third quarter 1981, p. 12; *QERS*, fourth quarter 1981, pp. 8 and 11.

73. Whether Syrian army units defected to the rebels' side remains an open—and politically explosive—question. Later accounts suggest that rebels had dressed in regular army uniforms and that this constituted the basis for early reports of defections. See "Des Combats entre les Frères musulmans et les forces de l'ordre," *Le Monde*, 12 February 1982; *Wall Street Journal*, 6 May 1982.

74. Umar F. Abd-Allah, *The Islamic Struggle in Syria* (Berkeley: Mizan, 1983), p. 192.

75. Thomas Mayer, "The Islamic Opposition in Syria, 1961–1982," *Orient* 24 (1983): 605.

76. Abd-Allah, *Islamic Struggle*, p. 193.

77. Mayer, "Islamic Opposition," p. 605.

78. Abd-Allah, *Islamic Struggle*, pp. 193–194.

79. Ibid., p. 193.

80. Perthes, "Syrian Economy in the 1980s," p. 43.

81. Ibid., p. 45.

82. Middle East Watch, *Syria Unmasked* (New Haven: Yale University Press, 1991), p. 20.

83. Ibid.

84. Hanna Batatu, "Some Observations on the Social Roots of Syria's Ruling, Military Group and the Causes for Its Dominance," *Middle East Journal* 35 (Summer 1981): 332.

85. Yahya M. Sadowski, "Patronage and the Ba'th: Corruption and Control in Contemporary Syria," *Arab Studies Quarterly* 9 (Fall 1987): 446.

86. Batatu, "Some Observations," p. 331.

87. Abd-Allah, *Islamic Struggle*, pp. 138–139.

88. Mayer, "Islamic Opposition," p. 601.

89. Raymond A. Hinnebusch, "Syria," in Shireen T. Hunter, ed., *The Politics of Islamic Revivalism* (Bloomington: Indiana University Press, 1988), p. 54.

90. Raymond A. Hinnebusch, "The Islamic Movement in Syria," in Ali E. Hillal Dessouki, ed., *Islamic Resurgence in the Arab World* (New York: Praeger, 1982), p. 152; Mayer, "Islamic Opposition," pp. 606–607.

91. Perthes, "The Syrian Private Industrial and Commercial Sectors," p. 211.

92. *MEED,* 5 February 1982.

93. *MEED,* 14 May 1982.

94. *MEED,* 26 February 1982.

95. *MEED,* 5 and 12 March 1982.

96. *MEED,* 26 March 1982.

97. *MEED,* 7 May 1982.

98. Perthes, "The Syrian Economy in the 1980s," p. 45 n. 34.

99. Ibid., p. 45.

100. Ibid., pp. 45–46.

101. *MEED,* 21 May 1982.

102. Kienle, *Ba'th v Ba'th,* pp. 160–161.

103. Ibid., p. 162.

104. *Middle East Contemporary Survey 1981–82,* p. 853.

105. *al-Ba'th,* 9 April 1982.

106. *Tishrin,* 15 May 1982.

107. *MEED,* 16 April 1982.

108. *MEED,* 28 May 1982.

109. *MEED,* 6 August 1982.

110. *MEED,* 7 May 1982.

111. *MEED,* 16 April, 21 May, and 4 June 1982.

112. *MEED,* 28 May and 4 June 1982.

113. Pedro Ramet, *The Soviet-Syrian Relationship since 1955* (Boulder, Colo.: Westview Press, 1990), p. 232.

114. Ibid., p. 149.

115. Efraim Karsh, *The Soviet Union and Syria: The Asad Years* (London: Routledge, 1988), p. 73.

116. These figures are taken from various annual issues of International Institute for Strategic Studies, *The Military Balance* (London: IISS, various dates).

117. Stockholm International Peace Research Institute, *SIPRI Yearbook 1989: World Armaments and Disarmament* (London: Oxford University Press, 1989), pp. 184–185 and 189.

118. Kais Firro, "The Syrian Economy under the Assad Regime," in Ma'oz and Yaniv, eds., *Syria under Assad,* p. 46.

119. Seale, *Asad,* p. 449.

120. Lawson, "Social Bases for the Hamah Revolt," p. 28.

121. See Alasdair Drysdale, "The Succession Question in Syria," *Middle East Journal* 39 (Spring 1985).

5. ABJURING CONFRONTATION WITH TURKEY, 1994

1. The rapprochement is surveyed in David Kushner, "Conflict and Accommodation in Turkish-Syrian Relations," in Moshe Ma'oz and Avner Yaniv, eds., *Syria under Assad* (New York: St. Martin's, 1986), pp. 90–92 and 99.

2. Ken Mackenzie, "Turkey: Focus on the Middle East," *Middle East International,* 5 March 1988, p. 14.

3. Ken Mackenzie, "Turkey: Ozal the Peacemaker," *Middle East International,* 16 April 1988, p. 11.

4. Ken Mackenzie, "Turkey, Iraq and the Kurds," *Middle East International,* 23 September 1988, p. 10.

5. Nadim Jaber, "The Kurds: The Unwanted," *Middle East International,* 21 October 1988, pp. 7–8; Ken Mackenzie, "Turkey and Iran: Turning Sour," *Middle East International,* 4 November 1988, p. 9.

6. Ken Mackenzie, "Turkey: The Kurds Again," *Middle East International,* 6 October 1989, pp. 12–13.

7. *Maghreb/Machrek,* no. 127 (January–March 1990): 181; *Middle East Contemporary Survey 1989,* pp. 642–643.

8. William Hale, "Turkey, the Middle East and the Gulf Crisis," *International Affairs* 68 (October 1992): 682–683.

9. Ken Mackenzie, "Turkey: Terrorism and Water," *Middle East International,* 15 December 1989, p. 13.

10. *Middle East Economic Digest (MEED),* 19 November 1993.

11. British Broadcasting Corporation, *Summary of World Broadcasts (SWB), The Middle East,* ME/1838 MED/6, 5 November 1993.

12. *MEED,* 26 November 1993; *Near East Report,* 22 November 1993.

13. *SWB,* ME/1833 MED/13, 30 October 1993.

14. *SWB,* ME/1838 MED/6, 5 November.

15. *Arab News,* 9 January 1994.

16. *Arab News,* 14 January 1994.

17. Amalia van Gent, "Turkey: Mideast Water and Islam," *Swiss Review of World Affairs,* January 1994. Ankara shunted more than one-third of the normal flow of the Euphrates into a new irrigation pipeline in early November 1994. See Hugh Pope, "Turkey: Consolidating Its Interests," *Middle East International,* 18 November 1994, p. 10.

18. Sami Kohen, "Turkey's Balancing Act in the Middle East," *Middle East International,* 18 March 1994, p. 19.

19. Hugh Pope, "Turkey: In for a Rough Ride," *Middle East International,* 29 April 1994, p. 14; Hugh Pope, "Turkey: Moving Away from the West?" *Middle East International,* 9 September 1994, p. 14.

20. *SWB,* ME/1839 MED/6, 6 November 1993.

21. *SWB,* ME/1840 MED/6, 8 November 1993.

22. *MEED,* 18 February 1994.

23. *Arab News,* 14 April 1994.

24. Kamal S. Shehadi, "Trading Places: The Balance of Power and Prospects for Iraqi-Syrian Rapprochement in the 1990s," *Beirut Review* 1 (Fall 1991).

25. See Eliyahu Kanovsky, "What's Behind Syria's Current Economic Problems?" *Middle East Contemporary Survey 1983–84.*

26. Volker Perthes, "The Syrian Economy in the 1980s," *Middle East Journal* 46 (Winter 1992): 40.

27. Ibid., p. 41.

28. *MEED,* 11 August 1989 and 23 February 1990.

29. *MEED,* 12 April 1989.

30. David Butter, "Syria's Under the Counter Economy," *MEED,* 23 February 1990, pp. 4–5.

31. Steven Heydemann, "Taxation without Representation: Authoritarianism and Economic Liberalization in Syria," in Ellis Goldberg, Resat Kasaba, and Joel S. Migdal, eds., *Rules and Rights in the Middle East* (Seattle: University of Washington Press, 1993), p. 84.

32. Ibid.

33. United Nations Development Program (UNDP), *Development Cooperation: Syrian Arab Republic, 1991 Report* (Damascus: UNDP, October 1992), pp. 40–41.

34. Perthes, "Syrian Economy in the 1980s," p. 44.

35. *Rapport 1990–1991 sur l'économie syrienne* (Damascus: L'Office Arabe de Presse et de Documentation, n.d.), p. A-25.

36. International Institute for Strategic Studies, *The Military Balance, 1991–1992* (London: Brassey's, 1991), p. 120; Elizabeth Picard, "State and Society in the Arab World: Towards a New Role for the Security Services?" in Bahgat Korany, Paul Noble, and Rex Brynen, eds., *The Many Faces of National Security in the Arab World* (London: Macmillan, 1993), p. 265.

37. *Rapport 1990–1991,* pp. A-1–A-2; *MEED,* 23 February 1990, pp. 4–5.

38. *MEED,* 16 March 1990; Patrick Clawson, *Unaffordable Ambitions: Syria's Military Build-up and Economic Crisis* (Washington, D.C.: The Washington Institute for Near East Policy, 1989).

39. *MEED,* 1 February and 12 April 1991.

40. *MEED,* 8 March 1991.

41. *MEED,* 18 January 1991.

42. *MEED,* 15 February and 21 June 1991.

43. *MEED,* 11 and 18 January 1991.

44. *MEED,* 12 April 1991.

45. *MEED,* 10 May 1991.

46. *Syrie et Monde Arabe,* February 1992.

47. *Economic Review of the Arab World (ERAW),* February 1991; *MEED,* 19 July 1991.

48. *ERAW,* April 1991.

49. *The Middle East,* September 1991.

50. *MEED,* 19 July 1991.

51. On Syria's ruling social coalition during the 1990s, see Elizabeth Picard, "Ouverture économique et renforcement militaire en Syrie," *Oriente Moderno* 50 (July–December 1979); Hanna Batatu, "Some Observations on the Social Roots of Syria's Ruling, Military Group and the Causes for Its Dominance," *Middle East Journal* 35 (Summer 1981); Raymond A. Hinnebusch, *Peasant and Bureaucracy in Baʿthist Syria* (Boulder, Colo.: Westview Press, 1989); Eberhard Kienle, "Entre jama'a et classe: Le pouvoir politique en Syrie contemporaine," *Revue du monde musulman et de la Méditerranée,* nos. 59–60 (1991).

52. See Fred H. Lawson, "Political-Economic Trends in Baʿthi Syria: A Reinterpretation," *Orient* 29 (December 1988); Perthes, "Syrian Economy in the 1980s," pp. 54–55.

53. Syrian Arab Republic, *Statistical Abstract 1987* (Damascus: Central Bureau of Statistics, August 1987), Table 37/16.

54. *MEED,* 8 June 1990. Syrian farm products found ready markets in the Arab Gulf states as well; see Heydemann, "Taxation without Representation," p. 92 n. 44.

55. Volker Perthes, "The Syrian Private Industrial and Commercial Sectors and the State," *International Journal of Middle East Studies* 24 (May 1992): 211. Slightly different figures are reported in Heydemann, "Taxation without Representation," p. 90.

56. Perthes, "Syrian Private Industrial and Commercial Sectors," pp. 212–213.

57. Ibid., p. 229 n. 40.

58. *MEED,* 12 October 1990.

59. Heydemann, "Taxation without Representation," pp. 89–90.

60. Ibid., p. 92.

61. Syrian Television Domestic Service, 8 March 1990 (FBIS, 9 March 1990).

62. Steven Heydemann, "Can We Get There from Here? Lessons from the Syrian Case," *American-Arab Affairs,* no. 36 (Spring 1991): 29.

63. Volker Perthes, "Syria's Parliamentary Elections: Remodeling Asad's Political Base," *Middle East Report,* no. 174 (January–February 1992): 18.

64. Ibid., pp. 16–17.

65. *al-Baʿth,* 22 July 1991 (FBIS, 30 July 1991).

66. Perthes, "Syria's Parliamentary Elections," p. 15.

67. *MEED,* 17 and 24 May 1991.

68. *MEED,* 5 and 12 July 1991.

69. *Syria et Monde Arabe,* March 1992.

70. *MEED,* 6 September 1991.

71. *MEED,* 18 October 1991.

72. *MEED,* 16 August 1991.

73. Fred H. Lawson, "Social Bases for the Hamah Revolt," *MERIP Reports,* no. 110 (November-December 1982).

74. Fred H. Lawson, "From Neo-Baʻth to Baʻth Nouveau: Hafiz al-Asad's Second Decade," *Journal of South Asian and Middle Eastern Studies* 14 (Winter 1990).

75. Perthes, "Syrian Economy in the 1980s," p. 47.

76. Ibid., p. 44 n. 31.

77. *MEED,* 28 December 1990.

78. *MEED,* 18 January and 15 February 1991.

79. *MEED,* 10 May and 28 June 1991.

80. *MEED,* 12 July and 2 August 1991.

81. *MEED,* 11 January, 19 April, and 14 June 1991.

82. *MEED,* 12 April 1991.

83. UNDP, *Development Co-operation,* p. 26.

84. *Syrie et Monde Arabe,* April 1992.

85. *Syrie et Monde Arabe,* May 1992.

86. *Syrie et Monde Arabe,* July and October 1992.

87. *MEED,* 15 February 1991.

88. *Current Digest of the Soviet Press,* 8 May 1991.

89. See Robert O. Freedman, "Soviet-Syrian Relations in the Aftermath of the Gulf War: A Preliminary Analysis," unpublished manuscript, June 1991.

90. *MEED,* 17 May 1991.

91. *Wall Street Journal,* 11 July 1991.

92. Economist Intelligence Unit, *Quarterly Economic Review of the Syrian Arab Republic,* first quarter 1992, p. 10.

93. *MEED,* 17 September 1993; *New York Times,* 12 December 1993.

94. G. H. Jansen, "Syria: Keeping the Lid On," *Middle East International,* 11 October 1991, p. 11; Kienle, "Entre jamaʼa et classe," p. 221.

95. *MEED,* 22 March 1991.

96. Ibid.

97. *MEED,* 12 April 1991.

98. *MEED,* 26 April 1991.

99. *MEED,* 8 November 1991.

100. *Wall Street Journal,* 29 October 1991.

101. *MEED,* 25 December 1992.

102. *MEED,* 19 March 1993.

103. *al-Jamahir* (Aleppo), 23 August 1993.

104. Cited in Heydemann, "Taxation without Representation," p. 95 n. 51.

105. Cited in ibid.

106. *MEED,* 8 May 1992.

107. *Syrie et Monde Arabe,* August 1992.

108. Damascus Radio Domestic Service, 2 December 1992.
109. *MEED,* 25 December 1992.
110. Interviews, Damascus, November 1992.
111. Interviews, Damascus, January 1993.
112. Syrian Television Domestic Service, 16 May 1993.
113. *MEED,* 28 August 1992.
114. *MEED,* 27 August 1993.
115. *MEED,* 11 and 25 September 1992.
116. *MEED,* 20 November 1992.
117. *MEED,* 22 October and 5 November 1993.
118. *MEED,* 4 June 1993.
119. *MEED,* 24 January 1992.
120. *MEED,* 28 February 1992.
121. *MEED,* 27 September 1991.
122. On the other hand, Syria's defiance of the sanctions imposed on Libya by the United Nations in the spring of 1992 primarily reflected efforts by forces associated with the party-state apparatus to reassert their steadily diminishing prerogatives in the face of the country's reemergent private commercial and agrarian bourgeoisie. Pointing out the dangers of a "new world order" orchestrated by Washington and London complemented the criticisms raised by representatives of the Ba'th-affiliated popular front organizations within the People's Assembly concerning the increasingly free hand being accorded private capital at home. Public sector managers and military commanders took advantage of the confrontation between Libya and the West not only to harness popular grumbling regarding the effects of economic liberalization but also to slow the rush of foreign goods and subsidiaries into the Syrian market.
123. *Syrie et Monde Arabe,* August 1992.
124. *Syrie et Monde Arabe,* September 1992.
125. Ibid.; *MEED,* 11 September 1992.
126. See Fred H. Lawson, "Domestic Pressures and the Peace Process: Fillip or Hindrance?" in Eberhard Kienle, ed., *Contemporary Syria: Liberalisation between Cold War and Cold Peace* (London: I.B. Tauris, 1994).
127. *MEED,* 27 November and 25 December 1992.
128. *Kifah al-'Ummal al-Ishtirakiyyah,* 17 December 1992; *Syrie et Monde Arabe,* December 1992.
129. *Kifah al-'Ummal al-Ishtirakiyyah,* 17 December 1992.
130. *Syrie et Monde Arabe,* December 1992.
131. See Picard, "State and Society in the Arab World"; Yezid Sayigh, "Arab Military Industrialization: Security Incentives and Economic Impact," in Korany, Noble, and Brynen, eds., *The Many Faces of National Security.*
132. *MEED,* 20 November and 25 December 1992.

133. Fred H. Lawson, "Libéralisation économique en Syrie et Irak," *Maghreb-Machrek,* no. 128 (April–June 1990).

6. DOMESTIC CONFLICT AND CRISIS ESCALATION IN A LIBERAL-DEMOCRATIC SYRIA

1. Dean V. Babst, "A Force for Peace," *Industrial Research* 14 (April 1972); Rudolph J. Rummel, "Libertarianism and International Violence," *Journal of Conflict Resolution* 27 (March 1983); Steve Chan, "Mirror, Mirror on the Wall: Are the Freer Countries More Pacific?" *Journal of Conflict Resolution* 28 (December 1984); Michael W. Doyle, "Liberalism and World Politics," *American Political Science Review* 80 (December 1986); T. Clifton Morgan and Sally Howard Campbell, "Domestic Structure, Decisional Constraints, and War," *Journal of Conflict Resolution* 35 (June 1991); T. Clifton Morgan and Valerie L. Schwebach, "Take Two Democracies and Call Me in the Morning: A Prescription for Peace?" *International Interactions* 17 (1992); Randall L. Schweller, "Domestic Structure and Preventive War: Are Democracies More Pacific?" *World Politics* 44 (January 1992); David A. Lake, "Powerful Pacifists: Democratic States and War," *American Political Science Review* 86 (March 1992); T. Clifton Morgan, "Democracy and War: Reflections on the Literature," *International Interactions* 18 (1993); Bruce Russett, *Grasping the Democratic Peace* (Princeton: Princeton University Press, 1993). Criticisms of this literature can be found in Raymond Cohen, "Pacific Unions: A Reappraisal of the Theory that 'Democracies Do Not Go to War with Each Other,'" *Review of International Studies* 20 (July 1994); David E. Spiro, "The Insignificance of the Liberal Peace," *International Security* 19 (Fall 1994); Edward D. Mansfield and Jack Snyder, "Democratization and the Danger of War," *International Security* 20 (Summer 1995).

2. Michael C. Hudson, "Democracy and Foreign Policy in the Arab World," *Beirut Review* 4 (Fall 1992): 5–6. See also Tabitha Petran, *Syria* (New York: Praeger, 1972), chap. 5; Elizabeth Picard, "La Syrie de 1946 à 1979," in André Raymond, ed., *La Syrie d'aujourd'hui* (Paris: CNRS, 1980); Fred H. Lawson, "Political Parties in Syria," in Frank Tachau, ed., *Political Parties in the Middle East* (Westport, Conn.: Greenwood Press, 1994).

3. Hudson, "Democracy and Foreign Policy in the Arab World," p. 7.

4. Syrian involvement in the 1948 war is detailed in Barry Rubin, *The Arab States and the Palestine Conflict* (Syracuse: Syracuse University Press, 1981), chap. 12; A. al-Nafuri, "al-Jaysh al-Suri fi Filastin: 'am 1948," *al-Fikr al-'Askari* 2–3 (July 1979); Salih Saib al-Juburi, *Mihnah Filastin wa-Asraruha al-Siyasiyyah wal-'Askariyyah* (Beirut: Matabi' Dar al-Kutub, 1970). On earlier Syrian relations with Palestine, see Philip S. Khoury, "Divided Loyalties? Syria and the Question of Palestine, 1919–39," *Middle Eastern Studies* 21 (July 1985).

5. Petran, *Syria,* p. 82; Gordon H. Torrey, *Syrian Politics and the Military, 1945–1958* (Columbus: Ohio State University Press, 1964), p. 74.

6. Petran, *Syria*, p. 86–87.

7. A. Aziz Allouni, "The Labor Movement in Syria," *Middle East Journal* 13 (Winter 1959): 67–68; Badr al-Din al-Siba'i, *al-Marhalah al-intiqaliyyah fi Suriyah* (Beirut: Dar Ibn Khaldun, 1975), pp. 88–94; 'Abdullah Hanna, *al-Harakah al-'Ummaliyyah fi Suriyah wa Lubnan, 1900–1945* (Damascus: Dar Dimashq, 1973), pp. 486–491. In sharp contrast to Syria's active industrial laborers, the comparatively quiescent farm workers were accorded no rights in the labor code. See 'Abdullah Hanna, *al-Qadiyah al-Zira'iyyah wal-Harakah al-Fallahiyyah fi Suriyah wa Lubnan* (Beirut: Dar al-Farabi, 1978), 2:430–431.

8. Samir Makdisi, "Fixed Capital Formation in Syria, 1936–1957," in Paul A. Klat, ed., *Middle East Economic Papers 1963* (Beirut: American University of Beirut Economic Research Institute and Dar al-Kitab, n.d.), p. 99; Edmund Y. Asfour, *Syria: Development and Monetary Policy* (Cambridge: Harvard University Center for Middle Eastern Studies, 1967), pp. 30–31.

9. See Ministry of National Economy, *Statistical Abstract of Syria 1961* (Damascus: Government Press, 1962), Table 8.

10. Petran, *Syria*, p. 84.

11. Ibid., p. 85.

12. Ibid., p. 84.

13. Martin W. Wilmington, "The Middle East Supply Center: A Reappraisal," *Middle East Journal* 6 (Spring 1952).

14. Petran, *Syria*, p. 82; Doreen Warriner, *Land Reform and Development in the Middle East* (London: Oxford University Press, 1962), p. 75.

15. Small farmers around Latakia rose in revolt soon after Syria's independence, and the district was pacified only after units of the regular armed forces were dispatched to the area. See Torrey, *Syrian Politics and the Military*, p. 82.

16. Ibid., p. 85.

17. Ibid., p. 78.

18. Elias S. Saba, "The Syro-Lebanese Customs Union: Causes of Failure and Attempts at Re-organization," in Paul A. Klat, ed., *Middle East Economic Papers 1960* (Beirut: American University of Beirut Economic Research Institute and Dar al-Kitab, n.d.), p. 101.

19. Patrick Seale, *The Struggle for Syria* (New Haven: Yale University Press, 1986), p. 32.

20. Torrey, *Syrian Politics and the Military*, p. 80.

21. Ibid., pp. 79 and 81.

22. Thomas B. Stauffer, "Labor Unions in the Arab States," *Middle East Journal* 6 (Winter 1952): 83–88.

23. Asfour, *Syria*, p. 70.

24. Petran, *Syria*, p. 88; Seale, *Struggle for Syria*, pp. 38–39. John F. Devlin gives 1950 as the year in which the Arab Socialist party was founded. See Devlin, *The Ba'th Party* (Stanford, Calif.: Hoover Institution Press, 1976), p. 64.

25. Seale, *Struggle for Syria*, p. 40; Petran, *Syria*, p. 88.

26. Devlin, *Ba'th Party*, pp. 13–14.

27. Ibid., p. 14.

28. Ibid., p. 48.

29. Torrey, *Syrian Politics and the Military*, pp. 78–79.

30. Petran, *Syria*, p. 93; Torrey, *Syrian Politics and the Military*, p. 93.

31. Muhammad Kurd 'Ali, *Memoirs of Muhammad Kurd 'Ali: A Selection* (Washington, D.C.: American Council of Learned Societies, 1954), p. 216.

32. Johannes Reissner, *Ideologie und Politik der Muslimbrüder Syriens* (Freiburg: Klaus Schwarz Verlag, 1980); Torrey, *Syrian Politics and the Military*, p. 82.

33. Torrey, *Syrian Politics and the Military*, p. 99.

34. Ibid., pp. 97–100.

35. Interviews, Aleppo, August 1993; Torrey, *Syrian Politics and the Military*, p. 100; Seale, *Struggle for Syria*, p. 31.

36. Torrey, *Syrian Politics and the Military*, p. 101.

37. Ibid., p. 93.

38. Ibid., pp. 101–102; Devlin, *Ba'th Party*, p. 49.

39. Dorothea S. Franck and Peter G. Franck, "The Middle East Economy in 1948," *Middle East Journal* 3 (April 1949): 202; Seale, *Struggle for Syria*, p. 32.

40. Chronology entry in *Middle East Journal* 2 (January 1948): 74.

41. This paragraph relies on Joshua Landis, "The Syrian Army: 1945–1947," paper presented to the Middle East Studies Association, Washington, D.C., December 1995.

42. Asfour, *Syria*, p. 31.

43. Franck and Franck, "Middle East Economy in 1948," p. 203.

44. Asfour, *Syria*, pp. 50 and 143 n. 25.

45. Saba, "Syro-Lebanese Customs Union," p. 97.

46. Ibid.

47. Asfour, *Syria*, p. 77.

48. Ibid., p. 31.

49. Torrey, *Syrian Politics and the Military*, p. 103.

50. Ibid., pp. 103–104; Devlin, *Ba'th Party*, p. 50; chronology entries in *Middle East Journal* 2 (January 1948): 74 and 2 (April 1948): 221.

51. Torrey, *Syrian Politics and the Military*, p. 104.

52. Devlin, *Ba'th Party*, pp. 50–51.

53. Torrey, *Syrian Politics and the Military*, p. 106.

54. Rubin, *Arab States and the Palestine Conflict*, p. 187.

55. Chronology entry in *Middle East Journal* 2 (April 1948): 221.

56. Ibid.; Devlin, *Ba'th Party*, p. 51.

57. Chronology entry in *Middle East Journal* 2 (July 1948): 337.

58. Chronology entry in *Middle East Journal* 2 (April 1948): 221.

59. Chonrology entry in *Middle East Journal* 2 (January 1948): 74.

60. Torrey, *Syrian Politics and the Military*, p. 104.

61. Ibid., p. 105.

62. Jack S. Levy, "The Causes of War: A Review of Theories and Evidence," in Philip E. Tetlock, Jo L. Husbands, Robert Jervis, Paul C. Stern, and Charles Tilly, eds., *Behavior, Society and Nuclear War* (New York: Oxford University Press, 1989), 1: 270.

CONCLUSION

1. See Stephen M. Walt, *The Origins of Alliances* (Ithaca: Cornell University Press, 1987); Michael Barnett, "Institutions, Roles, and Disorder: The Case of the Arab States System," *International Studies Quarterly* 37 (September 1993); Janice Gross Stein, "Deterrence and Compellence in the Gulf, 1990–91," *International Security* 17 (Fall 1992).

2. For complementary attempts to incorporate domestic politics into explanations for strategic choices, see Williamson Murray, MacGregor Knox, and Alvin Bernstein, eds., *The Making of Strategy* (Cambridge: Cambridge University Press, 1994); Richard Rosecrance and Arthur A. Stein, eds., *The Domestic Bases of Grand Strategy* (Ithaca: Cornell University Press, 1993); Alastair Iain Johnston, "Thinking about Strategic Culture," *International Security* 19 (Spring 1995); Elizabeth Keir, "Culture and Military Doctrine: France between the Wars," *International Security* 19 (Spring 1995).

3. Leo Hazlewood, "Diversion Mechanisms and Encapsulation Processes: The Domestic Conflict–Foreign Conflict Hypothesis Reconsidered," *Sage International Yearbook of Foreign Policy Studies*, vol. 3 (Beverly Hills: Sage, 1975); T. Clifton Morgan and Kenneth Bickers, "Domestic Discontent and the External Use of Force," *Journal of Conflict Resolution* 36 (March 1992).

4. Patrick James, *Crisis and War* (Kingston: McGill-Queen's University Press, 1988); Fred H. Lawson, *The Social Origins of Egyptian Expansionism during the Muhammad 'Ali Period* (New York: Columbia University Press, 1992).

5. David Ottaway and Marina Ottaway, *Algeria: The Politics of a Socialist Revolution* (Berkeley: University of California Press, 1970); Hugh Roberts, *Algerian Socialism and the Kabyle Question,* Monographs in Development Studies no. 8, School of Development Studies, University of East Anglia, June 1981, pp. 113–120; Mahfoud Bennoune, *The Making of Contemporary Algeria* (Cambridge: Cambridge University Press, 1988), pp. 97–98.

6. François Weiss, *Doctrine et action syndicales en Algérie* (Paris: Editions Cujas, 1970), chaps. 4–6; Ian Clegg, *Workers' Self-Management in Algeria* (New York: Monthly Review, 1971), chaps. 4 and 7.

7. Ottaway and Ottaway, *Algeria*, p. 97; Roberts, *Algerian Socialism*, pp. 254–256; Ramadane Redjala, *L'Opposition en Algérie depuis 1962* (Paris: L'Harmattan, 1988), pp. 147–158.

8. Bennoune, *Making of Contemporary Algeria*, p. 90; John Ruedy, *Modern Algeria* (Bloomington: Indiana University Press, 1992), p. 195.

9. Ottaway and Ottaway, *Algeria,* p. 62; Clegg, *Workers' Self-Management,* chap. 4.

10. Ottaway and Ottaway, *Algeria,* p. 64.

11. Bennoune, *Making of Contemporary Algeria,* pp. 99–100.

12. Ibid., p. 98; Marc Raffinot and Pierre Jacquemot, *Le Capitalisme d'état algérien* (Paris: Maspéro, 1977), p. 50.

13. David C. Gordon, *The Passing of French Algeria* (London: Oxford University Press, 1966), p. 83.

14. Ruedy, *Modern Algeria,* pp. 200–201.

15. Bennoune, *Making of Contemporary Algeria,* p. 100.

16. Ibid., p. 163.

17. Ottaway and Ottaway, *Algeria,* p. 98; Roberts, *Algerian Socialism,* pp. 258–259; Ruedy, *Modern Algeria,* p. 202.

18. Ottaway and Ottaway, *Algeria,* pp. 108–109.

19. Raffinot and Jacquemot, *Le Capitalisme d'état,* p. 69.

20. Ahmed Abdalla, *The Student Movement and National Politics in Egypt* (London: Al Saqi Books, 1985), pp. 189–192; Mahmoud Hussein, "The Revolt of the Egyptian Students," *MERIP Reports,* no. 11 (August 1972); Peter Johnson, "Retreat of the Revolution in Egypt," *MERIP Reports,* no. 17 (May 1973): 6–10.

21. Abdalla, *Student Movement and National Politics,* p. 180.

22. Ibid., p. 183.

23. Ibid., p. 186.

24. Ibid., p. 184.

25. Mark Cooper, *The Transformation of Egypt* (Baltimore: Johns Hopkins University Press, 1982), p. 84; Maurice Martin, "A Note on Worker Agitation in Egypt," *CEMAM Reports 1975: Religion, State and Ideology* (Beirut: Dar El-Mashreq, 1976).

26. David Hirst and Irene Beeson, *Sadat* (London: Faber and Faber, 1981), p. 143. See also Nadia Ramsis Farah, *Religious Strife in Egypt* (New York: Gordon and Breach, 1986).

27. Abdalla, *Student Movement,* p. 187.

28. Ibid., p. 188.

29. *Middle East Economic Digest (MEED),* 16 February 1973.

30. *MEED,* 2 February 1973.

31. *MEED,* 16 February 1973.

32. *MEED,* 23 February 1973.

33. *MEED,* 16 March 1973.

34. *MEED,* 27 April 1973.

35. *MEED,* 4 and 11 May 1973.

36. *MEED,* 23 March, 18 May, 1 June, 27 July, and 17 August 1973.

37. *MEED,* 27 July 1973.

38. *MEED,* 3 August 1973.

39. *MEED,* 17 and 24 August 1973.

40. *MEED,* 14 September 1973.

41. Malak Zaalouk, *Power, Class and Foreign Capital in Egypt* (London: Zed Books, 1989), pp. 57–58.

42. Hani Shukrallah, "Political Crisis/Conflict in Post-1967 Egypt," in Charles Tripp and Roger Owen, eds., *Egypt under Mubarak* (London: Routledge, 1989), p. 70.

43. John Waterbury, *The Egypt of Nasser and Sadat* (Princeton: Princeton University Press, 1983), pp. 127–138; Alvin Z. Rubinstein, *Red Star on the Nile* (Princeton: Princeton University Press, 1977), p. 282.

44. Saad El-Shazli, *The Crossing of the Suez* (San Francisco: American Mideast Research, 1980), pp. 173–175; Janice Gross Stein, "Calculation, Miscalculation and Conventional Deterrence I: The View from Cairo," in Robert Jervis, Richard Lebow, and Janice Gross Stein, eds., *Psychology and Deterrence* (Baltimore: Johns Hopkins University Press, 1985), p. 46.

45. Richard Ned Lebow, *Between Peace and War* (Baltimore: Johns Hopkins University Press, 1981), p. 234.

46. Hirst and Beeson, *Sadat,* pp. 156–164.

47. John Galvani, Peter Johnson, and Rene Theberge, "The October War: Egypt, Syria, Israel," *MERIP Reports,* no. 22 (November 1973): 8–10.

48. Barry Blechman and Douglas Hart, "The Political Utility of Nuclear Weapons," in Sean Lynn-Jones, Steven Miller, and Stephen Van Evera, eds., *Nuclear Diplomacy and Crisis Management* (Cambridge: MIT Press, 1990).

49. Chaim Herzog, *The War of Atonement* (Boston: Little, Brown, 1975).

50. Yaacov Bar-Siman-Tov, *The Israeli-Egyptian War of Attrition* (New York: Columbia University Press, 1980).

51. Russell J. Leng, *Interstate Crisis Behavior, 1816–1980: Realism versus Reciprocity* (Cambridge: Cambridge University Press, 1993), p. 63. See also Geoffrey Blainey, *The Causes of War* (New York: Free Press, 1973); James L. Richardson, *Crisis Diplomacy* (Cambridge: Cambridge University Press, 1994); Michael Brecher, *Crises in World Politics* (Oxford: Pergamon Press, 1993).

52. Leng, *Interstate Crisis Behavior,* p. 162; Glenn H. Snyder and Paul Diesing, *Conflict among Nations* (Princeton: Princeton University Press, 1977), pp. 480–484.

53. Janice Gross Stein, "International Co-operation and Loss Avoidance: Framing the Problem," in Janice Gross Stein and Louis W. Pauly, eds., *Choosing to Co-operate: How States Avoid Loss* (Baltimore: Johns Hopkins University Press, 1993), p. 21. See also Jack S. Levy, "Declining Power and the Preventive Motivation for War," *World Politics* 40 (October 1987); Robert Jervis, "Political Implications of Loss Aversion," *Political Psychology* 13 (June 1992): 193–199.

Index

Cornell Studies in Political Economy

EDITED BY PETER J. KATZENSTEIN

National Diversity and Global Capitalism, edited by Suzanne Berger and Ronald Dore
Collapse of an Industry: Nuclear Power and the Contradictions of U.S. Policy, by John L. Campbell
Power, Purpose, and Collective Choice: Economic Strategy in Socialist States, edited by Ellen Comisso and Laura D'Andrea Tyson
The Political Economy of the New Asian Industrialism, edited by Frederic C. Deyo
Dislodging Multinationals: India's Strategy in Comparative Perspective, by Dennis J. Encarnation
Rivals beyond Trade: America versus Japan in Global Competition, by Dennis J. Encarnation
Enterprise and the State in Korea and Taiwan, by Karl J. Fields
National Interests in International Society, by Martha Finnemore
Democracy and Markets: The Politics of Mixed Economies, by John R. Freeman
The Misunderstood Miracle: Industrial Development and Political Change in Japan, by David Friedman
Ideas, Interests, and American Trade Policy, by Judith Goldstein
Ideas and Foreign Policy: Beliefs, Institutions, and Political Change, edited by Judith Goldstein and Robert O. Keohane
Monetary Sovereignty: The Politics of Central Banking in Western Europe, by John B. Goodman
Politics in Hard Times: Comparative Responses to International Economic Crises, by Peter Gourevitch
Closing the Gold Window: Domestic Politics and the End of Bretton Woods, by Joanne Gowa
Cooperation among Nations: Europe, America, and Non-tariff Barriers to Trade, by Joseph M. Grieco
Pathways from the Periphery: The Politics of Growth in the Newly Industrializing Countries, by Stephan Haggard
The Politics of Finance in Developing Countries, edited by Stephan Haggard, Chung H. Lee, and Sylvia Maxfield
Rival Capitalists: International Competitiveness in the United States, Japan, and Western Europe, by Jeffrey A. Hart
The Philippine State and the Marcos Regime: The Politics of Export, by Gary Hawes
Reasons of State: Oil Politics and the Capacities of American Government, by G. John Ikenberry
The State and American Foreign Economic Policy, edited by G. John Ikenberry, David A. Lake, and Michael Mastanduno
The Paradox of Continental Production: National Investment Policies in North America, by Barbara Jenkins
Pipeline Politics: The Complex Political Economy of East-West Energy Trade, by Bruce W. Jentleson
The Politics of International Debt, edited by Miles Kahler
Corporatism and Change: Austria, Switzerland, and the Politics of Industry, by Peter J. Katzenstein
Cultural Norms and National Security: Police and Military in Postwar Japan, by Peter J. Katzenstein
Industry and Politics in West Germany: Toward the Third Republic, edited by Peter J. Katzenstein
Small States in World Markets: Industrial Policy in Europe, by Peter J. Katzenstein

The Sovereign Entrepreneur: Oil Policies in Advanced and Less Developed Capitalist Countries, by Merrie Gilbert Klapp

Norms in International Relations: The Struggle against Apartheid, by Audie Klotz

International Regimes, edited by Stephen D. Krasner

Business and Banking: Political Change and Economic Integration in Western Europe, by Paulette Kurzer

Power, Protection, and Free Trade: International Sources of U.S. Commercial Strategy, 1887–1939, by David A. Lake

State Capitalism: Public Enterprise in Canada, by Jeanne Kirk Laux and Maureen Appel Molot

Why Syria Goes to War: Thirty Years of Confrontation, by Fred H. Lawson

Remaking the Italian Economy, by Richard M. Locke

France after Hegemony: International Change and Financial Reform, by Michael Loriaux

Economic Containment: CoCom and the Politics of East-West Trade, by Michael Mastanduno

Mercantile States and the World Oil Cartel, 1900–1939, by Gregory P. Nowell

Opening Financial Markets: Banking Politics on the Pacific Rim, by Louis W. Pauly

The Limits of Social Democracy: Investment Politics in Sweden, by Jonas Pontusson

The Fruits of Fascism: Postwar Prosperity in Historical Perspective, by Simon Reich

The Business of the Japanese State: Energy Markets in Comparative and Historical Perspective, by Richard J. Samuels

"Rich Nation, Strong Army": National Security and the Technological Transformation of Japan, by Richard J. Samuels

Crisis and Choice in European Social Democracy, by Fritz W. Scharpf, translated by Ruth Crowley

In the Dominions of Debt: Historical Perspectives on Dependent Development, by Herman M. Schwartz

Winners and Losers: How Sectors Shape the Developmental Prospects of States, by D. Michael Shafer

Europe and the New Technologies, edited by Margaret Sharp

Europe's Industries: Public and Private Strategies for Change, edited by Geoffrey Shepherd, François Duchêne, and Christopher Saunders

Ideas and Institutions: Developmentalism in Brazil and Argentina, by Kathryn Sikkink

The Cooperative Edge: The Internal Politics of International Cartels, by Debora L. Spar

Fair Shares: Unions, Pay, and Politics in Sweden and West Germany, by Peter Swenson

Union of Parts: Labor Politics in Postwar Germany, by Kathleen A. Thelen

Democracy at Work: Changing World Markets and the Future of Labor Unions, by Lowell Turner

Troubled Industries: Confronting Economic Change in Japan, by Robert M. Uriu

National Styles of Regulation: Environmental Policy in Great Britain and the United States, by David Vogel

Freer Markets, More Rules: Regulatory Reform in Advanced Industrial Countries, by Steven K. Vogel

The Political Economy of Policy Coordination: International Adjustment since 1945, by Michael C. Webb

International Cooperation: Building Regimes for Natural Resources and the Environment, by Oran R. Young

International Governance: Protecting the Environment in a Stateless Society, by Oran R. Young

Polar Politics: Creating International Environmental Regimes, edited by Oran R. Young and Gail Osherenko

Governments, Markets, and Growth: Financial Systems and the Politics of Industrial Change, by John Zysman

American Industry in International Competition: Government Policies and Corporate Strategies, edited by John Zysman and Laura Tyson